POST-HELLENISTIC PHILOSOPHY

Post-Hellenistic Philosophy

A Study of its Development from the Stoics to Origen

G. R. BOYS-STONES

OXFORD
UNIVERSITY PRESS

Great Clarendon Street, Oxford, OX2 6DP,
United Kingdom

Oxford University Press is a department of the University of Oxford. It furthers the University's objective of excellence in research, scholarship, and education by publishing worldwide. Oxford is a registered trade mark of Oxford University Press in the UK and in certain other countries

First published 2001
First published in paperback 2020

Published in the United States of America by Oxford University Press
198 Madison Avenue, New York, NY 10016, United States of America

British Library Cataloguing in Publication Data
Data available

Library of Congress Cataloging in Publication Data
Data available

ISBN 978–0–19–815264–4 (Hbk.)
ISBN 978–0–19–885732–7 (Pbk.)

Preface

THE centuries immediately following the end of the Hellenistic age remain a murky area in the history of philosophy. While a great deal of work has been done in recent years to rehabilitate Hellenistic thought itself from the generally negative assessment of the nineteenth century, the thesis that later philosophy traces a decline into 'eclecticism' (cf. not least Zeller 1892: vol. iv/1) retains a programmatic hold over studies of the period. Three centuries of intellectual activity are held to mark out a kind of philosophical no man's land between the earlier systems from which they are taken to derive their material, and the glories of 'Neoplatonism' to which they look forward. Even John Dillon, who has done so much to map out the territory (esp. Dillon 1996) and to question the term 'eclecticism' itself (Dillon 1988), found the period interesting 'chiefly as a prologue to Plotinus' (Dillon 1996: p. xiv). However, if scholarship has managed to bring the post-Aristotelian schools within the pale, the possibility must exist that post-Hellenistic philosophy can be brought inside as well—perhaps, ultimately, that the no man's land it marks out at the doorstep of Plotinus can be reclaimed and the pale brought down altogether. It is the aim of the present study to explore that possibility. It looks at post-Hellenistic philosophy, in particular at the one distinctive and influential movement it produced, namely Platonism, and argues that, in this movement, philosophy changed for ever, and changed in a manner perhaps less visible for its very depth. For this change, I shall argue, was not one marked as such—in the first place, at least—by a radical departure from engagement with the doctrines of the Hellenistic schools; it was rather marked by a shift in the theoretical understanding of how philosophy itself should be done. The distinction between 'Neo-' and 'Middle' Platonism is based on superficialities: the real philosophical revolution had taken place by the end of the second century AD, and it is this revolution that the study traces.

Platonism, it hardly needs arguing, was about a return to the philosophy of Plato. But this return was the consequence, not the basis, of a theory: the consequence, as I argue, of a theory developed from work originally done in the Hellenistic Stoa on the nature of mythological and theological traditions. In Part I of the study I examine the Stoics' suggestion that these traditions might preserve fragments of the philosophical outlook which obtained among the very first generations of mankind, an outlook whose truth could be independently established. In Chapters 1–2 I examine the basis for this belief in the early Stoa, and in Chapter 3, the increasingly sophisticated methods developed by the later Stoics for isolating 'original' philosophical material from the traditions which preserved it. One of the most important of these methods was the cross-cultural comparison of theological traditions—an approach which called for further investigation into the purity and antiquity of the traditions with which it worked. As evidence for the development of interest in these questions, I look in Chapters 4 and 5 at the way it is reflected in the Hellenistic debate between Greek and Jewish intellectuals over the age and status of Jewish culture, and argue that the issue of Jewish antiquity arose as a theme in the polemic it involves only in the light of the work of the later Stoics.

In Part II I turn to the Platonists themselves. They, I argue in Chapter 6, adopted the Stoics' beliefs concerning the survival of ancient, privileged wisdom, and their methods for extracting it as well. But what made the Platonists Platonists was their additional belief that Plato had already made use of just this kind of approach himself. Plato's philosophy represented, they believed, a full and successful reconstruction and articulation of the primitive, privileged wisdom of early man—and that is why Plato came to stand as an authority for them. But if Plato's authority is explained on the basis of his sources and method, the *truth* of his philosophy is also made plausible by the Platonists through an account of post-Platonic history. In Chapter 7 I show that, working from the explosion of philosophical disagreement and debate after Plato's death, institutionalized in the foundation of a number of different philosophical schools, the Platonists argued that we should not (with the Sceptics) suspend judgement over where the truth lay at all, but rather conclude that a return to the study of Plato might provide the most promising route to discovering it. The difficulties and disagreements among schools which had diverged from the teaching of Plato only made it more plausible that Plato had been right in the first place.

Finally, I argue that the models which defined the Platonist approach to philosophy were adopted by Christian thinkers of the later first and early second centuries AD, and shaped the emergence of Christianity as a force in Western philosophy. Needing to respond to Platonist claims that the dissension within Christianity could be explained by their own divergence from the ancient tradition inherited through Plato, the Christians used the Platonists' own tools to develop the notions of 'orthodoxy' and 'heresy' by which a 'true' and unified Christian tradition could be distinguished from the dissension it later attracted. Furthermore, by arguing that Christianity was in philosophical continuity with Hebrew thought (as the apologists of the second century started to do), 'orthodox' Christians were able to lay claim to a Hebraeo-Christian tradition which was *older* in its turn than any pagan tradition. Indeed, they argued that the traditional theologies of the pagans themselves must now be viewed as later and decadent offshoots of their own. But all of this leaves the Christians one further question, explored in Chapter 9: if traditional pagan theology is to be explained as a corrupt divergence from Hebraeo-Christian thought, how did it come to give rise to the more positive tradition of Classical Greek *philosophy*? Since it was axiomatic to the argument used by the Christians that divergent traditions could only tend to the worse, the improvements apparent in the work of the philosophers were in need of explanation. The answer offered by the Christians was that, one way or another, pagan philosophy also depended for its existence on the prior existence and superior truth of the Christian tradition: that it was, for example, sparked into being by contact during the Classical period with Hebrew Scripture. This explains the much-maligned 'dependency theme' (as one commentator has called it); but, crucially, it explains why one should not allow the positive developments within pagan philosophy to blind one to the essential weakness of its approach. The same traits which had led the pagans to diverge from the original tradition led their philosophers to dispute all over again the insights they had gained from the Hebrews, and to fall once again into a disagreement which showed that, if the truth was discernible at all, it must lie within orthodox Christianity.

Having described what is contained in this study, I should say a word about what is omitted. I do not, on the whole, discuss evidence later than the late third century AD—or, more specifically, later than the Platonist Porphyry, or Origen in the chapters on Christianity. These two thinkers seem to me convenient resting-points in their respective traditions; and the theory I discuss has been sufficiently established by this point for it to be neither necessary nor profitable to extend the investigation further. But a word is needed on the scope of my discussion of earlier Platonism as well, from which several familiar names will be found to be absent. It is part of my argument that Platonism should not be defined primarily by its doctrines, but rather by its methodology (in the context of which its doctrinal development can then be understood). For this reason, I concentrate away from Platonists who are only known to us through doxographical fragments or works: this is the excuse I offer for the absence here of figures such as Albinus, Alcinous, Gaius, and Apuleius. I am encouraged in focusing my attention elsewhere (in particular on Celsus, Plutarch, Atticus, and Numenius, as well as, to a lesser extent, on Plotinus and Porphyry) not just by this theoretical consideration, but also by the failure of doxographical approaches to Platonism which have deployed these thinkers on the front line of their evidence—one thinks in particular of the now discredited theory which traced Platonism from Antiochus of Ascalon, through Arius Didymus, to Gaius and the school attributed to him (cf. Chapter 6 below, esp. n. 2). Quite generally, in fact, this study does not aim to be comprehensive; but it does aim to start uncovering the kinds of structure in terms of which a comprehensive investigation might operate.

I have accumulated many debts of gratitude in preparing this study: first of all to the President and Fellows of the British Academy, for the Post-Doctoral Junior Research Fellowship which allowed me to start it; and to the President and Fellows of Corpus Christi College, Oxford, for the concurrent award of a non-stipendiary Junior Research Fellowship which gave me the ideal environment for the work it involved. The book contains material that has been aired in papers variously presented to seminars in Oxford, Bristol, and (thanks to the generous invitation and hospitality of Karin Blomqvist) Lund Universities. I am especially grateful for the attempts made to steer me away from error by Michael Frede, Charles Brittain, Myles Burnyeat, John Dillon, Ian Kidd, David Levene, Ben Morison, David Sedley, R. McL. Wilson; and the anonymous readers at Oxford University Press.

May 2000 G.B.-S.

Contents

Abbreviations

AA	Josephus, *Against Apion*
ANRW	H. Temporini and W. Haase (eds.), *Aufstieg und Niedergang der römischen Welt: Geschichte und Kultur Roms im Spiegel der neueren Forschung* (Berlin: de Gruyter, 1972–)
DK	H. Diels and W. Kranz, *Die Fragmente der Vorsokratiker*, 6th edn. (3 vols.; Dublin and Zurich: Weidmann, 1954)
D.L.	Diogenes Laertius, *Lives of the Philosophers*
FGrH	F. Jacoby, *Die Fragmente der griechischen Historiker* (3 vols.; Berlin: Weidmann, 1926–30)
EK	L. Edelstein and I. G. Kidd, *Posidonius*, i. *The Fragments*, 2nd edn. (Cambridge: Cambridge University Press, 1989)
PHP	Galen, *Placita Hippocratis et Platonis* = *On the Doctrines of Hippocrates and Plato*
RE	G. Wissowa *et al.* (eds.), *Paulys Real-Encyclopädie der classischen Altertumswissenschaft* (Stuttgart: J. B. Metzler, 1894–1978)
Schürer	Schürer (1973–87)
S.E., *M.*, *PH*	Sextus Empiricus, *Adversus mathematicos* = *Against the Professors*, *Pyrrhoneae hypotyposes* = *Outlines of Pyrrhonism*
Stern	Stern (1974–84)
SVF	*Stoicorum Veterum Fragmenta*, ed. J. von Arnim (3 vols.; Stuttgart: Teubner, 1903–24); vol. iv (indexes) by M. Adler

PART I

Ancient Wisdom: Stoic Exegesis

1

The Outlook of Primitive Man: Beginnings of a Theory

1. *From Hesiod to the Cynics*

This is a study of ancient perceptions of truth and philosophy, of the discovery and transmission of wisdom. It explores, in particular, a radical shift of emphasis in philosophical research which came about when the guiding assumption of earlier Greek thought, that philosophy had to build up to the truth by tentative progression from first principles, was challenged by the conviction that another and safer route was possible: a route which led backwards to an ancient account of the world whose truth could be established objectively. A reconstruction of this ancient philosophy would bypass the uncertainties and dangers involved in the traditional, 'progressive' approach to philosophy, and would cut through the disagreements and errors it inevitably entailed. An account of the truth already existed: a philosopher need only unearth and decipher it. In Chapters 2 and 3 I shall explore through the work of the Stoics some of the issues surrounding the manner in which the philosophy supposed to have existed in a previous age might be reconstructed, before going on in subsequent chapters to look in detail at the influence that this programme of reconstruction had on philosophy at large. But there is at the beginning a more fundamental question to address, namely the grounds for a belief that an earlier philosophy existed for the reconstruction at all. Why might anyone have believed that a privileged understanding of the world could be found in the outlook of earlier generations?

In so far as the purpose of Classical philosophy was, ultimately, to understand man's relationship with the world, and the means of achieving happiness within it, it is naturally of interest to note that a belief in the peculiar happiness of earlier generations—or, more specifically, of the *first* generations—of mankind was one that had roots deep in Greek mythology.[1] Such a belief did not, to be sure, form the only model to emerge from the rich tradition of speculation over the matter: according to one account, for example, it was only the ingenuity of mankind itself, assisted by arts stolen from the gods by Prometheus, that made human life possible, let alone bearable, at all.[2] Yet it was a popular theme, explored in a number of ways. Hesiod provides early evidence for two of these, woven together at *Works and Days* 106–201: the myths of the races of man,[3] and of the Cronian age.[4] According to the former account, the first generation of man was created as a 'golden race', superior to the silver, bronze, and iron generations that followed;[5] in the latter, the human race was born into a period of bounty and ease under the benevolent rule of Cronus. As far as the theme of this study is concerned, however, the imagery of these accounts will be far more important than their message. Read as allegories for human nature or society, these myths tell us nothing

[1] Much of the material relating to the Greeks' view of early human history has been discussed in works concerned with the notion of 'progress' and 'decline' in Greek thought. A good source-book is Lovejoy and Boas (1935); cf. also Guthrie (1957), Edelstein (1967), and Dodds (1973). For the myths of Prometheus and of the races of man in particular, see Fritz (1947); Gatz (1967).

[2] The earliest trace of this myth occurs in Hesiod, *Theogony*, 561–9; cf. *Works and Days*, 47–52. See also [Aeschylus], *Prometheus Bound*, 436–506 (with Kleingünther 1933: 66–84; and O'Brien 1985). In Plato, *Protagoras*, 320 C–322 D (esp. 321 D–E), Prometheus is said to have passed on the gifts of Athene (i.e. wisdom) and Hephaestus (i.e. fire); and elsewhere these gods are directly responsible for the benefactions (both together at e.g. *Homeric Hymn* 20; Athene alone at e.g. Cornutus, *Introduction*, 20, 39. 12–40. 4 Lang).

[3] For the pre-Hellenic roots of this myth see Griffiths (1956) and (1958) (*contra* Baldry 1952 and 1956); West (1978), 172–7.

[4] See, apart from Hesiod as cited, the *Alcmeonis* fr. 7 Davies (at p. 140; cf. Kinkel p. 313): *κα[ὶ τῆς ἐπ]ὶ Κρόνου ζω[ῆς εὐ]δαιμονεστά[της οὔ]σης, ὡς ἔγραψ[αν Ἡσί]οδος καὶ ὁ τὴν [Ἀλκμ]εωνίδα ποή[σας] καὶ Σοφοκλῆς*. (For Sophocles, Davies cites a fragment of the *Inachus*, F 278 Radt.) The myth itself seems to be somewhat earlier than Hesiod: cf. Baldry (1952), 84–6.

[5] Between the bronze and iron ages Hesiod inserts into what was, presumably, the original scheme an additional, heroic race—which stands out not only because it is not named from a metal, but also because it, uniquely, is *better* than the race that went before it. The simpler scheme (without a heroic interlude) is found in Orphic tradition as well (see Orpheus fr. 140 Kern = Proclus, *On Plato's* Republic, 2. 74. 26–30 Kroll)—although it seems likely that this version of the myth is rather a reorganization of Hesiod's account than an independent witness for its earlier history (cf. Gatz 1967: 52–3; West 1983: 107).

at all about *early* man as such;[6] and read as historical theses they describe a state in which human happiness is made a function of external benefits wilfully supplied or withheld by the gods: they imply nothing about the way in which early man *understood* the world that could, even in principle, be of interest or use to later philosophers. It was, for example, the bounty of nature guaranteed by Cronus that made mankind happy under his beneficent rule, not the ethical life or outlook of early men themselves; the hardship of our own lives is likewise the result of the disruption of the natural world at large consequent on Zeus' accession.[7] And, while man's happiness is at least made a function of his own nature in the myth of the races of man, it is still not subject to human control or related to human understanding. The golden race, for example, was *created* golden, born as it were to privilege; the iron race to which we now belong is inferior because it was *created* inferior. The fault remains with god; there is nothing we can do to improve our lot or become more 'golden'. Far from being able to exploit the model provided for us by the golden race, we can only derive from a contemplation of their happiness the understanding that such a state is beyond the grasp of our own, 'iron' race altogether. All we can do is to wish, with Hesiod, that we had ourselves been created as different beings (*Works and Days*, 174–5).

But if the earliest mythological accounts placed human nature too much at the whim of the gods for a knowledge of our created state to be of much value to us now, later Presocratic speculation refigured (or even abandoned) the notion of divine 'creation' in a way that tended to deny a privileged status to our earliest ancestors at all.[8] As the 'physicists' started to look for stable

[6] Such interpretations might include that of Hesiod himself: at least the city described at *Works and Days*, 225–37, shortly after the myth of the races of man, implies the possibility of a 'golden' existence for contemporary man, so long as he practises justice. (In fact a great deal of the imagery associated in later literature with the golden age comes from this passage and not the earlier account of the golden race itself.) Cf. also Plato, *Republic*, 3, 415 A–C, and *Cratylus*, 398 A–B: here, the different *races* of mankind described diachronically by Hesiod stand for a synchronic description of the three main *types* of human character.

[7] Similarly again, in the myth of Pandora it is the gods who control our (un)happiness: cf. Hesiod, *Works and Days*, 69–105; *Theogony*, 570–612.

[8] This dichotomy admittedly simplifies the historical situation, and a range of possibilities lie between its poles: Empedocles, for example, was able to incorporate into his own account of human evolution something resembling a primitive golden age (cf. 31 B 128, 130 DK). Cf. also Vlastos's comment on the 'well-known inde-

principles which could be deduced as explanations of the world from the varied phenomena of our experience, an anthropomorphic model of divine agency gave way to a model in which god's activity was identified *with* (rather than located within) the universe at large,[9] leading to a radical rethinking of the nature of the relationship between mankind and god. The deity was depersonalized to an extent that excluded a notion of divine involvement with human affairs;[10] and, if this safeguarded us from the wilful spite of the gods, it removed, by the same token, any expectation that one generation might be shown their particular favour. Albeit for different reasons, there was in Presocratic thought no more basis than there was in the mythology that preceded it for believing that an investigation of earlier generations might provide any sort of pattern for life that later philosophers could follow.[11] In order for this to become possible, a different model again of divine activity would be needed: one which reasserted the interest of god in humanity without reverting to the anthropomorphism of the poets; one in which mankind was created as such, but created by a providential god whose nature would not allow him to create anything imperfect, or to change for the worse his creation.

It was just such a theory of providence that emerged in the fifth and fourth centuries BC; and the ethical implications of what is,

cision as between teleology and mechanism in Anaxagorean thought' (1946: 57). Vlastos points to 59 B 4 DK in particular, where the first men are not just born into a world where the earth provides them with plenty, but are even born with the trappings of civilization: *καὶ τοῖς γε ἀνθρώποισιν εἶναι καὶ πόλεις συνῳκημένας καὶ ἔργα κατεσκευασμένα ὥσπερ παρ' ἡμῖν.*

[9] An originative substance whose nature is supposed to account for movement and change in the universe, and, ultimately, for the formation of our world, is identified with the divine, e.g. by Anaximander (12 A 15 DK), Anaximenes (13 A 10 DK); cf. already Thales (11 A 22 DK); and later Heraclitus (22 B 32, 64, 114 DK—taking the 'divine law' to refer to the nature of the universe at large in the last fragment); Xenophanes (21 B 23–6 DK; [Aristotle], *On Melissus, Xenophanes, and Gorigas*, 3–4).

[10] God might, that is to say, arrange the universe as a whole for the best, but not in a way that takes account of what is 'good' for individual people or races within it. For the potential conflict between universal teleology and the parochial interests of humanity cf. Heraclitus, 22 B 102 DK.

[11] For Presocratic accounts of human evolution cf. e.g. Anaximander, 12 A 30 DK. Xenophanes is presumably rejecting a 'mythological' notion of divine involvement when he says that the gods left it to man to improve his own lot (21 B 18 DK; compare the situation later on in Democritus' wholly atheistic materialism: 68 B 144, 154 DK).

on the face of it, a primarily physical or theological theory were immense. For if man was *created* by a *providential* god, it follows that he must have been created happy; furthermore, it follows that his happiness must reside in the perfection of his own created nature. A providential god would not, for example, create a being whose happiness relied on the presence of external factors he was not prepared to guarantee. If, then, the first men were happy and later generations were not, the fault must lie entirely with them: they must have the same potential and the same advantages, and if *anyone* was ever happy (as the hypothesis of divine providence implies that they were), then *everyone* (under the same hypothesis) has the ability to be so. Within the context of this theory, Hesiod's myth of the *races* of man was reinterpreted as a history of the human moral condition:[12] from a serial taxonomy of human species more or less wilfully created and destroyed by the gods, the story became one of the *corruption* of a race, the decline of its members from virtue. According to this theory, we all have the potential to gain membership (metaphorically speaking) of the golden race that must once have existed: it is our own negligence that transmutes into a baser metal the gold within ourselves. But now, at last, the study of the earliest men becomes genuinely interesting and useful: if the first men lived happily as god had intended, they might in some sense constitute a pattern for us to follow. A historical interest in the life of the earliest men comes in this way to have real importance in the realm of ethical research.

One of the earliest ethical movements which exploited this opening was Cynicism, a school which grew out of the philosophy of Socrates. Perhaps the most characteristic feature of Cynical philosophy was its absolute denial that one's happiness relied in any way on one's physical circumstances: happiness, said the Cynics, should never be confused with pleasure, and physical comfort could only provide the latter—the former was constituted by virtue alone, a correct *mental* attitude to the world. And to support their claims they argued in this way: the life of early man, they supposed, must have been physically demanding, because man lacked at that time

[12] The formal reworking of Hesiod's myth into an account of the *ages* (rather than the *races*) of mankind was a Roman development: see esp. Baldry (1952), 87–90. But the interpretation that this relies on was current much earlier: we shall see that Aristotle's pupil Dicaearchus, for example, used the myth as evidence for a three-stage account of human history.

the various arts which we have developed precisely to make ourselves more comfortable; but god could not have created man imperfect or unhappy; therefore it follows that man can be happy even in the absence of physical comfort.[13] Indeed, the Cynics went further than this, reasoning that the hardship inherent in the life of early humanity actually *helped* people then to be happy, by ensuring that they would never confuse happiness with pleasure—a guard which their ingenious descendants lacked, much to their disadvantage.[14]

For the Cynics, then, the happiness of the first men was constituted not by any difference from us in their essential character, but by a difference in their outlook and approach to life: it was, in the end, their value system that made them happier. And in consequence, we find in the Cynics, perhaps for the first time, the implicit recognition that to reconstruct something of the thought processes of early man will be a way of finding a cure for our own moral malaise, of pushing forward our own philosophical understanding. According to the Cynics, primitive man knew how to live, if he knew nothing else, and the authority of his knowledge was as objectively certain as the fact of Providence itself—was, in fact, an obvious deduction from the existence of a provident god. With the Cynics, it starts to become clear why someone might have invested the outlook of the first men with an authority which made it worth reconstructing: whether or not the first men were aware of it at the time, they were already in possession of what was to become a large part of the object of later philosophical research.

2. *Two Theories of Primitive Happiness in Plato*

The Cynics supposed that the first generations of men must have been happy, and that their happiness must have been constituted

[13] In an encomium on the Cynical life (*Dissertation* 36 Trapp) written in the 2nd cent. AD, Maximus of Tyre suggested that mythology depicted the bounty of nature under the reign of Cronus not because nature ever was, in fact, more plentiful than it is now, but simply because early man lacked our sense of greed, and so was *content* with what there was.

[14] According to one report, Diogenes of Sinope, the founder of Cynicism, argued that we miss the point of the myth of Prometheus if we think that Zeus is the villain of the piece. In fact, he said, Prometheus deserved his punishment, as his introduction of the arts of 'civilization' enervated man and helped to cause his moral decline (Dio Chrysostom, *Oration* 6. 21–9).

by the purity of their outlook on the world; and I have suggested that this represents the simplest beginnings of a belief that, in theory at least, there are philosophical questions, in particular the question of what constituted human happiness, which could find a solution in a reconstruction of the thought of the earliest men. But the Cynics, it is important to note, did not think that early men were themselves in possession of *philosophy* as such, in so far as philosophy was a self-conscious, technical study which, by its nature, aimed at a *cure* for the disease affecting our understanding of the world. The first men had nothing to cure and, one supposes, no conception of the moral ills with which a person might be afflicted. Their privilege lay in their *innocence*: at least as much in their lack of false beliefs (e.g. false beliefs about the value of material comfort) as in the truth of their assumption that only virtue conduces to happiness. The Cynics in fact seem to have supposed that early man lived well not because of philosophy, but because he possessed a kind of *pre*-philosophical outlook. As we shall see, such a distinction (between a philosophical and a pre-philosophical life) was to become important in the thought of Plato and his successors as well; but, while it was an easy conclusion for the Cynics, it was one at which Plato only arrived at length and with some difficulty.

Plato, like the Cynics, believed in a provident god; like the Cynics, then, he could not assume that mankind was created in any way imperfect. If people became vicious and unhappy, that would have to be explained by their own corruption of the nature with which god had created them. However, Plato could not so readily suppose with the Cynics that the happiness of early mankind was constituted by the mere *absence* of false beliefs, for one very simple reason. Plato, unlike the Cynics, believed that all humans had, as part of their psychology, an *innate* tendency towards vice, a non-rational faculty of the soul which tended to pull men towards pleasure *rather than* virtue, and so to pull them away from happiness quite independently of any beliefs they might hold. So, for Plato, an important component of virtue became the *achievement* of virtue against this tendency: virtue could never be quite automatic, and even the earliest men could not be actually *unaware* of the possibility of vice, as the Cynics had supposed. Plato might have conceded that the rise of a technological civilization, with the culture of greed it brought with it, would make it *more difficult* to resist the inclination to vice; but the inclination itself had always been a part of human nature.

The problem to which this now gave rise is highlighted in the *Timaeus*, a dialogue which discusses the created nature of the world quite generally, but more particularly the place of mankind within it. And Plato's account of happiness in this dialogue is, as such, very straightforwardly linked to his psychological theory. Human motivation, he reminds us, is characterized by a struggle between reason and emotion (42 A–C), and happiness is the reward for the virtuous man, the man in whose soul reason (the pull to the good) wins out over passion. Someone who loses his soul to passion is condemned to unhappiness (and successively more degrading forms of reincarnation: 42 B–C). The moral point of this story is very clear: reason needs to be trained and exercised if happiness is to be achieved. Philosophy, to put this another way, is a prerequisite for well-being. But here is the problem: for it follows from all of this, either that the first men were philosophers, or that they were not happy. But how could the first men have been expected to become philosophers by their own efforts? yet how could god have created them if there was a reasonable chance they would fail to become happy?

The problem is one that is raised in the *Statesman* as well. In the course of this dialogue Plato draws on Hesiodic imagery to depict a world ruled in alternate cycles by Cronus and Zeus (*Statesman*, 269 C–274 D). The reign of Cronus is described (in obviously Hesiodic terms) as a kind of golden age, in which Cronus himself plays an active part in governing the world, and every region and group of men is under the tutelage of a heavenly daemon; in which the needs of men are provided for, food is available in abundance and without cultivation, clothes are unnecessary for the most part, and nature in general forms a benign and congenial environment. Furthermore, since every man has all that he needs, and since each generation of men is born anew from the earth without an accumulated heritage of political affiliation, savagery in general is unheard of and wars do not exist. There is, however, a literal and figurative reversal during the reign of Zeus: god relinquishes the helm, the daemons depart from the provinces that were in their care, and the world is left to fend for itself. At this point all of the hardships that we associate with life come about (272 D–273 D).[15]

The contrast between the eras of Cronus and Zeus is as stark as its imagery makes it familiar, so it comes as a surprise to the reader when the 'Eleatic Stranger' who directs the discussion asks the young Socrates in which of the two periods mankind was happiest—under the reign of Cronus or of Zeus? The answer seems so obvious that the question appears rhetorical; and yet, Socrates does not take it to be so. Indeed, he replies that he is in no position at all to answer it. And his surprising response is endorsed by the Eleatic Stranger himself, who *agrees* that he had not given us enough information to know (see 272 B–D): we have, he says, to drop the subject 'until we find someone qualified to tell us whether the men of the [Cronian] age were keen for knowledge and the cultivation of reason'—whether, in other words, they were philosophers. The Hesiodic imagery turns out to have been a red herring. Again, very clearly, the point is made that happiness depends on the cultivation of philosophy; no amount of physical comfort is an adequate substitute for that.

The *Statesman* offers no further comment, but leaves us instead with this hint at the problem we saw in the *Timaeus*. The first men (as all of us) need to develop philosophy in order to be happy—their happiness needs to be *won* through their own subjugation of their passions. Yet if the definition of happiness in these terms means that a man cannot be created with happiness (which has to come from his own struggles), it would seem to implicate god in the creation of a race which potentially at least might always be strictly imperfect. It is, in fact, to the *Timaeus* that we have to return to find Plato's first attempt at a solution. And the solution he proposes is this: god could not create a race of virtuous men without robbing them of the happiness that comes from *achiev-*

[15] There is no story of human improvement when the world reverts to the guidance of Cronus at the end of this age, since the human race is utterly annihilated as the world turns back (270 D–E), and a *new* race of men, unrelated to their immediate predecessors, is born afresh from the earth (271 A–C). (The species is continued into the age of Zeus through the act of procreation, which itself seems to be symptomatic of the general decline: 274 A.) Proclus, later on, interpreted the *Statesman* myth as representing two *aspects* of the world, rather than two historical stages of it: see *Platonic Theology*, 5. 6–8, esp. 7; and cf. Dillon (1995). For his own part, Dillon supposes that the whimsical features of the myth suggest that it is not to be taken seriously in its own right at all: it is rather a 'foil for his [i.e. Plato's] own more serious type of system-building' (1992: 33).

ing virtue; but what he could do was to create a race of men who were naturally *predisposed* towards philosophy. We can see from the very architecture of a human being, argues Plato, that in his natural state it is less than a matter of chance that a man would achieve happiness, without quite being a matter of necessity. From the eyes (which allow contemplation of the heavens in which philosophy finds its first impulse: 47 A–B) and the mouth (which through speech is a 'minister to intelligence': 75 E) to the lower belly and the bowels (designed to limit our intake of food and drink, and stop gluttony from making us 'unphilosophical': 72 E–73 A), everything inclines us to philosophy. There has to be a battle if the triumph of reason is to mean anything, but the battle between reason and emotion is, in man's natural state, weighted in this way in favour of reason. Vice necessarily remains a possibility for us; but, as Plato says, it is also a strictly *unnatural* state, a disease of the soul which only ever arises because of broadly external factors which disturb the original and natural order of things—bad education, for example, or bodily disorders which affect the capacity of reason (86 D–E). In the primitive absence of these cancers, everything was in favour of the first men. For all Plato's circumspection, it seems that he did in the end assume that providence made sure that the first men became philosophical—and so became virtuous and happy.

Yet all of this might leave us feeling slightly dissatisfied. The compromise of the *Timaeus* is slightly disingenuous, because the fact that vice can only creep in through *external* factors tends very strongly to the conclusion (which the compromise was intended to avoid) that early man *could not but* become happy, and that later men *could not but* become vicious any more than they could help succumbing to the influence of disease. However, if Plato's solution in the *Timaeus* has a disingenuous air, so too does the problem as described in the *Statesman*. Plato there said that we could not know on the information given whether mankind was happier under the reign of Cronus or under the reign of Zeus; and it is true that the abundance of material blessings which present themselves in the Cronian period might not weigh heavily in a philosophical assessment of the happiness of the age. But surely the absence of savagery and wars at that time points to a form of life which is in some sense, even some moral sense, superior to our own? Whether or not men were philosophers, the reader's natural instinct, to suppose that the Cronian age was the happier, is supported by more than a greedy hankering after material prosperity. Plato left one further account of human history, the last that he wrote, and in it he addressed these problems with a new and influential solution.

The model for the rise of human culture outlined in book 3 of the *Laws* is articulated, somewhat like that in the *Statesman*, around cycles of destruction and regrowth; but in the *Laws* the cosmic metaphors employed in the *Statesman* have been stripped away to leave a more literal historical thesis. Human culture, says Plato, is periodically wiped out by natural cataclysm, by 'floods, pestilences, and other causes' (*Laws*, 677 A). Some humans survive these disasters, but those who do can only be those who live well out of harm's reach in the mountains; and such people are by their very nature and removal from the centres of civilization unlikely to preserve elements of culture with themselves. Plato stresses this point: these survivors are wholly unversed in philosophy even to the extent (he says) of being ignorant of music (677 C–D). Human life as such is preserved through each cataclysm, but culture is destroyed in its entirety, so that each new cycle of history heralds a new 'primitive age' for mankind.

What is most striking in Plato's new account, however, is the enviable picture he paints of life in the primitive period at the beginning of each cycle. The men of this age, he says for example, are simple, and all their needs are catered for, so there is no poverty or strife or violence or envy (679 A–C). Indeed, he goes much further than this: their very ignorance and simplicity makes them 'more guileless, braver, more temperate, and altogether more just' (679 D–E: *εὐηθέστεροι δὲ καὶ ἀνδρειότεροι καὶ ἅμα σωφρονέστεροι καὶ σύμπαντα δικαιότεροι*). In stark contrast (or so, at least, it seems) to the *Timaeus* and *Statesman*, it is no longer philosophy that accounts for early man's happiness, it is, in a sense, its very absence. Rather as I suggested for the Cynics, Plato here supposes that primitive men acted well precisely because the possibility of acting badly never occurred to them: their piety was not founded on a theoretical understanding of god, and their virtue was likewise divorced from any enquiry into the nature of good and bad (679 C).

But then what has become of the claim, so central to Plato's ethical theory more generally, that virtue consists in the philosophical subjugation of the passions? The answer is suggested by the distinction I drew in discussing the Cynics between philosophical and 'pre-philosophical' virtue. For it turns out in *Laws* 3 that the 'virtue' of the early men is not *virtue* in its strictest sense at all, but *merely* the absence of vice, and on this distinction Plato's final solution rests. Plato is quite clear that virtue proper does not exist among these people—that it can only occur in the teleological context of a developed state (*Laws*, 3, 678 B). What Plato has done is to exculpate providence by allowing that man in his 'primitive', natural state (and by implication in his created state) was in no way imperfect, and that he lived with all the characteristics of virtue; but at the same time he maintains his creed that *perfection* as such, that *virtue itself*, requires philosophy. Philosophy still depends on effort and rewards those who pursue it; but for the first men at least, providence guaranteed a life of *pre-philosophical* happiness.

3. *Dicaearchus and Pre-philosophical Virtue*

Plato's discussion of early human history in *Laws* 3 was the last, and in many ways the most historically important, of his discussions of the matter, and his conclusion, that early man was possessed of an uncorrupt, but *pre*-philosophical view of the world, was, in the first place, the most widely adopted theory among philosophers who believed in the providential creation of man at all. This does not include Aristotle: as we shall see in the next chapter, he did adopt some aspects of Plato's cyclical account of human history, but he substituted for the work of providence a teleology which gave him reason to deny that mankind could be in any way better off at the beginning of a given historical cycle than at its end. But, oddly enough, it does include one of Aristotle's pupils. Indeed, Dicaearchus of Messene was one of the best-known advocates of something like the *Laws* theory of philosophical development, and placed it on a more explicitly theoretical basis than Plato himself had done.

We have only a modest collection of fragments representing the work of Dicaearchus,[16] but about a quarter of their total derive from one of his most original works, a cultural history of Greece (the title,

[16] See Wehrli (1944); Gaiser (1983), (1988). For Dicaearchus in general see E. Martini (1905); Wehrli (1968). The dates of Dicaearchus can only be conjectured on the basis of our knowledge that he was a pupil of Aristotle's and, more specifically,

Βίος Ἑλλάδος, more literally suggests a 'biography'), which traced the development of that nation from the earliest stages of human life down to Dicaearchus' own time.[17] It is, of course, the earlier stages of his history that interest us here, and Dicaearchus seems to have used as evidence for them the myth of the races of man as recorded by Hesiod (see fr. 49 Wehrli). This myth, he said, has been added to over the years, but its origins were presumably very ancient, and it seems to preserve at its core a reliable, and certainly a rational, account of the history of the early development of mankind.[18]

Following Hesiod, then, Dicaearchus identified the earliest stage of mankind as a kind of 'golden age'. But it was not, according to Dicaearchus, the unparalleled bounty of nature that gilded the times: claims in mythology to that effect are to be taken as a metaphor for the real situation, which was simply that men were content with such produce as nature did provide. It *seemed* an abundance to them, because they lacked the greed which characterizes our own attempts to force more and more out of the earth.[19] And this lack of greed, this contentment with what there was, meant that strife was unknown among men (they saw nothing worth fighting over); it

a contemporary of the Peripatetic Aristoxenus (fr. 8(*d*) Wehrli = Cicero, *Tusculan Disputations*, 1. 41). This suggests a floruit of around 310 BC (cf. E. Martini 1905: 547).

[17] It should be noted that Dicaearchus, like Aristotle, certainly believed in the eternity of the human race (cf. frr. 47–8 Wehrli), and, since there is no 'earliest period' of eternity, must have followed Aristotle (and, as it happens, Plato as represented in the *Laws*) in holding a cyclical account of human history. Cf. Wehrli (1944), 56, and Giglioni (1986), 641–3. We have one fragment from a book by Dicaearchus *On the Destruction of Man* (fr. 24 Wehrli = Cicero, *On Duties*, 2. 16) which suggests that, although natural disasters have been known to wipe out 'whole races of men', more lives are lost to warfare than to cataclysm. Perhaps, then, he believed that each race or nation of men was subject to its own cycles of growth and destruction—that there was no *universal* cycle of history, but a complex of more local cycles which operated more or less independently of each other.

[18] Fr. 49, 24. 10–11 Wehrli: *εἰ δεῖ λαμβάνειν μὲν αὐτὸν ὡς γεγονότα καὶ μὴ μάτην ἐπιπεφημισμένον, τὸ δὲ λίαν μυθικὸν ἀφέντας εἰς τὸ διὰ τοῦ λόγου φυσικὸν ἀνάγειν.* There is too little material surviving to reconstruct any more general account of the origins of mythology in Dicaearchus. It does, however, make sense to suppose that he believed, much as Aristotle before him and after him the Stoics (the theories of both will be discussed in the next chapter), that traditional stories in mythology took their rise from perfectly straightforward historical or philosophical observations made at some point in the distant past which became embroidered into the nation's folklore as they were handed down through the generations.

[19] Cf n. 13 for a similar argument employed by the Cynics.

also meant that illness was unknown, because men (perforce) lived and ate with due moderation.

Greed, however, could not long stay out of the picture when the opportunities for the exploitation of nature became apparent to man, and it was greed that powered the decline of humanity through its second and into its third, and most degenerate, state. Men turned to a nomadic existence as they realized they could find more food by, as it were, casting their net wider—and, indeed, by casting off their previous adherence to a vegetarian diet. Finally, they discovered artificial ways of forcing a greater abundance of food out of nature than it would ever provide on its own, and the decline of humanity was completed by the development of farming communities around which human life settled.

Dicaearchus was in no doubt that the earliest men were the happiest, and he thinks that their happiness was a function of their own outlook and attitude rather than the material circumstances of their world (which, in fact, were no better than are available to us today). Yet Dicaearchus left no place for philosophy among the earliest men: indeed, he seems to have thought that theoretical philosophy was something which took its rise only when society became so corrupt that intelligence became divorced from the practical sphere to which it was proper. The virtue and happiness of the first men could not possibly be explained by appeal to the presence among them of *philosophy* as such, because philosophy only arose in its theoretical form out of the corruption of a later age. Drawing, then, on the distinction that I traced in Plato's *Laws*, Dicaearchus attributed to early man a different kind of happiness: not the happiness which comes with a philosophical achievement of virtue (and which, in principle, is available to us), but a more innocent, unselfconscious, and, above all, *pre*-philosophical happiness, which could only come from a virtue that had no awareness of the possibility of vice. Dicaearchus was at pains to explain that we should say of early men that they *lived well*, and yet were not *philosophers* (fr. 31, 19. 15–17 Wehrli):

> Dicaearchus did not think that even these [Pythic sayings] were the words of *wise* men [σοφοί]: for he thought that the ancients did not engage in verbal philosophy. 'Wisdom' in their age meant the exercise of good deeds—only later did it turn into an art of jostling words [χρόνῳ δὲ λόγων ὀχλικῶν γενέσθαι τέχνην].

That Dicaearchus wanted to put the distinction we have already seen in Plato on a more theoretical footing is shown by his very precise use of language in this area—both here and also in fr. 30 (from D.L. 1. 40), where he says that even the 'Seven Sages' were not really *sages*, let alone *philosophers* in his sense at all: they were certainly intelligent, but they used their intelligence for practical rather than theoretical ends. 'Dicaearchus says that they [the Seven Sages] were not *wise* men or *philosophers*, but that they were *intelligent* men and *lawgivers* [συνετοὺς δέ τινας καὶ νομοθετικούς].'[20]

It seems from all of this that philosophy as we now understand it was developed rather later even than the final stage in the historical decline of mankind. As late in the agricultural age as the Seven Sages men could live 'well' without needing to theorize about *how* to live well, could run a good state without needing to wonder whether or how a man should engage in politics (οὐ γὰρ ἐζήτουν ἐκεῖνοί γε εἰ πολιτευτέον οὐδὲ πῶς, ἀλλ' ἐπολιτεύοντο αὐτοὶ καλῶς: fr. 31, 19. 20–1 Wehrli). The change in this state of affairs and the rise of philosophy tell us as much about earlier man as they do about ourselves. Dicaearchus maintained against his contemporary Theophrastus that the 'practical' life was preferable to the 'theoretical' (fr. 25 Wehrli = Cicero, *Letters to Atticus*, 2. 16. 3), but the age had become so corrupt, he thought, that philosophy was now the only refuge for the wise. And from all of this we can see how philosophy, made essential today, was superfluous in a former age which was blessed with a simpler route to happiness.

Dicaearchus, then, provides us with valuable evidence that the distinction between philosophical and pre-philosophical happiness did not die with Plato: that, despite the intervention of Aristotle, and even among Aristotle's own followers, the account remained strong into the Hellenistic era. And this is important because, as we shall see, its adoption and further theorization by the Stoics formed the basis for their development of a theory to reconstruct something of the privileged outlook it ascribed to primitive man.

[20] Cf. Cicero, *On Duties*, 3. 16, and *On Friendship*, 7: 'Subtler enquirers into the question refuse to number the so-called Seven [i.e. the Seven Sages] among the wise.'

4. *The Early Stoics on Early Man*

Our evidence for the early Stoics' adoption of a theory of pre-philosophical wisdom in the tradition of Plato's discussion in the *Laws* is all, regrettably, more or less indirect. Such considerations as there are, however, amount to a very strong case for the position that they too believed that the first generations of mankind possessed a unique and privileged, but pre-philosophical, understanding of the world. It seems plausible in the first place to suppose that the Stoics might have been sympathetic to a view commonly held, in some form, by the Cynics, by Plato, and even by some Peripatetics;[21] as I shall suggest further below, it is a view that in any case follows from their own theory of human rationality. But it is a view, furthermore, which explains the position adopted by Seneca in the 90th of his *Moral Epistles*.

Seneca, *Epistle* 90, is not directly about the early Stoics' views on early mankind: its immediate purpose is to attack the claims made by the *later* Stoic writer Posidonius concerning, primarily, the invention of the technological arts. Posidonius believed that these arts were developed by early philosophers; Seneca disagrees. This much is clear and not subject to doubt. But there is a great deal in the letter about the nature of early mankind more generally which forms the background to this discussion: and what is less clear is Seneca's stance on the matter. (Seneca naturally assumes rather more familiarity with the general issues of the debate among his readers than we can claim for ourselves.) But it seems to me reasonable to take the fact that Seneca is attacking Posidonius at all to suggest (at least as a starting-point) that his position on this matter comes close to that of the earlier Stoics; and that the early Stoics believed (unlike Posidonius) that the first generations of men lived in pre-philosophical innocence.[22] But in order to begin untangling Seneca's position, it will be helpful to present in outline the argument of the letter:

Introduction (1–3)

Philosophy is what allows us to live well.

[21] And it may be relevant to note that Zeno of Citium was philosophically active in Athens from 312 or 311 BC—just at the time of Dicaearchus' floruit (see again n. 16).

[22] With my reading of this letter, and my identification of Seneca's position with that of the early Stoics, compare Frede (1989), 2088–9.

Outline of the history of early man (4–6)

Stage 1: The first generations of men were uncorrupt (*incorrupti*), and lived under the direction of naturally pre-eminent leaders (this is why Posidonius says that they were under the rule of the wise) (4–5).

Stage 2: Vice steals in (6).

Criticism of Posidonius (7–35)

Posidonius: believes that philosophers invented the various arts—and afterwards withdrew from such banausic concerns (esp. 20–3, 30).

Seneca: argues that the arts were indeed the product of reason, but not of right reason (i.e. wisdom) as such. Nature is bountiful enough to allow us a good life without the need for technology; and wisdom is a matter of understanding and living in accordance with god and nature (esp. 7–19, 24–9, 35).

Conclusion: definitive sketch of early human history (36–46).[23]

Stage 1: the first men lived in *fortunata tempora*, before vice and luxury. They were not wise, but acted as wise men would. The earth was more fertile for being untilled. Men were not *sapientes* (nature does not bestow virtue: virtue has to be acquired), but they were 'lofty in spirit and (so to speak) fresh from the gods' (36–8 + 39–44).[24]

Stage 2: the rise of avarice and the decline of mankind into degeneracy (38–9).

As I have presented it, the argument of this letter is quite straightforward: Posidonius thought that mankind began in a kind of golden age, in which people were ruled well by philosophers. But the philosophers, in trying to make man's life more comfortable,

[23] There is a crux in 90. 36 at the point where this conclusion, as I am taking it, begins. The MSS read †*sicutaut*† *fortunata tempora*, emended by Bücheler to *secutast fortunata tempora*. This reading has been the most widely adopted, but it confirms the impression that the two periods that Seneca describes in what follows should be added to what comes before to create a three-stage account. However, it turns out that the *fortunata tempora*, which is clearly a pre-philosophical stage, would have to constitute the *first* stage on anyone's account—and it does not at all differ from what has gone immediately before. Numerous other emendations of the text have been suggested: cf. the discussion at Beltrami (1927), p. xl. My own understanding of the letter as a whole would suggest something like *sic erant fortunata tempora* (cf. Blankert 1940: 71). This would mark the beginning of a summary of Seneca's beliefs (and a two-stage account), which makes perfect sense in its own right, and which Seneca would now be in a position to expound after his refutation through the preceding chapters of Posidonius' version.

[24] Seneca's phrase (*a dis recentes*) has a number of precedents, where the metaphorical sense of the excellence of early men indicated is explained by a literal proximity to their divine roots. So Plato, *Laws*, 948 B 5–7; cf. *Critias*, 120 D–121 C; *Philebus*, 16 C 8; also Dicaearchus fr. 49, 23. 33–24. 3 Wehrli; and, later on, Cicero, *Laws*, 2. 27; *Tusculan Disputations*, 1. 26.

invented the various arts which led to the rise of avarice, the decline into decadence, and the general loss of virtue. Seneca, for the early Stoics, likewise believes that there were two stages to early human history, but (rather like Plato, for example) he thinks that none of the men in the first stage were philosophers as such:[25] they were not (he says) *wise* (*sapientes*) and were not (therefore) virtuous, strictly speaking;[26] but they lived well in a pre-philosophical sense, doing what wise men should do (*faciebant facienda sapientibus*: 90. 36). The *potential* for philosophy and virtue was given by god, says Seneca (echoing Plato, of course), but virtue itself, as something that had to be won, could hardly be expected to have existed among the earliest men (*non enim dat natura virtutem: ars est bonum fieri*: 90. 44). It follows that people invented the arts not because they were philosophers (perhaps, even, because they were not philosophers) but simply because they had the rational capacity to do so. But Seneca finishes in agreement with Posidonius over the second stage of history: that the invention of the arts had the effect of promoting avarice and vice, and of causing the decline of mankind into its present sorry state.[27]

[25] Cizek (1963: 205–7) supposes, as I do, that the pre-philosophical *fortunata tempora* described at 90. 36–8 represent early Stoic doctrine—but for rather different reasons. Cizek does not see this passage as history, but argues that it has an essentially moral import, and therefore comes from the writer of a Stoic Utopia. Since, as he thinks, Posidonius was not interested in political Utopias, he links the passage with Zeno's *Republic*.

[26] Part of the idea behind this may be that it only makes sense to talk about virtue where there is vice with which it can stand in contrast (a point made in Hine 1995). However, Seneca seems quite clear that these primitive men had a character that was *different* from the character of virtue. It is not just that it makes no logical sense to talk about virtue in the absence of vice; it is also (or rather) that virtue of its nature is something that has to be won *against* vice. So *Epistle* 90. 44: *non enim dat natura virtutem: ars est bonum fieri*. Similarly with philosophy (which is, of course, the 'art of becoming good' referred to here): it is part of the character of a sage that he has had to struggle to win his wisdom. So again 90. 44 (of the term *sapiens*): *in opere maximo nomen est*.

[27] Edelstein (1967: 137–8) has questioned whether the Stoics believed in a golden age at all on the basis of one of a series of arguments against the eternity of the world reported from Theophrastus by Philo of Alexandria (*On the Eternity of the World*, 130–1 =part of fr. 184 Fortenbaugh), but ultimately, he thinks, deriving from Zeno (and cf. *SVF* i. 106; also Zeller 1876; Pearson 1891: 110–14, ad fr. 56; Regenbogen 1940: 1539–40; Pohlenz 1959: ii. 44, ad i. 77. 28). This argument reaches its conclusion by appealing to the relatively recent invention of the arts: but the human race can be *no older* than the arts (since the arts are necessary for human survival); hence the world cannot be eternal. In fact it is not clear, even if this argument were Stoic in origin, that there would be any real conflict with

This is my reading of the letter, and it is, I think, by far the most straightforward way of taking it. According to this reading, Seneca believes (and provides evidence that the early Stoics believed as well) that the first generations of man lived in a state of pre-philosophical harmony with nature. But there are problems within the text that I have so far avoided—problems which threaten to undermine the opposition between Seneca and Posidonius on which my identification of the early Stoic view rests. For Seneca actually looks, at one point, as if he is *agreeing* with Posidonius' claim that early man was under the direction of sages—the opposite, as I am claiming, of what he (and the early Stoics) believed. At the beginning of 90. 7, after Posidonius' account of the earliest men, Seneca says just this: *hactenus Posidonio adsentior*. Now I have suggested that Seneca here—as often in his writings—is representing the views of the early Stoa; but it is true that his philosophy elsewhere is influenced by the later Stoic views of Panaetius and Posidonius, so it has struck many commentators as reasonable to use this remark to conclude that Seneca's views about the history of mankind as expressed in *Epistle* 90 need to be brought into greater conformity with those of Posidonius. Unfortunately it is not so easy to make this reconciliation. Perhaps the least complicated suggestion is to suppose that Seneca meant something weaker by the word 'wise' at the beginning of his letter than he did at the end, so that both passages (and both Seneca and Posidonius) concur in the belief that, in the early period of human history, there were philosophers *only in a loose sense of the word*.[28] But this reading cannot, I think, be

the account of early human history I am ascribing to the early Stoics (the claim for the equal antiquity of arts and men from which Edelstein deduces the absence of a pre-technical golden age might, for example, be a convenient simplification for the sake of the argument's rhetoric). And in any case Sedley (1998) has now convincingly shown that Theophrastus was (and in fact must have been, for reasons of chronology) using a *pre*-Stoic source. The Stoic language of the fragment is presumably due, not to its original formulation, but to Philo of Alexandria himself (cf. Sedley 1998: 333).

[28] So Hirzel (1877–83), ii. 286–8 with n. 1 at 288–9, followed by Blankert (1940), 89–96. One of Hirzel's arguments is that Seneca refers to Solon as a *sapiens* at *Epistle* 90. 6, although it is unlikely that Posidonius thought of Solon as a 'wise man' in the strictest sense, since we know that he thought even Socrates was only in a state of moral *progress* (see D.L. 7. 91). This is a suggestive argument, but not by any means a watertight one. It relies, for one thing, on the assumption that the reference to Solon in *Epistle* 90. 6 comes from the mouth of Posidonius—which need not be true, even if the argument it illustrates does. But, more than

supported. We know for a fact that at least some later Stoics believed that there were early human beings who were philosophers, and there are good reasons to think that Posidonius was one of them (this is something I shall discuss in Chapter 3). Furthermore, it is one thing for Seneca to allow himself broader strokes of his brush in the assumption that his audience would be familiar with the outlines of the debate, but quite another to allow so glaring an ambiguity to lie unexplained at the heart of his argument.

If Seneca and Posidonius cannot be reconciled in the belief that early men were *not* philosophers, then perhaps they can be reconciled in the view that they *were*? Another interpretation of the letter argues that Seneca and Posidonius *both* thought that some of the earliest men were philosophers, disagreeing only over the subsidiary question of whether philosophy, as such, was behind the invention of the arts. It is true (so this interpretation goes) that Seneca makes a distinction between early men who were philosophers and those who acted as virtuous men would without the need for philosophy, and it looks as if he is opposing the two views: but this impression is misleading. In fact, both Posidonius and Seneca believed both things: both thought that there were not two but *three* historical stages in the development of mankind. The first period is occupied by the 'scattered men' mentioned in 90. 7, and designated as the 'fortunate times' at 90. 36: this was a *pre*-philosophical period, when nature was so abundant that men were able to live without the support of formal communities; the second period was the golden age, characterized by the formation of communities for mutual protection and support, and placed under the leadership of the wisest men of the day; the third period was (and is) the age of vice and corruption. So why did we get the impression that there are *two* major stages of history (not three)? Because, according to this interpretation, Seneca tends to conflate the first two periods in his eagerness to focus on the real point at issue, namely the refutation of Posido-

this, it relies on the claim that this passage states Solon to have been wise. In fact it says something slightly more oblique: that Solon was 'one of the seven known for their wisdom' (*inter septem fuit sapientia notos*). The use of the word 'wisdom' here obviously need not rely on any particular philosophical standpoint: it might well be no more than a concession to the popular designation of the Seven Sages.

nius' claim that the wise men of the golden age were inventors of the arts.[29]

It is hard to believe that such a baroque reconstruction of Seneca's sequence of thought can be right: the solution it offers seems to be out of all proportion to the original problem. Indeed, it seems to me that both interpretations considered here have considerably overstated the difficulty in the first place. The root of this difficulty, to repeat, is that Seneca says he agrees with the Posidonian account of early man sketched in 90. 4–6. But does this have to mean that he agrees with *all* of it? The answer, it seems to me, is certainly not. At this stage of the argument the most important point introduced by Posidonius is not the specific claim that early men were philosophers, but rather his general model for the discussion of early human history: it is the belief in a golden age followed by a period of decline into vice initiated by the invention of the technological arts with which Seneca agrees, and not the claim that philosophers existed in the first of these periods. Indeed, the way in which Seneca introduces Posidonius' claim that they did makes it easy to see it as a parenthesis, an attempt to bracket it off from the main part of the narrative (with which, at this point, he is in agreement). At the beginning of the letter Seneca has described a 'golden age' when all people did as they ought, but the best of them acted as rulers—and *this*, he says, explains why Posidonius went on to believe (albeit wrongly) that they were actually philosophers (*illo* ergo *saeculo . . . penes sapientes fuisse regnum Posidonius iudicat*: 90. 5). When Seneca finally says that he agrees with Posidonius (in 90. 7), there is no pressing need to include this parenthesis in his agreement. He agrees with the model, with the claim that the best men ruled, with everything else, but not with this one parenthesis, which is there simply to explain (and so for now to explain away) Posidonius' false extension of the view that Seneca does hold. If it is objected that Seneca does nothing to refute this extension here, there is actually a very good reason for this. The issue in which Seneca is here interested is the question of whether philosophy was responsible for the invention of the arts, and he wants to be able to say that it was not, *whether or not there were any sages at this time anyway*. Sages, he says, would have had no incentive to invent the arts (90. 16); and even if they had

[29] So Bertoli (1982); cf. also Rudberg (1918), 51–70 (esp. 54); Heinemann (1921–8), i. 88–108; Pfligersdorffer (1982).

existed and done so, it would not have been *qua* sages that they did it (90. 31). Of course, the question of whether there were philosophers among early men will become relevant later on in the letter, and when it does, Seneca makes his position perfectly clear. When he summarizes his own beliefs at the end of the letter, he becomes very insistent in his description of early men living *like* sages, without *being* sages (90. 36); he becomes quite clear that man could not have been *created* wise (as Posidonius seems to suppose), but rather that wisdom is something that has to be won (90. 44).[30] In short, there is no real 'problem' in Seneca's agreement with Posidonius in 90. 7 at all: there is nothing here that cannot be explained by the natural logic and rhetoric of his argument.

Seneca, then, disagrees with Posidonius over the status of early man, and his disagreement seems best explained on the assumption that he is championing an earlier Stoic belief that the first generations of men lived in pre-philosophical innocence, in a privileged age before the rise of technology and the decline into vice and misery. The ascription of such a view to the early Stoics certainly has historical plausibility on its side, as I suggested above, since it would show how their views on this subject related closely to those of Plato, the Cynics, and Dicaearchus.[31] But it also makes excellent sense in the light of the Stoics' own theory of human nature and rationality. On a simple consideration of this, it turns out that the early Stoics (as we saw was the case with the Cynics) could hardly fail to believe that the earliest men had *no need* of philosophy.[32]

Earlier, I suggested that the reason why Plato had to face the question of whether early man possessed philosophy or not lay in

[30] The insistent polemic at the end of *Epistle* 90 makes good sense if it is aimed against the view I am attributing to Posidonius, that primitive men were (naturally) philosophers, but it lacks point if it is supposed to line up *with* Posidonius (i.e. with the supposed Posidonian view that the very first men were not philosophers).

[31] Hine (1995: 97–8) takes the unnecessary and cumbersome view that Dicaearchus was Seneca's immediate source for the idea of an age of pre-philosophical virtue—and that the idea played no part in earlier Stoicism at all; cf. also Theiler (1982) ii. 384–90 (ad fr. 448), esp. 390.

[32] Cf. Hays (1983), 5–20, who also suggests a theoretical basis for Stoic allegorical exegesis in the Stoic theory of concept formation. However, he fails to explain why an earlier people should have *more reliable* concepts than we do, and in fact seems to concede that the best the Stoics could hope for is the reconstruction of ancient *opinions* ('perceptions of reality' at 15; similarly Long 1992: 65).

his view of human psychology. According to Plato, we have a non-rational part to our soul which requires the control of reason to counteract its tendency towards indulgence and vice. But the Stoics, like the Cynics, believed that the soul was wholly and purely rational, and that vice was the product of false belief alone. And if we look at the way in which the Stoics thought that rationality develops in the human mind, it becomes all the clearer that there would be no openings for the introduction of false beliefs in the earliest men. According to the Stoics, rationality quite generally is constituted by a certain corpus of concepts. As rational animals, we are all in some way 'programmed' to acquire these concepts in the course of our natural development—hence they are called 'common concepts' (*κοιναὶ ἔννοιαι*), and are sometimes referred to as 'innate' or 'inborn' (cf. Plutarch, *On Stoic Self-contradictions*, 17, 1041 E; *On Common Conceptions*, 24, 1070 C). But, as we acquire these concepts, connections between them are supposed to be formed (for example, our concept of god is linked with our concept of benevolence); the connections result in 'theorems' (*θεωρήματα*), which provide the framework in terms of which all of our thinking can take place. But these theorems now have propositional content ('god is benevolent'), so it turns out that for someone to be rational at all already means that this person has a basic propositional understanding of the world. What is more, if the process happens naturally and as it ought, this understanding will be infallibly true. There is no motive at all in the natural situation for the development of philosophy as such, since a true and adequate understanding of the world is developed by entirely natural and unselfconscious means.

In an ideal situation, as I say, the rationality and understanding we acquire would be infallible, an undistorted reflection of the rationality which underlies the construction of the cosmos. But one of the very features of the Stoics' theory that ensures that this will be so also explains how it is that no one today does acquire such a pure rational outlook. We acquire our rationality by the interaction of an innate predisposition to form concepts with empirical information furnished by the world itself; but while this guarantees the connection between our rationality and the nature of the world in an ideal situation, it also means that we are prone to develop false ideas if our environment is itself distorted. For example, if we are brought up among people who already hold wrong beliefs, or imbue us with a false sense of the value of things, then that distortion will be reflected in our own rationality. (This, of course, is one reason why we know that the first men naturally acquired a perfect outlook: we know that there could not have been any influences in their upbringing which worked against nature.) And it is only when this happens, when rationality is distorted and our lives become unnatural and miserable as a result, that the incentive for philosophy arises, since philosophy is supposed to be a way of reorganizing our concepts into the correct articulation. There is, in short, no real need of philosophy until vice has made its appearance, so that in this way too we can see that there is good reason to doubt that the first men practised philosophy: somewhat like early man in Dicaearchus, they *lived* well, and as they lived well it did not occur to them to theorize about life.

5. *Conclusion*

Such evidence as we have all points to the fact that the early Stoics believed that mankind existed in rational, but pre-philosophical, harmony with the world. And with the Stoics even more than with Dicaearchus, Plato, and the Cynics, it is possible to see very clearly, on a highly theorized level, how this view implies the infallibility of their outlook. What might at first have seemed a surprisingly optimistic claim for our primitive ancestors turns out to be a straightforward deduction from what might naturally be supposed about god and, in the case of the Stoics, from a more technical consideration of the nature of human rationality as well. This answers the question I raised at the beginning of this chapter, namely how anyone could believe that an earlier generation of mankind might be expected to have had a privileged understanding of the world. But now the more difficult question is left: how might it be possible to find out what these men believed? Neither Plato nor Dicaearchus attempted to answer this question; for both of these philosophers, it seems, a contemplation of the history of human development might identify symptoms, or even causes, of mankind's decline into vice—to that extent it was useful; but there was no going back to an earlier stage of thought: philosophy would have to tackle the answers on its own.[33] The Stoics, however, came to

[33] It is worth making this point because it is easy to assume that Plato shows

believe that there did exist a channel through which thought which had its roots among the earliest men was, to a greater or lesser extent, preserved; and their development of a theory to exploit this channel represented the first important step towards the new theory of philosophy that was to be developed later on by the Platonists.

the respect that he does for a culture such as that of Egypt because he thinks that the antiquity of its wisdom points to a basis in a more privileged age. In fact he does not. Plato supposes that philosophy in Egypt took its rise some time after the end of the one period when man might have had a privileged understanding of the world, and that it is worthy of respect simply because it has been under development for much longer than the Greek philosophical tradition (this is explained by Egypt's geographical immunity to many of the cataclysms that affect other areas: cf. *Timaeus*, 22 D–E). Naturally the Egyptians invented and worked certain things out before the Greeks did: Plato suggests that the Egyptian god Theuth was the inventor of writing and the various branches of mathematics which, we would have to suppose, were thus a relatively late introduction into Greece: *Phaedrus*, 274 C–275 B; cf. *Philebus*, 18 B–D. But Egyptian philosophy is far from perfect, and Plato seems to think (and the author of the *Epinomis*, if different, says quite explicitly) that the very conservatism of the Egyptians, which protects them from the decadence evident in other cultures, at the same time prevents them from developing any branch of philosophy to perfection at all: see *Epinomis*, 987 D (and cf. Plato, *Laws*, 2, 656 D–657 B, for the conservatism of the Egyptians; also *Republic*, 4, 435 E–436 A, where the Greeks as a whole are characterized as 'lovers of learning' and *contrasted* to this extent with the Egyptians). Cf. also Aristotle: he considered the Egyptians important for their development of astronomy (*On the Heavens*, 2. 12, 292^{a}6–8); mathematics (*Metaphysics*, *Α* 1, 981^{b}21–4); even some aspects of political thought (*Politics*, 7. 10, 1329^{b}2–3; and see further *On Philosophy*, fr. 6 Rose, with Jaeger 1948: 128–9 for his interest in pre-Hellenic thought). But he explains these achievements, not by the ancient roots of the culture, but by the rather more mundane fact that the Egyptians were the first civilization to develop a class with the leisure for these studies (cf. again *Metaphysics*, *Α* 1, 981^{b}21–4). Aristotle himself held a 'progressive' view of Greek philosophy—and believed that he stood near the teleological pinnacle of its achievement himself (see esp. fr. 53 Rose=Cicero, *Tusculan Disputations*, 3. 69; cf. Edelstein 1967: 124–5).

2

The Recovery of Primitive Wisdom in Early Stoicism

1. *Introduction: Aristotle*

In the course of his discussion of the movers of the heavens in *Metaphysics Λ* 8, Aristotle breaks off to make the following observation (1074^{a}38–^{b}14):

> Fragments of the thought of the ancient, the very ancient thinkers have been handed down to us in the form of a myth, to the effect that these [sc. the planets] are gods, and that the divine embraces the whole of nature. The rest has been added later in a mythological form to influence the beliefs of the vulgar, for the benefit of the laws, and for pragmatic reasons. And they say that these [gods] are human in shape or are like some other animals, and add other things consequent on and similar to what has been said. If we separate out and take only the first claim, that they thought the first substances to be gods, we must regard it as a divine saying, and reflect that, since every art and philosophy has probably been repeatedly developed to the utmost and has perished again, these beliefs of theirs have been preserved as relics. To this extent only, then, can we see the opinion of our ancestors and of the first men.

This rather curious claim, that fragments of a perfected philosophy can be found at the heart of traditional mythology, may seem bold; but in fact it makes perfect sense when it is seen in the context of Aristotle's beliefs about the world in general and the course of human history in particular.[1] In fact, his account of human history has many points of contact with the theory suggested by Plato in

[1] Other texts relevant to Aristotle's belief that ancient wisdom can be recovered or duplicated include *On the Heavens*, 270^{b}16–20; *Meteorology*, 339^{b}27–30; and *Politics*, 7. 10, 1329^{b}25–9.

Laws 3: like Plato, for example, Aristotle believed that human history was cyclical, and that civilization was built up over the ages, only to be destroyed by natural cataclysm and set back to square one.[2] But underlying the structure they share is one significant difference: Aristotle's system as a whole was driven by a teleology in which a later stage of man's development must always be superior as such to an earlier state. Civilization, for Aristotle, was the end of human activity and also its perfection, so that, according to Aristotle, in disagreement with Plato, there could be *nothing* exceptional about the state of mankind at the beginning of each historical cycle: people at that time were not so much *pre*-philosophical as *un*philosophical, 'no better,' he says, 'than the ordinary or even the foolish people of today' (*Politics*, 2. 8, 1269ᵃ4–8).[3] So where are the ancient scraps of wisdom he finds in mythology supposed to have come from? Presumably from philosophy perfected *before* the last cataclysm: for the same teleological model that makes fools of humanity in its primitive state will tend to make finished philosophers among them in the end.[4] True, it is not the philosophers who survive (philosophers live in the heart of the civilization that is destroyed); but neither, thinks Aristotle, would those who did survive suffer from the total cultural amnesia envisaged by Plato (and necessary, in fact, for his account of their pre-philosophical innocence). The survivors might, for example, be expected to have known and preserved popular apothegms into which some of the wisdom of their time had been distilled (Aristotle, fr. 13 Rose):

Whether a 'saying' [παροιμία] counts as something wise: Why not? Aristotle says about them that they are remnants of an ancient philosophy [παλαιᾶς

[2] See esp. Aristotle, fr. 13 Rose, from his lost work *On Philosophy*. For a possible reconstruction of Aristotle's theory of the development of human culture see Grilli (1953), 4–6.

[3] This perhaps overstates the opposition a little: after all, Plato and Aristotle agreed on the most important point, which was that real or 'perfect' virtue was only possible in a fully developed political environment; and we saw in ch. 1 that Dicaearchus was able to incorporate a belief that the earliest men were pre-philosophically 'virtuous' into an Aristotelian framework. But if there is an overstatement here, it is more Aristotle's than mine: it is he who seems to insist that, if teleology takes us to a better state, it must have brought us from the opposite extreme.

[4] As we saw, Dicaearchus thought that a reliable account of the early development of mankind could be extracted from Hesiod's myth of the races of man (cf. fr. 49, 24. 10–11 Wehrli): this looks (reasonably enough) like exegesis in the same tradition as Aristotle. But note that it is history Dicaearchus reconstructs, not philosophy; and note that Hesiod's myth cannot represent a remnant of *pre*-cataclysmic insight, since it refers to the period *after* the cataclysm.

εἰσι φιλοσοφίας . . . ἐγκαταλείμματα] saved by their brevity and acuity when it was lost in the great destructions of mankind.

Through popular and memorable sayings, then, fragments of the advanced philosophy of a former civilization survived into our own cycle of history, and became preserved in the mythologies which grew up around them.

There is no evidence that Aristotle developed his theory of the survival of ancient wisdom very far, or even that he thought it could be fruitfully developed. There remains, after all, a limit to how much philosophy might be preserved in these 'sayings'—and the exegesis of mythology in an attempt to extract fragments of pre-cataclysmic wisdom from it is one enterprise which seems to have been absent from the Peripatetic syllabus.[5] But the theory is remarkably suggestive as a way of explaining the rise of mythological traditions and the peculiar mixture of wisdom, wit, theology, and fiction they contain. One would not have had to accede to Aristotle's particular account of human history to find his theory of mythology attractive: all one would need to believe is that, in mankind's dim and distant past, there had been people who somehow or other had a superior understanding of the world and the gods, and that the mythological tradition might be traced to the echoes of their wisdom. We know (from the last chapter) that the Stoic view of human history would be at least compatible with this; the Stoics also, as we shall see, displayed an interest in the philosophical exegesis of mythology, apparently claiming that it could be made to yield weighty insights into nature. Having read Aristotle, we do not

[5] Despite Jaeger's claim (1948: 130) that Aristotle 'laid the foundation of a collection of Greek proverbs' for just this reason. There are a number of difficulties with Jaeger's assertion. For one thing, it does not go without saying that Synesius (the author of the fragment just quoted) was quite accurate in attributing to Aristotle the strong-sounding claim that sayings are the 'remnants of an ancient philosophy'. Presumably Aristotle thought at best that *some* sayings were survivals, and the *Metaphysics* passage quoted earlier shows that early wisdom can become assimilated into quite a different medium by the time it reaches us. It is true that Aristotle wrote one work on (or a collection of?) sayings (D.L. 5. 26); but we have no evidence at all for its purpose. We do know, however, that collections of sayings made by pupils of Aristotle could contain wisdom with roots within our own historical cycle (as explicitly, for example, the saying mentioned by Dicaearchus at fr. 49, 24. 25–7 Wehrli); and that the genre was not in any case restricted to the Peripatetics (so e.g. Chrysippus at D.L. 7. 200; cf. frr. at *SVF* iii, p. 202; but for other Peripatetic collections of *Sayings*, see e.g. Theophrastus at D.L. 5. 45, with fr. 738 Fortenbaugh; cf fr. 710 Fortenbaugh; also Clearchus frr. 63–83 Wehrli).

require very much imagination to suppose that these two facts must be linked.[6]

2. *The Early Stoics and the Allegorical Exegesis of Mythology*

The Stoics' belief that traditional Greek mythology contained insights of value to the philosopher is something which has for a long time been a focus for scholarly interest, but which has, until recently, been almost universally misunderstood. Part of the problem has lain in the fact that the Stoics' approach to recovering these insights—in particular, the allegorical exegesis they applied to the older Greek poets—placed them as such in a tradition of reading the poets that went well beyond the philosophical and temporal confines of the Stoa. The ancients themselves believed that allegorical exegesis of Homer originated in the sixth century BC with Theagnes of Rhegium, but it may have had roots even earlier than this,[7] and the practice continued in an unbroken tradition that stretched well into the Middle Ages. And it is true that there is, throughout this tradition, a surprising level of continuity in the kinds of interpretation offered:[8] no wonder, then, if historians of the

[6] Cf. Long (1992), esp. 53, 65. The Stoics, he says, believed in a process of 'cultural transmission': from mythology they thought that they could recover 'evidence of how early people interpreted the world'. The connection between Aristotle's theory and that of the Stoics was already noted by Wehrli (1928: 56–8), but dismissed by Tate (1929*a*: 44–5), partly on the grounds that Aristotle thought that very little ancient wisdom could be recovered from mythology (but this is irrelevant to the theoretical question), and partly on the assumption that the Stoics would, like Aristotle, have had to hold a cyclical theory of human history in order to explain the existence of earlier wisdom. But this, as I have already indicated, and shall explain further below, is simply not true: the Stoics' theory of rationality itself, along with their belief in divine providence, could be used as the basis for an explanation of how an earlier state of mankind had access to superior insight.

[7] For Theagnes see 8 fr. 2 DK with Pépin (1958), 95–8, Détienne (1962), 65–7, and Lamberton (1986), 32, variously arguing that he may have been influenced by Pythagorean readings; and more generally for the Presocratics, Buffière (1956), 85–123. Cf. also Pherecydes of Samos (7 A 9, B 1a, 13a DK) for more early examples of allegorical exegesis (cf. Most 1993 for a foretaste of the method, if not the purpose, in Homer himself). Finally, for 'philosophical' views of the poetry of Homer among the Presocratics see Anaxagoras and Metrodorus (D.L. 2. 11); Democritus (68 B 21 DK; cf. B 18); and Plato's reference to 'those who read Homer allegorically' (ἐν ὑπονοίαις: *Republic*, 378 D; cf. Xenophon, *Symposium*, 3. 6).

[8] Cf. e.g. Pherecydes (7 B3 DK), where Zeus becomes Eros when he creates the world, a doctrine remarkably similar to Cornutus, *Introduction*, 25, 48. 5–9 Lang—although perhaps not coincidentally, as Kirk, Raven, and Schofield (1983: 62 ad fr. 54) suggest that this fragment contains 'palpably Stoic interpretation'. Pherecydes' principle that one god might be called by different names according to function (καὶ

subject have assumed that there was a certain continuity in the theory and motivation behind the practice as well. Furthermore, since a Homeric scholion tells us that Theagnes developed the approach as a means of rehabilitating the poems of Homer in particular, and defending them against charges that they presented a false picture of the gods (see 8 fr. 2 DK), and since some of our later texts are explicitly apologetic in their intent (the *Homeric Questions*, written in the period of the early Roman Empire, and attributed to someone named as 'Heraclitus', is a good example of the genre), it has naturally been supposed that this had always been the purpose of allegorical exegesis. Allegorical exegesis, according to this account, was meant either to justify the apparently rather blasphemous accounts of the gods sometimes found in ancient poetry,[9] or perhaps to vindicate the poets' account of the world which, in the eyes of contemporary science, had come to look rather jejune.[10] *A fortiori*, this is what the Stoics were doing as well: their interest in Homer and Hesiod, and the allegorical interpretations they offered of their poems, were a way of justifying their position at the centre of Greek culture—and were perhaps, as the Epicureans insinuated, a way of appropriating their authority for the doctrines of Stoicism too.[11] But if this account provides a convenient and unified historical model for our understanding of Greek allegorical exegesis, there are serious reasons to doubt that it is true. As we shall see below, there is very good evidence against the possibility that the Stoics viewed their exegesis as a form of apologetic; but there are also reasons to doubt that their predecessors viewed it in quite the way implied by this characterization either. The Presocratics certainly argued over how to read Homer, but it would be downright misleading to suggest that those who interpreted his theology more favourably did so *because he was Homer*—because they believed that Homer must stand beyond criticism. Despite the rather unhelpful

γὰρ Δὶς καὶ Ζὴν καὶ Δὴν καὶ Ζὰς παρὰ Φερεκύδῃ κατὰ κίνησιν ἰδίαν: 7 B 1 DK) was extended by the Stoics to the claim that *all* gods are in some sense aspects of one god (*SVF* i. 536, ii. 1070).

[9] Cf. (in addition to Pépin and Lamberton, cited in n. 7) Zeller (1892), iii/1. 345; Détienne (1962), 34, 61–3; Pfeiffer (1968), 9–10; also Buffière (1956), 20–1.

[10] Cf. Long (1992), 44; Most (1997) (for the Derveni papyrus in particular).

[11] So Tate (1929*b*), 144; Pépin (1958), 105, 125; Lamberton (1986), 11–16. For the Epicurean precedents to this argument see Philodemus, *On Piety*, col. 6. Cf. Cicero, *On the Nature of the Gods*, 1. 41 (which obviously relies on this passage), with Long (1992), 49–50; Obbink (1994), 111–14.

comparison (still regrettably common) between the role of ancient poetry in Greek society and the place historically held by the Bible in our own, Homer simply did not have a claim to this kind of authority *ex officio*, as it were.[12] If some of his interpreters were able to champion his theology against criticism, this is not because they felt that they had to defend it at all costs; it was rather because of what they believed Homer had, as a matter of fact, meant.[13] To put the point bluntly, they believed that Homer was a philosopher, that his interests were their interests, that a principle of charity would demand that one should look for ways of reading him which made best sense of his work. And if such a view of the ancient poets seems strange to us, we should remember that there was no early literature with which 'poets' such as Homer could be contrasted in a way that would allow the Presocratics to draw a distinction in their case between 'mere' poetry on the one hand and what would later be called 'philosophy' on the other. Indeed, the distinction between the aims of these two branches of wisdom was not clearly defined even in the fifth century, when physical and moral speculation was still commonly written in verse.[14] The Presocratics talked about Homer and

[12] Herodotus supposed that Homer and Hesiod were responsible for framing the Greek pantheon, 'giving names to the gods, determining their offices and powers, and describing their appearance' (*Histories*, 2. 53). But, if Herodotus takes them to have been iconographically influential, there is no suggestion even here that their account of the gods was philosophically privileged. And it is worth noting that other artists felt no compulsion to follow Homer's precedents in their depiction of mythological events: see Snodgrass (1998) (for visual arts); Fowler (1987), 3–39 (for early Greek lyric).

[13] It is in this context important to note that there is no evidence of any attack on Homer which *predates* the supposed response of Theagnes. Cf. Pépin (1958), 93–5, and Tate (1929*b*), 142 ('allegory was originally positive, not negative, in its aim'). We are of course *told* that Theagnes read Homer allegorically for apologetic purposes (8 fr. 2 DK); but we are told it by a source some 800 years later than Theagnes himself, one which does not even purport to be quoting him. Again, in Plato, *Republic*, 378 D, we are told *only* that there are some who read Homer 'allegorically' (ἐν ὑπονοίαις), *not* that they do this to answer his critics. It is Plato himself who hints at the potential for apologetic in these exegetes by bringing their interpretations into dialogue with his *own* criticisms of the poet.

[14] Cf. Most (1999). Note that Heraclitus in one fragment treats Hesiod with Pythagoras, Xenophanes, and Hecataeus as if all four lay in the background of his own tradition of thought (22 B 40 DK). Even Plato (though in this case, perhaps facetiously) links Homer with Heraclitus and Empedocles in point of physics (*Theaetetus*, 152 E); and Aristotle (presumably not facetiously) starts his discussion of the history of philosophy with 'the ancients' (who, he thought, held a view of nature very like that of Thales: *Metaphysics*, *Α* 3, $983^{b}27$–$984^{a}2$), and discusses Hesiod's cosmology in the same breath as that of Parmenides (*Metaphysics*, *Α* 4, $984^{b}23$–32).

Hesiod—and Orpheus too—as *wise men*, men who, they assumed, were engaged in a project similar to their own.[15] If their exegesis could be turned to apologetic use later on, that is only because of this *prior* understanding of how the 'poets' should in any case be read.

And whatever the truth of Presocratic exegesis, it does not, in any case, follow that the Stoics were pursuing a similar approach. Indeed, the opposite seems to be the case: whether the Presocratics viewed Homer as divinely infallible or wisely philosophical, it is clear that the Stoics were reacting *against* them. For the Stoics explicitly *denied* that the poets were wise in any sense at all.[16] As we shall see below and in context, the Stoics complained about the 'superstition' with which the poets filled man's life (Cicero, *On the Nature of the Gods*, 2. 63); they criticized Hesiod's morality (Plutarch, *On Stoic Self-contradictions*, 14, 1039 F), and they said that to believe or even to repeat Homer's stories is 'utterly stupid: they are full of nonsense and the height of absurdity'. We should, they say, 'scorn and repudiate these myths' (*On the Nature of the Gods*, 2. 70–1; cf. *SVF* ii. 1076, p. 315. 17–19). It already looks very much as if one thing the Stoics were trying to do was to rewrite the history of philosophy that they inherited from their predecessors, and in doing so to make a much clearer (perhaps a more Platonic?) distinction between poetry on the one hand and philosophy on the other. The starting-point for an understanding of the Stoics' approach to the ancient poets is their rejection of the Presocratic assumption that their works were works of philosophy. They were

[15] To take, for example, the Presocratic exegetes of Homer mentioned in n. 7: Anaxagoras and Metrodorus *only* said that issues of virtue, justice, and physics were *dealt with* by Homer, not that the *Iliad* and *Odyssey* were, so to speak, 'biblical' authorities on the questions; and Democritus likewise suggested only that Homer was *wise*, not that he was always correct. For Orpheus as a speculator rather than prophet (and one, what is more, who was drawing on a tradition of speculation that preceded him), cf. the Derveni Papyrus col. XVIII. 7–9 Laks and Most: 'For Orpheus called wisdom Moira. This seemed to him to be the most suitable of the names that all men have given . . .'

[16] Cf. esp. Long (1992). We might also note with Most (1989: 2023–6; cf. Frede 2002) against Steinmetz (1986) that the Stoics were not narrowly concerned with the exegesis of the poets anyway. In fact they were interested in traditions concerning the gods however preserved, whether in literary form or in 'epithets, cult practices, and artistic descriptions'. This is something that is clear from Cornutus alone (cf. Most 1989: 2024 with references), but for which we also have ample evidence in the earlier Stoa. One notorious example is Chrysippus' exegesis of a pornographic painting: *SVF* ii. 1071–4.

poets *instead*, engaged in a different and less noble occupation altogether.

Yet for all their absurdity, the poets *were* worth the bother of interpreting, and the Stoics found insights in them of great philosophical significance and even, at times, sophistication (Cicero, *On the Nature of the Gods*, 2. 70–1):

> It is utterly stupid to repeat and believe these stories; they are full of nonsense and the height of absurdity. But, though scorning and repudiating these myths, we shall nevertheless be able to understand as the god who pervades the nature of each thing, Ceres (permeating earth), Neptune (the sea), and so on . . .

It has been suggested that the Stoics believed they could find scraps of wisdom in mythology simply because they believed that rationality (λόγος) pervades the structure of the whole universe, that the whole world is, in some sense, an expression of god: *a fortiori*, then, it is unsurprising if aspects of this rationality somehow force themselves through the works of even the most imperfect of men; the poets, simply in virtue of being rational, would according to the Stoics have inevitably hit upon the truth at times. But this explanation lacks cogency[17]—and is in any case refuted by the fact that what wisdom there was to be found in ancient poetry had its roots in an earlier period, and was discernible *despite* the additions of the poets (Cicero, *On the Nature of the Gods*, 2. 63):

> From another approach too, a philosophical one indeed [*physica*], come a number of deities who, clad in human form, have furnished the poets with legends and have filled man's life with all sorts of superstition. This subject

[17] Cf. Pfeiffer (1968), 237–8: 'As the λόγος (reason) is the fundamental principle of everything, it must manifest itself in poetry also, though hidden behind the veil of mythical and legendary tales and pure fiction.' Not only is this too vague to carry conviction, it also fails to explain why the Stoics believed (as we shall see they did) that poetry contains *privileged* elements of truth rather than just rational opinion. Pohlenz, who obviously realized that the poets are supposed to have taken over earlier insights, suggested that they originated by a similar process, but at a much earlier period, when the cosmological Logos was purer (1959: i. 97: 'der Logos sich in alter Zeit am reinsten entfaltet habe'; cf. Lovejoy and Boas 1935: 261). But it is not clear that Logos is at its 'purest' at the beginning of each cycle of world history (nor for that matter that it is at the end, *pace* Most 1989: 2021–3). And in any case, it is badly misconceived to link the purity of Logos viewed from a cosmological perspective to the state of human rationality. The early Stoics did not even claim (as we shall see that the later Stoics did) that the first men were more intelligent than us.

was handled by Zeno and was later explained more fully by Cleanthes and Chrysippus.

The poets, by *contrast* with some *earlier* thought, could only invent, and their inventions only obscured in superstition the truths which had come down to them. In a passage reporting the Stoics' account of the various origins of the traditional pantheon, one whole division is devoted to poetical fabrication (*SVF* ii. 1009, p. 300. 27–30):

> The sixth heading [under which the Stoics group the origins of our concepts of the gods] covers the inventions of the poets. For Hesiod, when he wanted to provide fathers for those gods who existed already, added to their number these progenitors: 'Coeus, Crius, Hyperion, and Iapetus' [*Theogony*, 134].

All of this is clear evidence that we have to draw a sharp distinction between the naming of gods undertaken by pre-mythological thinkers and the superstitious extension of this process in the poets who came later. In other words, the Stoics thought almost exactly what Aristotle had said, in the passage quoted at the beginning of this chapter. According to Aristotle too, ancient philosophical insights had become encased in 'mythological form', bundled up in many absurdities (such as the anthropomorphic descriptions of the gods) from which they have to be 'separated out'. The Stoics, to repeat, did not follow the particular account of the history of the world given by Aristotle, but this does not at all preclude them from thinking within their own model of human history that some earlier generations of men had achieved great insight into the working of nature. The real question, though, is who?

One of the reasons why it is so obviously plausible to pursue an explanation of the Stoics' account of mythology by reference to Aristotle is that the Stoics clearly did believe that the earliest generations of men were in a better position to understand the world than any of their successors had been—this was something I discussed in the last chapter. The trouble is that it is extremely unlikely that the Stoics thought that it was the very first men (those purest in outlook) whose thought was preserved in mythology. This becomes clear from another consideration of the kind of wisdom that the Stoics thought they could find embedded in the poets. For the Stoics thought that they could recover pre-mythological thought which showed a deep *technical* understanding of the role of gods in nature. One example of this comes in Cicero, *On the*

Nature of the Gods, 2. 63–4, where the Stoics (Zeno, Cleanthes, and Chrysippus have just been named) say that they can find the insight that aether (itself not something easily accessible to observation) was ultimately responsible for the generation of the whole of nature. This insight, according to the early Stoics, is captured in the poetic account of the mutilation of Caelus:

> For since the ancient belief filled Greece that Caelus was mutilated by his son Saturn, and Saturn himself was bound by his son Jupiter, [we can see that] subtle reasoning about nature [*physica ratio non inelegans*] is embedded in impious fables. Their meaning was that the highest, celestial element of aether, i.e. fire, which by itself generates all things, lacks that part of the body which requires union with another for procreation.

Physica ratio non inelegans: the ancients in the period we are now discussing were in their own way worthy physicists, and arrived at significant truths about god and nature. But this means that they cannot be identified with the very first men, because (according to my reconstruction in Chapter 1) these men articulated no philosophical views or theories. At the very time when man had the purest epistemic relationship with nature, he would have had least to say *about* nature. What we need to do now, then, is to suggest how the Stoics might have thought that these men turned to self-conscious reflection on nature, and developed from their unpolluted rationality the understanding which became embedded in the mythological and poetic tradition.

The obvious period in which to look for the emergence of reflective understanding among men is not the first period of human development, but the beginning of the second. For at this point, it seems, men had started to want more from nature than it gave of its own accord, and, in their desire to manipulate things to this end, they would need to develop and articulate an understanding about the way in which nature works.[18] And the identification of this period as the one in which the insights preserved in mythology were first articulated is supported by the fact that all, as it turns out, or most of the insights recovered by the Stoics through alle-

[18] It is not a sign of *corruption* that these men wanted to improve their material situation, even though we know that they had enough already (Seneca, *Epistle* 90. 16): the Cynics might have thought this (also Dicaearchus), but physical comfort is actually something 'preferable' in the Stoics' scheme of things. On the other hand, it was an ill-advised venture which was to have disastrous effects for humanity: one reason to think that it was not the work of *philosophers* as such.

gorical exegesis embodied precisely the kinds of concern that men would have had at this period: many of them, for example, relate to just the kinds of natural phenomena which would be of concern to someone who wanted to develop the art of farming, the technological art *par excellence*.[19] Furthermore, it turns out that many of the 'gods' assimilated into the poetic tradition were in origin *human benefactors*—they had been, that is, not gods at all, but the men responsible for inventing the technological arts. So, for example, the man who invented the art of viticulture became the god Dionysus in mythology.[20] In this case, of course, we have a kind of historical record rather than the preservation of a technical insight: but it does show that it is in this period, the period in which the arts (and especially farming) were invented, that the roots of the poetic tradition lay.[21]

At this point it is worth going back to the Stoics' theory of rationality, to try to give some content to the claim (examined in Chapter 1) that an uncorrupted rationality would give a person a true outlook on the world. For it might be supposed that early man succeeded in having a true outlook only because his rationality was constituted by a relatively narrow compass of thought about the world, itself of a relatively trivial nature; that the purity of his outlook was secured more by the absence of false beliefs than the presence (implicit or explicit) of true ones. In this case, no amount of reflection on his rationality would yield much secure information of use to later philosophers. But in fact the Stoics must have believed that reflection on an undistorted rationality would allow the articulation of an extremely rich body of knowledge. This is

[19] For the pre-eminence of farming among the arts cf. Xenophon, *Oeconomicus*, 5. 17. The third age in Dicaearchus' history was characterized by the development of farming (fr. 49, 24. 34–5 Wehrli); cf. Seneca, *Epistle* 90. 37 (quoting Virgil). Also Seneca, *Medea*, 333–4; and the relocation of lines 309–11 to follow 333–4 suggested by some editors (e.g. Leo 1879 ad loc.) creates a suggestive juxtaposition of farming and observation of the heavens: 'parvo dives, nisi quas tulerat | natale solum, non norat opes; | nondum quisquam sidera norat | stellisque quibus pingitur aether | non erat usus . . .'

[20] Cf. again *SVF* ii. 1009, p. 300. 31–7 (Heracles, the Dioscuri, and Dionysus); and the Stoic Persaeus at *SVF* i. 448 (including Demeter and Dionysus).

[21] Note that this argument does not involve adding a third stage into the Stoics' early history of man as sketched in ch. 1. This is rather a transitional period between the two, which is allowed by Seneca himself when, speaking of the technological arts, he says that they *have been* born while vice *is still emerging* into the world (*Epistle* 90. 9: *ista nata sunt iam nascente luxuria*).

something that can be seen from a more detailed account of the way in which our concepts are acquired.

One of the most important of natural concepts acquired as part of the process of becoming rational is the concept of 'god'. The Stoics insist that we all acquire this concept: indeed, they are able to argue in reverse that the fact that we all have a concept of god is evidence for god's existence. However, the Stoics also insist that the 'common concept' of god possessed by us all is, as such, evidence *only* that god exists; it cannot be used further to demonstrate what god is *like* (Cicero, *On the Nature of the Gods*, 2. 13; S.E. *M.* 9. 61). If this were the end of the story, it would tell us at least that primitive man possessed a concept of god; but there would be no reason to suppose that any amount of reflection on this concept later on would put him in a privileged position to gain insights into the *nature* of god. He would (like us all) know that god exists, but would have no special basis for developing an understanding of what he was like. However, this is not the end of the story. In fact it turns out that someone who has gained a 'common' concept of god, and who has not (as we have) been corrupted by spurious or false beliefs about the nature and operation of god, would be able, on reflection, to discover a number of reliable ideas *about* him. The limiting claims made by the Stoics for the scope of the argument from the common concept of god to his existence do nothing to undermine this position. For the argument they use is not a simple appeal to a *consensus omnium*, as often seems to be supposed: the Stoics did not conclude without elaboration from the premiss that 'everyone believes in god' to the conclusion that god must exist (cf. Obbink 1992). Rather, having noted that everyone has the *concept* of god, what they argued was that this concept (ἔννοια) had the kind of causal history that meant it was engendered in such a way as to make it a '*common* concept' (κοινὴ ἔννοια) in the technical sense—a concept that, in terms of the Stoic theory of rationality, is one of the privileged items of *a priori* knowledge given us by nature. So it is only in virtue of believing that the universal concept of god has *in addition* the right kind of causal history (one which guarantees its truth) that the Stoics thought they could use it to prove the existence of god.

If the Stoics' argument had been simply that 'everyone has a concept of god, therefore god exists', it would not have cut much ice with the Sceptics. Sceptics do not at all want to deny that they, or however many other people, have a *concept* of god. They simply believe that the concept may be a false or an inaccurate one, and that there is no more reason to believe in the existence of god (or the god represented to us in our concept of god) than there is to believe in the existence of Hippocentaurs (or whatever other mythical creatures one might have a concept of). And the reason why Sceptics could class their concept of god with their concept of the Hippocentaur as a more difficult case than, for example, their concept of the colour red is that it is much easier to understand how the concept of red *might* have been engendered such that it represents some real feature of the world. Whatever the Sceptics' ultimate position on the existence of red things, they can at least accept the force of the claim that we have received impressions of red things from the moment of our birth. It is very much otherwise with god. One can, for all sorts of reasons, doubt that 'red' things exist; but at least we seem to see them; gods, on the other hand, like Hippocentaurs, seem to be the product of an *imagination* that fabricates concepts of mythical beasts quite generally.

The Stoics, however, had two strategies against this argument. One was to say that there must be some kind of difference between our concept of god and our concept of a Hippocentaur, just because the notion of, and certainly the belief in, god is much more widespread (*On the Nature of the Gods*, 2. 5). But secondly, they countered the objection that we have never *seen* a god by pointing out that, as a matter of fact, we see god every day: we see god and the operation of god throughout nature (and we should again recall that the Stoic god is identified with nature and the world itself: cf. *On the Nature of the Gods*, 1. 39; *SVF* ii 945, p. 273. 25–8). There are, for example, particular natural phenomena which obviously betray the divinity of the world and which *would* explain the natural formation of a concept (in the sense of *κοινὴ ἔννοια*) of god. Cleanthes, in fact, 'gave four reasons to account for the formation in men's minds of their ideas of the gods' (*On the Nature of the Gods*, 2. 13–15; and cf. also *SVF* ii. 1009–10; S.E. *M*. 9. 60):

> He posited as one reason . . . that which arises from foreknowledge of future events; next, one which we have drawn from the magnitude of the benefits which are perceived in the moderation of the climate, in the fertility of the earth, and in a vast abundance of other benefits; the third reason is the awe inspired by lightning, storms, rain, hail, etc. etc. The fourth and greatest reason is the regularity of the motion and revolution of the heavens, the

sun, and the moon, and the individuality, variety, beauty, and order of all the stars . . .

The argument from the obviously divine quality of natural phenomena shows that no one has any reason to doubt that there is a perfectly good causal explanation in nature for the formation of his concept of god. Furthermore, since it would be absurd to believe that we could systematically extract false concepts (concepts with no extensional value at all) from our pre-rational experience of the world, the Stoics argue that the concept of god which we all develop by the means outlined must be a 'common concept' (κοινὴ ἔννοια), and must therefore be true.

From this analysis of the Stoics' argument for the existence of god, it is clear that a person does not just acquire a bare concept *that* god exists. Since he acquires that concept through qualitative manifestations of god, his concept will allow him to form reliable theorems about *what god is like* as well.[22] Or at least it will if there is no risk that his formation of the concept of god was contaminated by unnatural sources. When the Stoics say that the 'common concept' of god can be used to prove god's existence, but not what god is like, they are speaking to an audience of fools, of the mentally corrupt. They do not mean that the concept of god is too thin to allow anything to be said on its basis about god's nature, but that *our* concept of god was acquired in unnatural surroundings—prompted by a contemplation of the heavens, perhaps, but infected by our reading of Homer as well. *We* are not in a position to use our concept of god to form secure propositions about god's nature, just because the context in which we acquired that concept was distorted. We might well even hold beliefs about god on the basis of our concept of god that contradict beliefs held by other people on the basis of theirs. All we can be really certain of is that our common possession of the bare concept 'god' itself guarantees it as a common concept,

[22] It is significant that Cleanthes' numerous arguments for the divinity of the cosmos on the basis of his identification of fire and life come, in *On the Nature of the Gods* (see 2. 23–31), once again under the heading of god's *existence*, not his *quality*. It is worth comparing Plutarch, *On Stoic Self-contradictions*, 38, where Chrysippus is reported to have attacked Epicurus for removing 'providence' from his notion (ἔννοια) of god. Again, the idea would be that our experience of providence in the natural world is one of the primary causes of our development of the concept of god in the first place: for this reason, to deny the existence of providence is to question the basis for our concept of god itself.

guarantees that it has some natural basis whatever distortions it has variously suffered, and guarantees therefore *that* god exists.

Primitive man, however, was free of the corruption we suffer. When he turned to consider his concept of god, we know not only that it would provide him with a rich source of information *about* god, but also that in spelling out that information there would be nothing to make him go wrong. And this, in the end, is what allows us to answer the question of how the men at the beginning of the second period of human development were able to arrive at such accurate and useful insights into nature, and why the reconstruction of their beliefs is of importance to the Stoics later on. According to the Stoics, if these early men came to the study with the natural concept of god (and no more than that), they would be bound to articulate a true understanding of those aspects of nature in which they were interested. In developing agriculture, for example, they would be interested in the stars and in the weather. But as we have seen, these two aspects of the world are crucial for the natural development of our concept of god (they comprise the greater part of the third and fourth sections of Cleanthes' analysis cited above). They would be interested in the fertility of the earth, and the enormous, not to say providential, benefits that nature seems organized to provide for man. This was likewise the second of Cleanthes' divisions. Since in the acquisition of their concepts they would naturally have seen the divinity in all of this, it is no wonder if, when they came to reflect on them, they named the stars, the earth, and the heavens as aspects of god; but at the same time none of this challenges their assumption that it is all the creation of one god. God, for them, is identified with the nature from which they had always gained their concept of him. This is all correct (according to the Stoics); and it is all the natural starting-point for the technological thinkers. And my claim is that it is the insights of these thinkers that the early Stoics thought they could recover by their exegesis of mythological texts.

On the reconstruction I suggested in Chapter 1 on the basis of Seneca, *Epistle* 90, the first age of man was, according to the early Stoics, a pre-technical, pre-philosophical age in which man 'automatically' did what was right without the need for reflection on the nature of virtue; the second age came with the invention of arts (agriculture foremost among them), on the basis of more self-conscious reflection on their outlook. In this chapter I have considered how a technical understanding of the world might have emerged during the first stages of this period. This could not have been a perfect *philosophy*—Seneca is clear about that; and the ultimate tendency of this understanding to lead men away from virtue rather than towards it rather supports his insistence. But, as being based on a conception of nature that had not *yet* been subject to that corruption which was the ultimate result of the new civilization, it constituted a privileged and secure understanding of nature. Only when decadence really took a hold on mankind was the purer outlook on which this understanding rested finally lost, and what had been discovered by the technologists turned into the fictions of their debased successors, the poets. Eventually, a striving after the truth, and, one supposes, some consciousness of the unhappy state of man, led to the rise of modern philosophy, culminating in Stoicism. But early Stoicism has an inbuilt disadvantage: one is supposed to 'straighten out' one's rationality so as to arrive at a consistent understanding of the world, and consequently of one's place in it. The study of physics is therefore central to their programme. And yet, how can a Stoic be certain of the truth of Stoic teaching if he himself is approaching it with distorted rationality (a distorted view of the world)? At least part of the answer, and part of the reason why the early Stoics seem to have expended so much effort in interpreting the myths, is that these myths retain fragments of physical doctrine from a time when men were not encumbered by the corruptions of the later age. Such exegesis therefore had much more than the academic interest it might have held for Aristotle (if he had pursued the question at all); it would provide invaluable confirmation of Stoicism itself.

3

Primitive Wisdom and Stoic Exegesis after Posidonius

In the last chapter I looked at the way in which the early Stoics thought that the outlook of the first men came to be articulated into a technical understanding of nature, and at how scraps of this understanding were subsequently preserved as the seeds of the mythological tradition; and I suggested that the Stoics thought the recovery of these fragments was worthwhile in so far as they could be used as evidence to support the general direction in which Stoic philosophy was developing. But the full historical impact of this theory was, as I hope to show, not confined to its implications for the Greeks' understanding of mythology, or for the Stoics' ability to support the truth of their doctrines on the basis of it. By suggesting that authoritative philosophical insights might be obtained by a student of the past, the theory would ultimately lead to a revolution in the way that philosophy itself was done: as I shall argue in Chapters 6 and 7, the Stoics' theory of the transmission through readily accessible cultural traditions of a primitive and authoritative wisdom would form the basis of the new approach to philosophy developed by the Platonists of the second century AD. But a great deal more needed to be done before the Stoics' theory could support such a radical programme. In practice, the early Stoics were very conservative in their estimate of how much ancient wisdom could be recovered: what there was came from thinkers who were not philosophers in the strictest sense, its transmutation into allegorical form was in large measure accidental, and its transmission lay in the hands of men who neither understood its importance nor cared about preserving its purity. However, all of these difficulties were soon to be addressed, in the work of the later Stoics: as we shall see in this chapter, they came to hold very different beliefs about the nature of early philosophy, and developed sophisticated exegetical approaches to overcome some of the difficulties thrown up by its transmission. Prominent in our evidence for this development is the first-century-AD Stoic Cornutus; but, as we shall see, much of his work relied on the critical revision of early Stoicism effected in the first century BC by Posidonius of Apamea and, in particular, on the revised account of early mankind that he gave.

1. *Posidonius on Early Human History*

The core of Posidonius' revision of the history of mankind was touched upon in Chapter 1, in the discussion of Seneca, *Epistle* 90 (which is our most important evidence for Posidonius' views as it was for those of the early Stoics).[1] From this letter I argued that we could see that, where the earlier Stoics had held that primitive man was in a unique state of *innocence*, a state of uncorruption from which even philosophy was absent, Posidonius seems to have made the claim that philosophy formed a very important part of early human activity. When men were first created[2] they were brought together into communities by philosophers,[3] and thereafter readily submitted to their rule (*Epistle*

[1] For discussions of Posidonius' theory of the development of mankind see esp. Rudberg (1918), 51–70; Reinhardt (1921), 392–401 (also 1953: 805–8); Heinemann (1921–8), i. 88–108; Grilli (1953); Laffranque (1964), 494–508; Cole (1990).

[2] Posidonius seems to have followed the earlier Stoics in thinking that they originated from a process of *gēgenesis*: see *SVF* i. 124 for the early Stoics (also ii. 739, although this passage does not name the Stoics), and S.E. *M.* 9. 28, for the 'younger Stoics' (and cf. Cornutus, *Introduction* 18, 31. 19–20 Lang). Heinemann (1921–8: i. 89 with n. 3, to 90 with n. 1) more tendentiously adduces passages from Cicero and Philo (e.g. *On the Special Laws*, ii. 160: γηγενεῖς τε καὶ ἐκ γηγενῶν) as evidence for Posidonius on this point. Cf. also Rudberg (1918), 52–3.

[3] The pre-communal state of the very first men, the *sparsi* of Seneca, *Epistle* 90. 7 (quoting Posidonius on this point; and cf. Cornutus, *Introduction*, 20, 39. 12–40. 4 Lang, discussed below; also perhaps Polybius 6. 5. 6–10), has been taken to contradict the Posidonian claim at *Epistle* 90. 4 that the '*first men* and those who sprang from them' lived in communities under the leadership of sages. One solution to this, developed from the conflation, discussed in the last chapter, between the pre-communal period mentioned here with the pre-*philosophical* period championed by Seneca later on in the letter, is suggested by Pfligersdorffer (1982: 312): 'die Menschen dieses Zeitalters werden daher eben *primi mortalium* genannt, ungeachtet dessen, daß bei Poseidonios das Stadium der *sparsi* bereits vorangegangen ist, die ohne *consortium* lebten und daher für die spezifisch "menschliche" Entwicklung noch nicht in Betracht gekommen sind.' Again, this seems to be a complicated

90. 5):

In that age, which they call 'golden', Posidonius thinks that the government was in the hands of sages. They were restrained in their own actions, and protected the weaker from the stronger . . . And no one had the inclination or the excuse for injustice: they were good subjects under good rulers, and a king could threaten nothing worse against someone who was disobedient than that he should be ejected from the kingdom.

If the nature of Posidonius' innovations on the early Stoics is fairly clear, what may not be so clear is why he made them, why it was not enough for him to maintain the position that early man lived in a state of *pre*-philosophical innocence. But the reason for this is actually not very far to seek, and is based on the more fundamental revisions made by Posidonius in the fields of psychology and ethical philosophy. The early Stoics (like the Cynics before them) were able to claim that men could live well in a pre-philosophical state, because there was no obvious force recognized by them that might lead man in his natural state to act *badly*. There was certainly no internal force that could have this effect, since the Stoics thought that the human soul was entirely rational, and that, as long as nothing interfered with the natural development of rationality in a man, he would always and naturally act as he ought, in accordance with reason. But this view was challenged by Posidonius: although the details of his psychological theory remain somewhat unclear to us, it is absolutely certain that Posidonius thought that there were non-rational as well as rational forces governing human motivation.[4] The immediate significance of this is that Posidonius, somewhat

response to a contradiction that might anyway be more apparent than real. The *sparsi* seem in fact to constitute, not a substantive first period of human history, but rather a brief stage of transition between the emergence of individuals from the earth and their coming together into communities. The *sparsi* certainly cannot be taken to constitute a pre-philosophical period of human existence, since it was their possession of philosophy that brought them together into communities in the first place.

[4] See fr. 142–8 EK and generally, for the difference between Posidonius and Chrysippus, Glibert-Thirry (1977). The difficulty is to know quite where these 'forces' (δυνάμεις) were located: Galen tempts us to compare them to the 'parts' of the soul as described by Plato, but Posidonius explicitly rejects terminology that could have this implication, and it seems more likely that he described them, very roughly, as different *kinds* of desire, rather than the desires of different *parts* of the soul. But see on this Kidd (1971), 203–6, and especially now Cooper (1998); cf. also Gill (1998). For the historical question of the relationship between Posidonius' psychological theory and that of Plato, see Vander Waerdt (1985).

like Plato, thought that the appearance of vice did not depend, or did not solely depend, on *external* corruption, but tended to have an *internal* source as well. And Posidonius actually went further than Plato in describing the consequences of this. In Chapter 1 I showed that even Plato, in the *Timaeus*, thought that vice could not take hold among men without the corrupting influences of external causes (mal-education or disease)—which ultimately allowed him (in the *Laws*) to claim that man lived in a state of pre-philosophical virtue in the period before these causes had their effect. But Posidonius thought that right from the start all people (including, that is, the very earliest people) were drawn towards vice at least as much as towards the good. This means that Posidonius could not think, as the early Stoics did, that the earliest men were safeguarded from vice just because they were a long way from the corrupting influences of high civilization. On the contrary: since all men have within themselves the seed of vice, providence would *have* to endow man with philosophy to ensure that he did not naturally and immediately start acting viciously, contrary to reason. Seneca himself gives us evidence that this must have been the way that Posidonius thought, making it clear in *Epistle* 90 that Posidonius' early philosophers are the only force that stop men in general from going to the bad. In the passage quoted above (*Epistle* 90. 5) we are told that men obey their rulers, but only because they realize that it is to their advantage: and Seneca does not fail to mention that there is a sanction available in case anyone should become disobedient, that of being excluded from the benefits of society. In a telling line from the same passage, Posidonius says that the philosopher kings 'protected the weaker from the stronger'—and thus implies that, in the absence of the philosophers, the stronger would naturally want to take advantage of the weaker. And we have more direct evidence that Posidonius linked his psychological theory with his understanding of how corruption and vice found their way into human society. Galen tells us that he criticized the early Stoics precisely on the basis that if, as they thought, the only source of vice were external, there would be *no* way of explaining the decline from the golden age at all.[5] If these external influences are powerful enough to overcome our own motivation towards virtue, he says, then we would all be evil in any case; but if, on the other hand, our psycho-

[5] See fr. 35 EK with commentary at Kidd (1988), 174–8; and compare fr. 169. 35–48 EK with Kidd (1971), 206–8.

logical motivation towards the good is stronger than any external influences could be, then 'who persuaded the first human beings to be conquered by the weaker force?'[6]

Posidonius does not think either that vice comes in afterwards to human beings from outside, without a root of its own in our minds, starting from which it sprouts and grows big, but the very opposite. Yes, there is a seed even of evil in our own selves; and we all need not so much to avoid the wicked as to pursue those who will prune away and prevent the growth of our evil.

The presence of sages in the golden age is essential, then, just to ensure as far as possible that no one is ever allowed the opportunity to become vicious. But what, then, of their philosophy? How far was it developed, and how much might survive? Oddly enough, Posidonius seems to have had rather little to say on the matter—or, to be more accurate, he had rather little to say on the question of their achievements in theology or theoretical philosophy, and hardly anything at all about the survival of their insights into these questions through mythological traditions. Posidonius certainly did suppose that the early philosophers developed and employed an understanding of nature and causality, and there is some reason to believe that he claimed a higher achievement for them in these areas than modern man could attain to even in theory.[7] But in practice his discussions seem to have focused on the development of the various practical arts which this wisdom made possible, and not on the transmission of the wisdom itself. We hear of the early philosophers' role in the development of farming (Seneca, *Epistle* 90. 21), architecture (7), metalwork (13), and even weaving (20);[8] but nothing about their view of the gods or the stars,

[6] Fr. 35. 5–7 EK. The passage that follows is the translation by Kidd (1999: 93) of fr. 35. 18–24 EK.

[7] See S.E. *M.* 9. 28 = Posidonius fr. 305 Theiler (and cf. commentary at Theiler 1982: ii. 182–3): 'Some of the younger Stoics think that the first, earth-born men greatly surpassed the men of today in intelligence (as one may learn from a comparison of ourselves with the ancients), and that they were heroes, possessing in the keenness of their intellect as it were an extra organ of sense, to apprehend the divine nature and discern certain powers of the gods.' This fragment does not mention Posidonius by name, and it is not printed in EK. However, Kidd (1988: 971) mentions it in his commentary on fr. 284 EK, and says of it that it 'seems to refer to Posidonius'. Cf. also Hirzel (1877–83), ii. 289 n.

[8] For the importance of an understanding of nature and causality even in these arts cf. Seneca, *Epistle* 88. 21–3. Here the inventor (in this case the inventor of stage machinery) is distinguished from the spectator: the spectator marvels at the

for example.[9] And the reason for this seems to be that Posidonius saw no very strong reason to suppose that theoretical philosophy had been much preserved even in the guise of mythology. Weaving, metalwork, agriculture, and so on were the tangible legacies of the early philosophers, but he thought that there was little to be gained from supposing that fragments of wisdom had somehow survived the decline of philosophy itself. And even where ancient wisdom could be discovered embedded within the mythological corpus, Posidonius thought that it might be discerned only when the doctrine in question had been sufficiently proved already (cf. fr. 156 EK). But if Posidonius himself did not have much time for the reconstruction of philosophy through myth, his developments in the understanding of early human culture enabled his successors to establish a much more substantial basis for the study than was available even to the earlier Stoics.

2. *Cornutus and Early Human History*

Lucius Annaeus Cornutus was a Stoic philosopher of the first century AD, and a much more important figure all round than the extent of his remains, or of modern interest in him, tends to suggest. He appears to have been born in Leptis, Libya—although quite when we do not know.[10] We do know that he lived and worked in Rome under Nero, by whom he was exiled, probably around

invention *because he does not understand the causes* ('his imperitorum feriuntur oculi omnia subita, *quia causas non novere,* mirantium'). Seneca himself agrees that the sage knows about natural causes: *sapiens enim causas naturalium et quaerit et novit* (88. 26); but he disagrees, here as in *Epistle* 90, that this means that the sage *as such* will, even in the first place, be the same person as the artisan (see 88. 24–8).

[9] It is worth noting that Posidonius viewed theoretical philosophy, not only as a prerequisite for the development of the arts, but as itself a kind of art: see fr. 90 EK (=Seneca, *Epistle* 88. 21–8) with Kidd (1988), 359–65; also Kidd (1978). Kidd shows that Posidonius included philosophy within the division of the arts labelled *artes liberales* by Seneca: as Seneca tells us, the *artes liberales* are those *quibus curae virtus est* (*Epistle* 88. 23). (What we would call the 'liberal arts' are actually represented in this scheme by the *artes pueriles.*) This *pace* Reinhardt (1921), 49–56, and Lafranque (1964), 362–7; cf. also Pohlenz (1959), ii. 105–6 (ad i. 214, 18).

[10] For Cornutus generally see G. Martini (1825); Reppe (1906); Nock (1931); Hays (1983); Most (1989). A fuller account of his approach to allegorical exegesis will be found in Boys-Stones (2002*a*). His name is generally taken to indicate that he was a freedman of Seneca the Elder, or of one of his relatives (so Marx 1894: 2227; cf. Reppe 1906: 7; Nock 1931: 996; Hays 1983: 30). His birthplace is given as Leptis by the *Suda* (s.v. *Κορνοῦτος*); but Stephanus suggests that he worked in Thestis (s.v. *Θέστις*) and Tergis (s.v. *Τέργις*).

AD 65.[11] He seems to have had a special interest, and a special eminence, in literary studies (especially grammar and rhetoric). He was consulted by Nero, praised by Cassius Dio, and taught the poets Lucan and Persius.[12] Allusions to his lost works show the breadth of his interests: he wrote commentaries on Aristotle's *Categories*, and on Virgil; a work *On Figures of Speech*; one *On Pronunciation* or *On Spelling*; and one called *Rhetorical Skills*. He is said, in a disputed passage, to have written a satire himself, and we possess commentaries on Persius and Juvenal which bear his name.[13] But the one authentic work of his that survives is his *Introduction to Greek Theology*: an allegorical investigation into Greek mythology. And there is reason to believe that we are especially fortunate that it should be this work that survives, because Porphyry, looking back down a century of Platonist allegorical interpretation, seems to have thought of Cornutus as one of the most important theorists in the field. At least, when he criticizes Origen for interpreting the Bible allegorically, he says that it was the approach of Cornutus, and Cornutus' Stoic contemporary Chaeremon, that he used; and he places these two at the head of his list of allegorical exegetes which otherwise names only Platonists and Pythagoreans (Porphyry, *Against the Christians*, fr. 39. 30–5 Harnack):

[Origen] was always consorting with Plato, and was conversant with the writings of Numenius, Cronius, Apollophanes, Longinus, Moderatus, Nicomachus, and the distinguished men among the Pythagoreans; and he made use of the books of Chaeremon the Stoic and Cornutus, from which

[11] Cf. Cassius Dio 62. 29. 2–3 with the *Suda*, s.v. *Κορνοῦτος: καὶ πρὸς αὐτοῦ* [i.e. *Νέρωνος*] *ἀναιρεθεὶς σὺν Μουσωνίῳ*. Musonius (assuming, as seems likely, that this is a reference to the Stoic philosopher Musonius Rufus) was exiled by Nero in AD 65. Reppe (1906: 7–9) notes that, if *ἀναιρεθείς* in the passage just quoted from the *Suda* means 'exiled', it would be a hapax for that work; but its usual meaning of 'executed' would not answer to the independent evidence we have for the fates of either Cornutus or Musonius Rufus. The reason for Nero's displeasure with Cornutus is given by Cassius Dio as his refusal to flatter Nero's literary pretensions: but cf. on this question Hays (1983), 31–2; Most (1989), 2035–43.

[12] See the *Life of Persius*; Persius, *Satire* 5 (which is dedicated to Cornutus); Aulus Gellius, *Attic Nights* 2. 6. 1; and Cassius Dio 62. 29. 2.

[13] For the works of Cornutus (certain and dubious) see Nock (1931), 996–8 and 1004–5. His work on the *Categories* is mentioned by Simplicius (*On the Categories*, 62. 27–8 Kalbfleisch, with numerous allusions elsewhere) and by Porphyry (*On the Categories*, 59. 10–11 Busse), who also refers to the *Ῥητορικαὶ τέχναι* (*On the Categories*, 86. 23–4 Busse). Aulus Gellius mentions the *De figuris sententiarum* (*Attic Nights*, 9. 10. 5) and the commentary on Virgil (2. 6. 1; cf. also Charisius, *Art of Grammar*, i. 127. 19–21 Keil). The *De enuntiatione vel orthographia* is known from an excerpt in Cassiodorus (see *On Orthography*, vii. 147. 24–154. 11 Keil).

he learnt the allegorical [μεταληπτικόν] mode of the Greek mysteries and applied this to Jewish writings.

But if Cornutus was an important figure in the history of allegorical interpretation, he is, by the same token, extremely important for our understanding of the development of the Stoic theory of the transmission of primitive wisdom after Posidonius. For Cornutus provides us with evidence that the later Stoics not only exploited his conclusions about the nature of early man to suggest that a much purer vein of wisdom might have survived from the primitive age, but also developed a highly sophisticated methodology for isolating it. In short, Cornutus gives us first-hand evidence for the manner in which the later Stoics opened the way for a reconstruction of ancient wisdom that might, in theory at least, be full enough and sure enough to advance philosophical knowledge, not just to support it.

Cornutus' *Introduction* is a practical handbook of exegesis: there is very little in it that is explicitly theoretical. However, a substantial amount can be inferred from the little there is. In particular, it quickly becomes clear that Cornutus based his exegesis on an account of the development of philosophy among early men which was very much in the Posidonian mould. For a start, we know that Cornutus agreed with Posidonius against the early Stoics on the most important issue that differentiated them, namely the question of whether there were philosophers as such among the first men (cf. 35, 75. 18–76. 5 Lang). Indeed, not only did Cornutus make the strong, 'Posidonian' claim that there were philosophers at this period, he also gave a surprisingly 'strong' explanation of how they came to be philosophers. In the course of a discussion of the epithet 'Giant-slayer' as applied to Athene, he explained that the *very* first of our ancestors were brutal, violent, and antisocial people represented in mythology by the Giants. But these were tamed by the gods, who 'prodded them and reminded them of their rational concepts [ἔννοιαι]', and thus made them into the social *and philosophical* beings who formed the basis and origin of the social structures we have inherited. So *Introduction*, 20, 39. 12–40. 4 Lang:

It has been handed down that Athene distinguished herself in the battle against the Giants, and was accordingly called Giant-slayer. Now it is likely that the first men, born from the earth, were violent and hot-tempered in their dealings with each other, being utterly incapable of reaching an agreement or of fanning the spark of community spirit which was in them. But the gods, as if spurring them on and putting them in mind of their rational concepts, prevailed, and the cultivation of reason utterly subdued them and brought them into line—to the extent that you might have thought it had routed and destroyed their old natures. After the change, they and their offspring became different people, living together in communities, thanks to Athene, Guardian of Cities.

The death of the Giants symbolizes the 'death' of pre-civilized mankind—the development of the race from its 'scattered' existence to its adoption of community life, as described by Posidonius (cf. again Seneca, *Epistle* 90. 7). In Posidonius, of course, it was philosophy, not the gods, as such, that brought men together; and, although this might look like a more economical account, it should be possible to see why Cornutus might have thought it necessary to refine it. After all, Posidonius based his claim that there were philosophers among the earliest men on the belief that philosophy would somewhere be needed among them as a counterbalance to man's natural tendency towards vice. But if the philosophers constituted the only influence which worked against the rise of vice in men, it is not at all clear how *they* had avoided vice to become philosophers themselves. Posidonius might have said that the gods *made* man philosophical to start with (it was Seneca arguing against him who insisted that the substance of virtue was derived from the process of *becoming* virtuous: cf. again *Epistle* 90. 44–5); but in that case Cornutus' account would not be so different from Posidonius' as it first might have seemed. The intervention of the gods would take place at slightly different stages, but it would take place one way or another in both.

The differences between Cornutus' and Posidonius' accounts of the very early stages of human existence are clearly not substantial: the two accounts are, on the other hand, very thoroughly and obviously united at a theoretical level—united in particular against the version of the earlier Stoics. But Cornutus now goes further than Posidonius. He agrees with him that there was an early stage of human history when men were, at least intellectually, 'fresh from the gods', and possessed a philosophy that was all the more certain for it. But he goes on to make a claim about these early philosophers which was not made by Posidonius, and could hardly have been made by the earlier Stoics at all. Not only were there privileged philosophers among early men, according to Cornutus; but they appear to have given self-conscious expression to their philosophy in allegorical form. This is what he says in the final paragraph of his work, in a passage addressed to its young dedicatee (35, 75. 18–76. 5 Lang):

And so, my child, the rest of the material handed down in myth which appears to be about the gods you are now in a position to refer to the principles I have set out, convinced that the ancients were no ordinary men, but capable of understanding the nature of the cosmos *and inclined to use symbols and riddles in their philosophical discussions of it* [συνιέναι τὴν τοῦ κόσμου φύσιν ἱκανοὶ καὶ πρὸς τὸ διὰ συμβόλων καὶ αἰνιγμάτων φιλοσοφῆσαι περὶ αὐτῆς εὐεπίφοροι].

Cornutus believed that the philosophers' wisdom had been transmitted through and mishandled by the poets, as the early Stoics had also argued; but the fact that he (unlike they) could believe that the philosophy was originally expressed in allegorical form means that his description of its reception is slightly different as well. For, whereas the early Stoics believed that the reflective understanding of nature that developed from the outlook of early man was corrupted from the very moment of its reception by the poets, whose misunderstanding actively remodelled it into mythology, Cornutus thought that this stage of corruption, this remodelling, at least, could be avoided. The philosophers expressed themselves in allegories: and it was just those allegories that the poets took over as the basis for their stories. After that, the process is much the same: the poets gradually embroidered these sometime allegorical 'myths' into greater and more entertaining narratives (17, 27. 19–28. 2 Lang):[14] 'One must not . . . unthinkingly accept fictional accretions which have been added to the genealogies passed down in the mythologies by people who did not understand what they hint at, and treated them as they would made-up stories.'

The difference between the early and later Stoics as reflected in Cornutus might seem trivial, but its importance should not be underestimated. For the fact that the early philosophers in Cornutus' account had themselves handed their thought on in allegorical form has a limiting effect on how badly the poets can corrupt it. It

[14] For the possibility of recovering fragments (his word is ἀποσπάσματα: cf. 17, 26. 17 Lang) of the original philosophy from poetry see esp. 17, 31. 12–17 Lang: 'You can obtain a more perfect exposition ⟨of the gods' genealogy⟩ than Hesiod's. For I think that he has transmitted some things from the ancients, but has himself added other things of a more mythical nature. In this fashion he has corrupted a great deal of the primitive philosophy.'

is no longer the case that they make stories *out of* other people's philosophical insights; they rather adopt those insights *as* their stories. In Cornutus they simply embroidered, where in the earlier Stoics they transmuted as well. And what this means, of course, is that when we successfully identify an 'original' fragment of early thought within a poetic tradition, we might (according to Cornutus) be supposed to have identified the very philosophy of the ancients. Allegorical interpretation will now be just that, interpretation of ancient allegories—and not the reconstruction of thought from a story into which it was only changed later.

In sum, Cornutus understood his allegorical exegesis in a broadly Posidonian framework: he thought that the first men understood and thought about nature, expressing their insight in allegory; that these allegories, which were taken to be mere fictions by the poets, formed the basis for their own stories, which were built around them; that, in time, a whole mythological tradition grew up (expressed as well in cultic practice and by oral transmission as in the texts of poets); and finally that, for someone who knew where to look, the original elements of philosophical allegory could be separated out again and interpreted to give a direct insight into what was, *ex hypothesi*, the truth. The question now, of course, is how certain we can be of isolating those primitive allegories from within the body of myth; and it is in this field that Cornutus reflects some of the most important and influential work to be done among Stoics in the generations immediately after Posidonius.

3. *Cornutus' Exegetical Method: The Reconstruction of a Tradition*

One of the most prevalent features of Cornutus' discussion of his material is his use of etymology. Indeed, this is so prevalent that it led Long to call Cornutus 'an etymologist, not an allegorist' (1992: 54). However, this might be to miss the point slightly. It is true that etymology as such is not allegory as such, and it is true that 'only rarely does Cornutus offer an interpretation of any extended episodes in early Greek poetry' (ibid.). But the *Introduction to Greek Theology* is not supposed to be an allegorical exposition of Greek myth; it is supposed to provide the material and method for someone who wants to pursue his own allegorical investigations. It is an introductory guide to such an exposition (cf. again 35, 75. 18–76. 5 Lang), and the role of etymology is surely to provide the materials needed by the expositor. What is presumably so interesting about the possibility of applying etymology to the names of the gods is the simple fact that these names are the one aspect of mythology that one can more or less confidently trace back to the earliest period of the tradition. A name is not like a story: unless you think that its etymology is important to its place in a narrative (and the whole point is that the poets did not), there will, on the whole, be no poetical reasons to tamper with it. The poets will have taken the names of the gods as they received them, and whatever they did with the allegories based around these names, it is unlikely that they would have meddled with the names themselves.[15] But this gives the allegorist a firm starting-point for his project because, once he has identified the names given to the gods by the first philosophers, and understood to what aspect of nature or god they were referring by these names, he can start to look at how the names occur in mythological traditions. In some of the cases where the name occurs, it will be there because someone other than the original philosophers has made up a story around this name. But precisely because their intention was to entertain rather than to communicate anything philosophical, it should be possible for the philosopher to see where this happens. In the clearest cases there will be no way in which sense can be made of the story if the etymological *meanings* of the names involved are substituted for the names themselves. If, on the other hand, a passage of Homer (for example) makes sense as a piece of cosmology when the names of the characters involved are understood by their etymologies, then Cornutus will have reasonable grounds to claim that that passage might itself be 'original' in this way. This method is far from infallible—but then Cornutus does not claim infallibility for it. Indeed, he is much more tentative in his approach than he is often given credit for, frequently refusing to choose between competing etymologies when there is no solid ground to do so (cf. Most 1989: 2027–8). Even when he thinks that etymologies can be established, he advances philosophical allegories identified on the basis of them with some show of diffidence: 'It *seems* [ἔοικε] that an ancient fragment has been preserved,' he will say (17, 26. 16–17 Lang); or 'perhaps' a passage

[15] The poets are capable of making up their own names (*SVF* ii. 1009, p. 300. 27–9): but that is something different again, and something which will in any case emerge from the investigation of their origins which is implied in the study of etymology.

'hints at something like' the relevant piece of doctrine (18, 32. 14 Lang).

Etymology is important for Cornutus, that is clear. But it is by no means the only exegetical tool available to him, and, viewed historically at least, it was certainly not the most important. For Cornutus realized in addition that, if the kernel of Greek mythology was constituted by the allegories put forward by the primitive philosophers, it might also be the case that the mythologies of other nations contained at their core *the very same allegories.*[16] Compare, for example, *Introduction*, 17, 26. 7–12 Lang: 'Many and various myths about the gods arose among the ancient Greeks, as others among the Magi, others among the Phrygians, and again among the Egyptians, Celts and Libyans and other races...'

This might not look to be a very startling observation. The similarities between different theological systems had long been noted, and identifications and syncretizations between the gods of different cultures expounded as early as Herodotus,[17] so it is clearly not true that the later Stoics were the first people to consider foreign mythologies, and to use cross-cultural comparisons to arrive at a better interpretation of the gods. However, where they do seem to have been original was in their development of what we might call a proper science of comparative mythology. As we can see, Cornutus did not just note similarities or dependencies between different theological systems, he actually used a comparison of them to isolate shared elements, to strip away their poetical accretions, and to reconstruct their common source—the common source being, of course, the original allegorical philosophy from which they all took their rise.

There is not a great deal of reference to non-Greek mythology in Cornutus' work—which is, after all, an *introduction*, and an intro-

[16] It seems likely that Cornutus (as perhaps Proclus later on: see *Platonic Theology*, 5. 7, 27. 2–4 Saffrey and Westerink) believed that all men were descended from the same primitive community—and therefore that all ancient traditions had their roots in the same corpus of primitive philosophy. But this is no more than likely: it is possible, for example, that Cornutus rather believed that the mythologies of different nations simply went back to philosophers who had the same view on the world, and who would naturally tend to find their way towards the same models of allegorical exposition.

[17] Cf. esp. *Histories*, 2. 49–50; also 2. 104 for the shared practice of ritual circumcision among the Colchians, Egyptians, Ethiopians, Phoenicians, and the 'Syrians of Palestine'. Closer to Cornutus' own time, cf. Varro, esp. *Divine Antiquities*, 16, 150 Cardauns, and *Latin Language*, 5. 57–74 with Boyancé (1955), 58; Pépin (1958), 298; Hengel (1974), 160.

duction to *Greek* theology at that. But the theory that involves it is clearly there. This is Cornutus' discussion of the myth of the rape of Kore (*Introduction*, 28, 54. 12–21 Lang):

> There was a myth that Hades kidnapped the daughter of Demeter which came about because of the disappearance of the seeds under the earth for a certain time. But the dejection of the goddess and her search throughout the cosmos were made up and added on later. For among the Egyptians Osiris, who is sought and rediscovered by Isis, suggests the same sort of thing. Among the Phoenicians there is Adonis, who is alternately above the ground and below the ground for six-month periods (Demeter's produce being thus called 'Adonis' from the fact that it 'pleases' [ἁδεῖν] men).

The details of Cornutus' argument here are (as often) not easy to reconstruct: he can hardly be saying (on the reading of the passage that otherwise seems to me most natural) that the Egyptian and Phoenician narratives prove that the 'grief of Demeter and her search through the cosmos for her daughter are fictional accretions to the original myth': Isis did grieve and search for Osiris; and, although no search was necessary for Adonis, his death was certainly grieved (witness Bion's *Lament for Adonis*; Theocritus, *Idyll* 15, esp. 100–44). It seems, then, that the explanatory clause ('For among the Egyptians . . .') should be made to refer back to Cornutus' interpretation of the myth as a whole, and may be glossed as follows: 'We know that the myth of Demeter and Kore contains elements of ancient wisdom (referring, as it happens, to the crop-cycle), and we know *this* because the Egyptians and the Phoenicians have traditional stories with much the same narrative structure.' But in any case, what is really important is what is beyond any doubt: that Cornutus is inviting us to compare mythologies from different cultures in an attempt to uncover their philosophical core; that this passage introduces us to a method of comparative mythology which can be used to identify the presence of primitive elements within the mythical structures that have grown up around them. And the significance of this insight cannot be exaggerated. Taken together with the later Stoics' theory of the nature of early philosophy, also reflected in Cornutus, it amounts to the claim that it is possible, not just to suggest a philosophical basis for the stories of the poets, but actually to isolate with some certainty, and from a much wider database than the earlier Stoics seem to have employed, the philosophical allegories of the earliest men. A much more objective and much more direct insight into the wisdom of the privileged age might now be thought possible. The profound impact that this view had can be seen in the Platonists' adoption of the theory in the later first century AD—indeed, I shall argue in Chapter 6 that their adoption of this theory helped define the Platonist movement itself. But *we scarcely find evidence for anything like it before Cornutus*: that is to say, we have *no* examples of this kind of exegesis before Cornutus at all,[18] and no evidence even for the general approach earlier than the Stoics of the generation immediately preceding him. When Porphyry placed Cornutus (with Chaeremon) at the head of his list of allegorical exegetes, we might well take him to have been honouring the influential position that he occupied in promulgating the later Stoic understanding of the transmission of wisdom, and the possibility of founding a philosophy on the basis of a reconstruction of it.

The exegetical methodology reflected in Cornutus was, as I say, to become very important for the development of Platonism and, through Platonism, for the course of later philosophy as a whole. But before turning to look at the use that was made of Cornutus' theory later on, there is one more point that needs to be made out of all of this. For once it is realized that there are a number of theological traditions which preserve elements of the original and privileged philosophy, the exegete will naturally need to know quite *which* of the many traditions in the world are to be counted in this number. If a theological tradition can be shown to be relatively recent, with little or no connection with the earliest philosophy, then clearly it will be of little interest to the philosopher in this context. Again, it will make a difference whether a mythological system (say that of the Greeks) is thought to come down directly from the earliest days, or whether it in turn derives from another surviving theology (say that of the Egyptians). In this case, by a principle analogous to that known to textual critics as the *eliminatio*

[18] As arguments *ex silentio* go, a good case is provided by the 2nd-cent.-BC ethnographical writer Apollodorus, who hardly seems to have mentioned non-Greek theologies at all in his work *On the Gods*—an extensive and highly influential work that was used by Cornutus himself. We have a good number of fragments (*FGrH* 244: cf. in particular frr. 95–9, 126, and 135–6 for material in Cornutus), but only *one* (fr. 104) mentions gods of only *one* other race (the Egyptians); and even here Apollodorus mentions them only to Euhemerize them out of existence. And this from a man interested enough in other peoples to write a twelve-book ethnographical commentary on Homer's Catalogue of Ships (frr. 154–207).

descriptae, the exegete will know that he can ignore the younger tradition and concentrate on the older—but he will, of course, have first to establish that one tradition *is* younger and derivative, and this might be a matter for disagreement.

These questions did not, as it happens, provoke a very lively debate in many areas: presumably the native theologies of most of the nations were considered to be at least ancient and pure *enough* to be of some help. However, there was one area in which debate did arise, and arose with unusual passion, and that was in the encounter between the Jews and Greeks in Egypt. In the next two chapters I shall consider the debate that arose between them: apart from the importance that it had in foreshadowing the argument over priority which was later conducted between the Christians and Platonists (discussed in Chapters 8–9), it will also provide evidence for the evolution of thought within the Stoa that I have so far been tracing, and shed light on the importance of the developments of the later Stoics as reflected in Cornutus. For, as we shall see, the nature of this debate had changed radically by the first century AD, when it became centred precisely on the issue of what intellectual credibility the respective traditions could be thought to have, based on argument and counter-argument as to their derivation and the depth of their roots in primitive antiquity.

4

Antiquity in Graeco-Egyptian Anti-Semitism

1. *The Early Hellenistic Period*

The distinctive character of Jewish culture attracted the attention of the Greeks a long while before the two peoples ever came into close contact. The Jewish practice of circumcision, for example, and the forms observed in their sacrifices were early on noted by the Greeks as something alien, intriguing, and in any case distinctly un-Hellenic.[1] Such knowledge as the mainland Greeks had of the Jews (and this knowledge was probably not in the first place very extensive or profound) suggested an exotic people to them, one linked in their minds with the Magi and Gymnosophists.[2] But in the Ptolemaic city of Alexandria the Greeks were to encounter Jewish culture at first hand, and in a way that demanded a more considered response: and while attitudes towards the distant cultures of the Magi and Indian sages remained aloof, perhaps, but increasingly benign, the Greeks' response to the Jews hardened there into a more systematic form of cultural anti-Semitism.

The reasons for this reaction are, of course, enormously complex;[3] but one issue stands out in particular, and that is the de-

[1] Herodotus mentioned the practice of circumcision amongst the 'Syrians living in Palestine' (*Histories*, 2. 104), and Theophrastus in his work *On Piety* discussed the Jews' mode of sacrifice as something 'from which the Greeks would recoil' (fr. 584A, 261–3 Fortenbaugh).

[2] Aristotle's pupil Clearchus, for example, suggested that the Jews, like the Magi, were descended from the Indian Gymnosophists: see fr. 6 Wehrli (=Josephus, *AA* 1. 177–82, quoting from Clearchus, *On Sleep*, 1); and cf. D.L. 1. 9 (which includes a reference to Clearchus, *On Education* =fr. 13 Wehrli). See also Lewy (1938), 217–18.

[3] It has a literature to match: but for the wider historical and sociological con-

termination of the Jewish community as a whole to preserve its traditional beliefs and practices in self-conscious opposition to the syncretized theology of the Graeco-Egyptian hegemony. By their refusal to compromise with the customs and beliefs of the Greeks, the Jews were (at least, the Greeks felt that they were) implicitly questioning their validity; and this, from the pagan point of view, was tantamount not just to 'godlessness', but actually, because theology was so central to the Greek conception of polity, to subversion, a refusal to accept the *political* norms of Alexandrian life.[4] And in a sense, of course, the Jews *did* want to deny the validity of Graeco-Egyptian religious beliefs. They maintained that their own religious differences did not, as a matter of fact, lead them to question or transgress the strictly civil laws of the society in which they lived; but not only did they steadfastly refuse to abandon their own traditions, they refused in addition to countenance any offer of a syncretism designed to include them. The form of their religion was for them not just a matter of political expression, but of philosophical truth; and in that case, it could not be appropriate to adopt any other theology.

The Greek response to this position is highly informative for the development in thinking about philosophy and cultural traditions which I have been tracing in previous chapters, for it changed as the debate moved on, and it changed in ways that seem to me explicable precisely by appealing to the work of the Stoics. One of the consequences of the theory of primitive wisdom and its transmission developed by post-Posidonian Stoics was that a cultural tradition could be reckoned as philosophically more or less valid according as it preserved more or less intact its connection with primitive wisdom. In the light of this theory, one way of attacking the philosophical integrity of a culture would be to show that it had

text in which the rather narrow discussion of this chapter and the next should be set, see esp. Tcherikover and Fuks (1957–64) (i. 1–93 for a historical overview); Tcherikover (1959); Schürer, iii. 38–60 with 151–3; Kasher (1985); Feldman (1993). Particularly clear surveys (of rather different kinds) are given by Momigliano (1971) and Barclay (1996: pt. 1). Greek and Latin texts referring to the Jews are collected in Stern. Discussion of the various authors in Stone (1984), and especially in Schürer, vol. iii.

[4] But for all their antipathy to Jewish culture, it is not clear that we should view the Greeks as strictly *racist* in their dealings with the Jews. A Jew, for example, prepared to renounce, or to act as if he renounced, his ancestral religion might be accepted without prejudice into the heart of political life. See on this Barclay (1996), pt. 1.

somehow diverged from the oldest traditions, that it had corrupted or lost altogether its connection with primitive wisdom through innovations introduced into it later on. It seems to me no coincidence, then, that the relative antiquity and purity of the Jewish and Graeco-Egyptian traditions started in the later first century BC to become an important theme in the debate between them. So important, that it has often been read back by historians into earlier stages of the debate; in fact, however, it was entirely absent until then.

None of this is to say that the history of the Jewish people and their theology was not of interest to earlier Greeks. But the polemical conclusions drawn from them were, in the first place, of a very different nature, because born of a very different understanding of the nature of philosophical progress at large. When the fourth-century-BC philosopher and historian Hecataeus of Abdera, for example, criticized the innovations at the heart of Jewish culture, he did so not because of a belief that a more ancient, less corrupted theology would preserve elements of a primitive philosophy more purely.[5] He did so for almost the opposite reason, namely because he thought that those innovations had isolated the Jews from the course of philosophical *progress*. He makes his point by drawing a contrast between the early history of the Greek and Jewish nations. Both peoples, he says, were descended from the same racial and cultural origins,[6] and their common ancestors had dwelled for some time in Egypt—which, in Hecataeus'

[5] For Hecataeus in general see Schwartz (1885); Susemihl (1891–2), i. 310–14; Jacoby (1912); Fraser (1972), i. 496–505 with notes at ii. 719–27; Schäfer (1997), esp. 203–6 for his anti-Semitism. Hecataeus' remarks on the Jews as discussed here came from his *Egyptian Studies* (cf. Diodorus, *Library*, 1. 46. 8, for the title). The influence of this work was enormous, and increased by the fact that it apparently provided the basis for Diodorus' well-known account of Egypt in his *Library of History*: see *Library*, 1. 10–98, with Schwartz (1905), 670–2. It is through Diodorus, via Photius, that Hecataeus' account of the Jews' relationship with Egypt is preserved (Photius, *Library*, 244, 380^{a}7–381^{a}8 = Diodorus, *Library*, 40. 3 = Hecataeus, 264 fr. 6 Jacoby). A work specifically *On the Jews* was also attributed to Hecataeus, but is normally assumed to be spurious (cf. ch. 5 n. 8). The present fragment is generally taken to be genuine, although ironically Photius ascribes it to the impossibly early Hecataeus of Miletus (see 381^{a}8), in what must be a *lapsus calami* (*pace* Dornseiff 1938: 76 n. 1). It contains what is possibly the first reference to the 'Jews' as such in Greek literature, though the fragment of Theophrastus cited in n. 1 might be slightly earlier (cf. Stern, i. 8–9; 1973; but *contra*, Jaeger 1938: 134–53; Murray 1970; 1973).

[6] See Diodorus, *Library*, 40. 3. 2 (and cf. *Library*, 1. 28. 2–5, with Feldman 1990).

eyes, as in those of Plato and Aristotle shortly before him, was a nation whose long tradition of research had put it in the vanguard of philosophy at the period he is discussing.[7] But, while the Greeks—which is to say, that portion of the original 'Graeco-Judaic' stock who went on to establish the Greek nation after their expulsion from Egypt—embraced what they had learnt in Egypt, and went on to take that learning further, the Jews, he says, were embittered by their experience, and became increasingly misanthropic, retreating instead into a new theology of isolation (esp. Diodorus, *Library*, 40. 3. 4). The Jews in Hecataeus' account are a people who had been given, but had *rejected*, the same opportunities for philosophical advance as the Greeks, choosing instead to develop their own culture in despite of the rest of the world.

But if Hecataeus' attack on the philosophical basis of Jewish theology was conducted from within the context of a model of philosophical history very different from that implied by the work of the later Stoics, he at least recognized Jewish claims that their theology should be judged by the standards of philosophy in the first place. In this, he went further towards accommodating their position than the anti-Semitic historians of the centuries immediately following him. For them, the Jews' theology, like their own, was to be judged on primarily cultural grounds, and the strategy they adopted in attacking what they too saw as the isolationist position of the Jews involved a focus on the perceived *political* implications of their practices and beliefs. Philosophical validity was not, in other words, an issue for them under any model; social compatibility was all. And so, through historical narratives constructed to demonstrate the subversive and destructive influence in Egypt of the ancestors of the Jews, these writers attempted to argue for the dangers of showing tolerance to what they saw as an alien and antagonistic culture in their midst. And for the purposes of comparison with later, Stoicizing accounts of the Jews, it is worth noting that their need to stress that Jewish culture *was* alien rather attracts writers of this period to emphasize the

[7] For Plato and Aristotle see again ch. 1 n. 33; and, for their view of Greek philosophy as a further development of this tradition, esp. [Plato], *Epinomis*, 987 D, as cited there: 'We may take it that, whenever Greeks borrow anything from non-Greeks, they finally carry it to a higher perfection . . .'

foreign (but thereby, incidentally, the *prior*) roots of their religion.

Tutimaeus. In his reign, I know not how, god blew against Egypt, and men undistinguished of race came unexpectedly from the east, emboldened to invade the country, which they took easily by force without battle.

So begins the account of the Jews written by the third-century-BC Heliopolitan priest Manetho[8]—an account which goes on to develop a characterization of the Jews almost entirely in terms of the supposed antipathy of their race at large towards other cultures. The eastern men 'undistinguished of race' tyrannized Egypt, according to Manetho: they razed temples to the ground, and attempted to purge the country of her native inhabitants. They were finally expelled from Egypt when the kings of the Thebais rose up against them—but only moved their activities elsewhere. These people crossed the desert to Syria, and there terrorized the Assyrians as well. But, according to 'fables and current stories about the Jews', some of their number returned to Egypt later on, to support an uprising of maimed and leprous Egyptians of whom the then king, Amenophis, was trying to purge the country:[9]

They appointed as their leader Osarsiph,[10] one of the priests of Heliopo-

[8] Josephus, *AA* 1. 75–6; but see all of *AA* 1. 73–105 for Manetho's account, drawn from his *Egyptian Studies* (*Αἰγυπτιακά*)—a work which rivalled Hecataeus' for its subsequent influence. For Manetho's life and works generally see *Suda*, s.v.; Fruin (1847); Susemihl (1891–20), i. 608–16; Laqueur (1928) (1080–9 for Manetho's use by Christians); Waddell (1940), pp. vii–xxx; Schürer, iii. 595–7. There has been some debate over whether the account of Manetho in Josephus has been infected by material originating with a later anti-Semitic editor of Manetho. See e.g. E. Meyer (1904), 71–7; (1908), 34 n. 5, and the even more elaborate reconstruction of Laqueur (1928: 1064–80), who argues that Manetho's original work was later infected by *two* sources, one pro-Jewish, one anti-Semitic, and thus purges Manetho of any deliberate references to the Jews at all. Cf. also *FGrH* iiic ad Manetho (no. 609), esp. note on p. 84; Waddell (1940), pp. xvii–xix; Weill (1918), 68–76 and (on *AA* 1. 250 in particular) 101; Fraser (1972), i. 505–9 with ii. 730–1 n. 105; Gager (1972), 113–18, esp. 116. But for a more conservative view see Tcherikover (1959), 362–3; Schäfer (1997); and cf. Barclay (1996), 33 with n. 44: 'it is possible that some of these judgements have been influenced by the doctrinaire conviction that such anti-Jewish statements could not have arisen this early'.

[9] Josephus, *AA* 1. 238–40; but see all of 1. 227–51. This passage is generally contrasted with the earlier 'historical' account discussed above (cf. e.g. Schürer, iii. 595)—although in fact the two extracts make perfect sense read as parts of a single narrative.

[10] For this name see Reinach (1930, pp. xxx–xxxi) who suggests that it represents

lis, and swore to obey him in everything. He set down as his first law that they should not worship the gods, nor abstain from any of the sacred animals held in special reverence in Egypt, but should sacrifice and consume them all; and that they should not have contact with anyone except those who had taken their oath. After laying down these and many other laws absolutely opposed to Egyptian custom, he ordered all hands to repair the walls of the city and make ready for war with Amenophis the king.

Absolutely opposed to Egyptian custom. This is the key to Manetho's attack on the Jews. The Jews had no right to claim tolerance for their religion in Egypt—not because it lacked intrinsic philosophical value as such (that question did not arise), but rather because it was taken by Manetho to embody misanthropy, and, in particular, an essential (and apparently irrational) antipathy to the customs of the Egyptians. The Jews of Manetho's day claimed that their religious observances were perfectly compatible with due respect for the laws of the land; Manetho's argument was that a nation's religious and political life were much more closely linked, and a people who rejected the one could only be doing so for reasons which would lead them to despise the other as well.

Much the same approach to the Jews can be seen in the tradition of anti-Semitic history which continued after Manetho into the second and early first centuries BC. We have several examples of the genre: notable, and notable especially for the extremes of his account, is the second-century-BC writer Lysimachus,[11] who argued that the Jews were expelled from Egypt because of a leprous disease they contracted which offended the Sun, and led to persistent failure of crops (Josephus, *AA* 1. 304–11). Again, Lysi-

Joseph, with 'Osiris' substituted for the first syllable on the basis of an identification between Osiris and Yah; van der Horst (1987: 50 n. 8 to fr. 1, with references) suggests a compound formation from Osiris and Sepa. At *AA* 1. 250 Josephus tells us that Manetho identified Osarsiph with Moses: but for sceptical views of his report see Weill (1918), 101, and Laqueur (1928), 1071–2.

[11] Fragments of Lysimachus at *FGrH* 621. If he is identified (*pace* Jacoby) with the Alexandrian Lysimachus who wrote the *Theban Paradoxes* and the *Home-comings* (*FGrH* 382), then his dates can be set with slightly more precision between *c.*175 BC and the early 1st cent. AD: see Gudeman (1928), 32–9; Fraser (1972), ii. 1092–3 n. 475. He seems in any case to have written later than the late 3rd cent. (since at fr. 11 Jacoby he quotes the late 3rd-cent. author Mnaseas—for whom see *Suda*, s.v. Ἐρατοσθένης; Schürer, iii. 597–8); but earlier than Apion (the obvious implication of Josephus, *AA* 2. 20: cf. Schürer, iii. 600).

machus makes a great deal of the Jews' antipathy to the gods and established religion of Egypt: not only did their diseased state offend the Sun and pollute the temples in the first place, but the Jews who escaped the subsequent purge readily agreed to follow the advice of their leader, Moses, to, among other things, 'overthrow any temples and altars of the gods which they found [*θεῶν τε ναοὺς καὶ βωμούς, οἷς ἂν περιτύχωσιν, ἀνατρέπειν*]' (1. 309). In the land 'now called Judaea' they maltreated the native people and burnt down their temples as well. In brazen celebration of their sacrilegious proclivities, the Jews went on to found a city called *Hierosyla* ('Temple-Pillage')—a city which was only renamed *Hierosolyma* ('Jerusalem', suggesting, in Greek, a *holy* city) when a sense of shame caught up with later generations. And again, we can see that Lysimachus' one argument against the Jewish position (behind the straightforward slanders) is his claim that the Jews' isolation from the religious norms of the country in which they lived could only have come from a sort of misanthropy, an antipathy to their hosts which, given licence, could easily break out again into violence against the city.[12]

2. *Anti-Semitism in Post-Posidonian Literature*

We learn almost all of what we know of the anti-Semitic writing of the Hellenistic age from the work of a single author, the first-century-AD Jewish historian Josephus.[13] In his work *Against Apion* he takes the reader through the works of a number of authors writing in Greek about, and mostly against, his people—his purpose being, of course, to refute their suggestion that the Jewish adherence to their religion was a function of their misanthropic refusal to accommodate the differing customs around which different nations were structured.

Or at least, one might have expected that to be his purpose.

[12] Cf. also in the early 1st cent. BC Apollonius Molon, who is mentioned twice by Josephus in the same breath as Lysimachus (at *AA* 2. 145 and 236) and who presumably shared similar views with him. See, on Apollonius, Brzoska (1896); Fraser (1972), i. 505–11; Schürer, iii. 598–600.

[13] The most important exception to this is Hecataeus, of whose history Josephus seems to be entirely ignorant. (Josephus knows the more philo-Semitic but presumably pseudepigraphic work *On the Jews*: see *AA* 1. 183–204; but, ironically, this is less helpful to him in establishing the antiquity of the Jews than the history itself might have been. See further ch. 5 with n. 8.) As far as Josephus is concerned, then, Manetho was the earliest anti-Semitic historian of Egypt: see *AA* 1. 223.

Against Apion is certainly an apologetic work, and it does address specific historical inaccuracies and unfounded racial slanders identified by Josephus in the texts that he cites. But his *purpose* in citing these texts is rather more specific than this. Consider, for example, his response to Manetho's account (*AA* 1. 104; cf. 1. 252):

> Manetho has thus furnished us with evidence from Egyptian literature on two most important points: first that we came into Egypt from elsewhere, and secondly that we left it at a date so remote in the past that it preceded the Trojan War by nearly a thousand years.

Or again, in replying to Lysimachus, Josephus points out that Lysimachus left it unclear whether he thought that the Jews constituted a clearly defined race of 'foreigners' in Egypt, or whether, in fact, they only 'became' a race when they were expelled (*AA* 1. 314). For Josephus, in other words, the issue of the antiquity and origins of his race was one which outweighed all others in importance. To a modern reader of his work, his focus on this apparently rather academic point seems strangely inappropriate as a response to the slurs that actually were directed against his race by historians such as Manetho and Lysimachus. Indeed, my argument is that it would have seemed unintelligible as a response in the eyes of those writers themselves: Manetho and Lysimachus were clearly not interested in the racial or cultural antiquity of the Jews, an issue which they would presumably have considered irrelevant to their polemical stance. However, we should not, of course, be measuring Josephus' arguments against the assumptions of Manetho or Lysimachus or their audience, any more than we should measure them against our own: rather, we need to look at them in the context in which Josephus himself was writing. As we shall see, by this time the situation had started to change: for the anti-Semitic writers in Josephus' immediate background had started to view traditional theology in the philosophical terms of the later Stoa, and *had*, as a consequence, started to introduce theories of racial antiquity into the heart of their polemic.

At an earlier stage, as I have stressed, the antiquity of a theological tradition had, as such, no bearing on its philosophical validity. Indeed, it is mistaken to think that the Greeks in general viewed 'philosophical validity' as an appropriate measure for theological traditions at all at this time: the pursuit of philosophy and the reception of religious forms were on the whole taken to be quite distinct matters, the former a progressive science, the latter a more or less stable expression of cultural identity.[14] So Judaism might *either* be considered in the light of a system of cultural mores, and attacked (as by Manetho and Lysimachus) as inappropriate for citizens of Egyptian society; *or* it might be considered in the light of a philosophical tradition—but then attacked (as by Hecataeus) for its isolation from contemporary advances. No Greek at this stage viewed it as *both*—as (what the Jews themselves presumably thought) a culture embodying an ancient philosophical heritage. But this above all is what the researches of the later Stoics changed. Someone like Cornutus, writing in the first century AD, could look *through* mythological traditions to a time in the primitive age of mankind when there was already a perfect philosophy, fully formed; and in consequence he could think that the antiquity and conservatism of a culture such as that of Egypt might mean that it best preserved this philosophy. Cornutus' Stoic contemporary Chaeremon (of whom more below) was a student of Egyptian theology, which he used, not as a starting-point for further innovation, but actually as the immediate object of philosophical enquiry. Plato wanted to build on the beginning made in Egyptian philosophy (Hecataeus criticized the Jews for failing to do so); but Chaeremon wanted to recover the beginnings of their theology as itself embodying the highest philosophical wisdom. For Cornutus and Chaeremon, and the later Stoics more generally, a cultural tradition was undoubtedly an expression of national identity; but it was *also* possible to judge it in terms of its philosophical value. And this development in the approach to traditional theology had a profound effect on the Greek attitude towards cultural dependency. If, for example, Egyptian theology was taken to preserve in relatively pure form elements of primitive wisdom, then any change made to their theology would, of course, be a change for the worse. If a people had inherited the theology of Egypt *and altered it at all*, then the objective, philosophical validity of their theology would *to that extent* be compromised. So here was a new basis for attacking the

[14] The Greeks were taken by Herodotus to have derived both their gods (cf. *Histories*, 2. 4, 50) and the seeds of their philosophy (cf. *Histories*, 2. 123) from Egypt—but there is no suggestion that the two things go together, that the inheritance of a theology implies reception of the philosophy or vice versa.

uncompromising position taken by the Jews in Alexandria. For, if Jewish theology could be accounted for as a wholesale *corruption* of Egyptian theology, then its philosophical validity could be compared—objectively and unfavourably—with its supposed ancestor.[15]

It was, as I suggested in the last chapter, the work of Posidonius that formed the basis for later Stoic thinking on the importance of cultural history in the reconstruction of primitive wisdom. For this reason alone, and although there is no reason to think that Posidonius himself was responsible for framing the theory developed on the basis of his work, it is unfortunate that his own views on the status of the Jewish race are particularly hard to discern. He certainly discussed the Jews: Josephus informs us that he (with Apollonius Molon) provided material for the work of the eponymous target of his own books *Against Apion* (*AA* 2. 79); but it is unlikely that this information can lead us to any more specific details of his views.[16] If the very fact of his association with Apion suggests an anti-Semitic slant to Posidonius, it should be set against the rather more positive attitude adopted in Strabo's account of the Jews, for which Posidonius is also likely to have been a source.[17] In fact, as far as we are concerned (and also, as it happens, as far as Josephus himself is concerned), the first indication of a shift in

[15] It is worth remembering that earlier Greeks traced their own mythological and philosophical traditions (as variously Herodotus and Hecataeus), and at times even their racial origins (cf. Plato, *Timaeus*, 21 E 6–7; Anaximenes of Lampsacus, 72 fr. 20 Jacoby), back to Egypt, without any sense that they were thereby undermining the validity of Greek culture. It was only later on that such models (though still employed: cf. perhaps as late as the 6th cent. AD Charax, 103 fr. 39 Jacoby) came to be viewed as potentially damaging to them—*in so far*, that is, as they might imply the Greeks' reception of a philosophically inferior theological tradition. Cf. especially Plutarch's criticisms of Herodotus for his 'malicious' claims that Greek theology derived from Egyptian (*On Herodotus' Malice*, 857 C–F; and further ch. 6).

[16] Two anti-Semitic fables from Apion have sometimes been traced back to Posidonius (Josephus, *AA* 2. 79–96 = Posidonius fr. 278 EK); but Josephus tells us only that Posidonius was *a* source for Apion, not *the* source for these tales (the first of which is in any case at odds with Diodorus 34/35. 1. 3, which is more likely to be Posidonian in source). See further Kidd (1988), 948–51.

[17] Strabo, *Geography*, 16. 2. 34–9: note in particular that Moses is claimed here for an Egyptian priest, but that the Jews' later innovations in religious practice (e.g. the move to monotheism from Egyptian polytheism) are clearly meant to canvass our respect. Assuming Posidonius was a (or the) source for this passage (and cf. Heinemann 1919), it acts as some confirmation that the link between cultural dependency and cultural inferiority was not forged *by* him even if it was developed on the basis of his work.

attitude towards the significance of the Jews' racial descent in anti-semitic history comes from the early first century AD with the work of the Alexandrian philologist and historian Apion himself.[18] And the importance of Apion in this context is perhaps confirmed by (and explains) the disproportionate amount of time which Josephus devotes to refuting his claims in his work on the antiquity of the Jews[19]—the work which, for this reason, has become known as *Against Apion*.[20]

The anti-Semitic slant of Apion's historical account of the Jews is hardly unexpected in the light of his historical antecedents. But, at least as far as Josephus is concerned, *Apion's* anti-Semitism in particular was epitomized by the fact that he consciously argued for the position that the Jews were Egyptian in origin, only gaining a new national identity when they left (were, in fact, expelled from) Egypt. According to Apion (whose account of the exodus is recorded by Josephus at *AA* 2. 8–32), the Jewish race could trace its roots back to Egyptian fugitives led into the wilderness by a native of Heliopolis called Moses.

There is some direct evidence that Apion was interested in the comparative relationship of nations recognized by him for their antiquity—we have fragments which point to his interest in comparing Greek theology and Roman custom with Egyptian wisdom, for example; and evidence that he wrote an ethnographical study of some kind.[21] We know, furthermore, that Apion was familiar with

[18] Apion's dates are *c*.30–25 BC to AD 50. On Apion generally see Cohn (1894); Motzo (1912–13); Jacobson (1977); Schürer, iii. 604–7. Apion's career has certain points of similarity with that of the Stoic Chaeremon (see further below): they both held the headship of the Alexandrian school; and both represented Greek interests against the Jews in embassies to the emperor—Apion in AD 39–40, on an embassy whose Jewish representative was Philo of Alexandria (see Josephus, *Antiquities*, 18. 257–60).

[19] Josephus devotes the first 144 paragraphs of *AA* 2 to his refutation. Contrast 92 paragraphs on Manetho (1. 73–105+227–87), 16 on Lysimachus (1. 304–20), and 15 on Chaeremon (1. 288–303).

[20] The original title of Josephus' work seems to have been *On the Antiquity of the Jews* (*Περὶ τῆς τῶν Ἰουδαίων ἀρχαιότητος*: cf. e.g. Origen, *Against Celsus*, 1. 16). The first writer to refer to the book as 'against Apion' seems to have been Jerome: cf. *Epistle* 70. 3 ('duos libros scripsit [sc. Josephus] contra Apionem'), with Schürer, i. 55.

[21] In his book *On Apis* he argued that the goddess Aphrodite represented in the Greek tradition exactly what Athor represented in Egyptian theology (see *Etymologicum Magnum Auctum*, 26. 7=Apion, 616 fr. 20 Jacoby); and elsewhere he linked the ancient Greek and Roman custom of wearing a ring on the fourth finger of the left hand to facts thrown up by Egyptian medical science (see Aulus Gellius, *Attic*

and used the work of the Stoic Posidonius, and presumably had contact in any case with such Stoics as were active in the Alexandria of his day.[22] His new claim that the Jewish race was descended from Egyptian stock cannot, against this background, be viewed as a matter of purely incidental interest: it seems clear that Apion, under the influence of the later Stoic theory that the most ancient cultural traditions held a privileged intellectual status, argued for the youth of the Jewish nation as a way of denying the philosophical validity of its theology. According to Apion, the best that could be said of this theology is that it was an offshoot and corruption of the Egyptian culture the Jews had abandoned. Josephus informs us that one class of Apion's criticism of the Jews was constituted by 'accusations against our [Jewish] temple-rites and our laws in general',[23] and it looks very much as if the specific nature of his accusations was precisely that these rites and laws were degenerate derivatives of Egyptian religion (and to that extent philosophically worthless, we are supposed to understand). Moses, according to Apion, was already supposed to have erected fantastic temples in Heliopolis, which seem meant to suggest travesties of Egyptian originals:[24] oriented towards the east *because Heliopolis is*, for example (*ὧδε γὰρ καὶ*

Nights, 10. 10). The ethnographical study is the *Ἱστορία κατ᾽ ἔθνος* attributed to him by the *Suda* (s.v. *Ἀπίων*)—although Cohn (1894: 2804) argues that this title does not represent a study distinct from the *Egyptian Studies* from which Josephus quotes (cf. e.g. *AA* 2. 10).

[22] For Posidonius' influence on Apion see Josephus, *AA* 2. 79. There were Stoic philosophers active in Alexandria at the time when Apion was writing—a change from the situation in the 3rd cent., when the lack of their presence at all led Ptolemy to invite Cleanthes or one of his pupils to court there (see D.L. 7. 185: both Cleanthes and Chrysippus declined the offer, and Sphaerus went in their place). In the 2nd cent. we hear of one Stoic in Alexandria, a pupil of Diogenes of Babylon called Chrysermos, who is known to us only from the *Index of Stoics* col. 52. 4–6 Dorandi (but the Chrysermi had been an important Alexandrian family at least since the 3rd cent.: cf. e.g. Staden 1989: 523–8). Later Alexandrian Stoics include Arius Didymus in the 1st cent. BC, and Chaeremon in the 1st cent. AD.

[23] See *AA* 2. 6–7. Josephus tells us that Apion's attacks on the Jews could be arranged into three categories, the other two being his history of the exodus and his account of the position of the Jews in contemporary Alexandria.

[24] Cf. Gager (1972), 123, on Apion's reference here to the 'native customs' (*AA* 2. 10: *πατρίοις ἔθεσι*) by which Moses was guided: they were, he suggests, 'the practices of his native Egyptian religion which he adopted as the basis of the new cult in Jerusalem'. It might be noted that Gager (ibid.) supposes that the temples described here were established in Jerusalem, not Heliopolis. This is perhaps a more attractive possibility; but Josephus' text gives no indication that Moses has left his native country at this point.

Ἡλίου κεῖται πόλις: *AA* 2. 10–11); but with pillars *instead of obelisks* (ibid., with the suggestion of a deliberate corruption of Egyptian architectural form). They were set up to trace the course of the sun—a fact which should, perhaps, recall the primacy in Egyptian mythology of the sun-god Atum-Re, and presumably reflects the Heliopolitans' particularly close association with him. Apion's claim that the Jews worshipped an ass's head (*AA* 2. 80–8) might similarly have been intended to suggest a travesty of the Egyptians' veneration of certain animals. Apion, like his anti-Semitic predecessors, criticized the cultural exclusivity of the Jews of his own time, and in particular the refusal of Jews living in Alexandria to worship the gods of the Egyptians (*AA* 2. 65–7). But for Apion it was not merely their exclusivity that made their position offensive. It was also the fact that their religion, far from being the philosophically superior theology they claimed, was in fact a corruption of an older and purer antecedent whose legitimacy they were now refusing to accept as a basis for civic life in its own native territory.

Apion's most important claim to originality in his historical account of the Jews lay, then, in his use of the supposed fact of their Egyptian ancestry as a way of undermining the possibility that the distinctive elements of their own tradition contained anything of (antiquity and therefore of) philosophical value. And I have suggested that this is the single most important reason why Josephus devotes such a long time to the refutation of Apion. In his discussion of earlier Greek historians of the Jewish people he often seems to miss their point, as we have seen: in particular, he rejoices in their 'inability' to prove the youth of the Jewish race when it was clearly never their intention to attempt it. But this turns out to be part of a wider strategy on his part: by discussing these historians from the perspective of the later debate, Josephus was hoping to isolate the position of Apion, to undermine his 'proof' of the youth of Jewish culture by suggesting that his predecessors had already tried and failed to do the same. Josephus clearly understood the nature of the development in the argument with Apion, and in particular the significance in his own intellectual world of the claim of Jewish dependency on (and descendence from) the Egyptians.

And yet, one might think that there is an alternative to this explanation: that Josephus attacks Apion at such length simply because of the extremes of anti-Semitism to which Apion went. However, although Apion was certainly anti-Semitic, he was not the only, and he was not the most extreme, anti-Semitic historian among those whom Josephus considers. Lysimachus is far more trenchant and abusive than Apion, yet he earns little more than a tenth of the time Josephus devotes to the refutation of Apion. On the other hand, Josephus also attacks with some vigour at least one thinker whose account of the Jews seems, by comparison, to have been almost conciliatory. This is the account given by Apion's younger contemporary, the Stoic philosopher Chaeremon[25]—someone whose views are of great relevance to this study, not just in general terms because of his school affiliation, but also because we know that he in particular took a great deal of interest in the allegorical exegesis of ancient theologies, and in the issues of antiquity and transmission the study required.[26]

Chaeremon was no philo-Semite in his political life: apart from anything else, we know that he took a leading role in an embassy to complain about the Jews to the emperor Claudius (as Apion had earlier taken part in representations to Caligula).[27] But the depiction of the moral character at least of the Jews' antecedents in his account (preserved, again, by Josephus: see *AA* 1. 288–92=

[25] Chaeremon was probably born in the first decade of our era, and died perhaps around AD 80 (and in any case before AD 96). On his life and work quite generally see esp. Frede (1989); also Schwartz (1897). Fragments at *FGrH* 618; with commentary in Schwyzer (1932) and, more recently, in van der Horst (1987). Cf. also Stern, i. 417–21. Stern (i. 421) tendentiously suggests that 'Although Josephus . . . blames Chaeremon for being vague, it stands to reason that he did not have Chaeremon's original work before him, but only some fragments from a collection that may have been made by a Hellenistic Jew.'

[26] I have already noted (in ch. 3) that Chaeremon was placed with Cornutus at the head of Porphyry's list of allegorical exegetes whose work was used by Origen (Test. 9 van der Horst=Porphyry, *Against the Christians*, fr. 39. 30–5 Harnack). For Chaeremon's interpretation of allegory found in the Egyptian tradition see esp. frr. 2, 5, 6, 7, 10, 12 van der Horst; cf. frr. 15D, 17D, 18D, 19D, 20D, 25D, 28D van der Horst; for his comparison of Greek and Egyptian theology see Test. 12 van der Horst; also fr. 18D van der Horst. In fr. 2 van der Horst Chaeremon deals directly with the vexed question of the relative antiquity of the Chaldean and Egyptian philosophical traditions.

[27] We do not know so much about the later representation, but it apparently concerned 'the same sort of quarrel with the Jews that Apion had conducted in the time of Caligula' (so Schürer, iii. 603). Our evidence for Chaeremon's involvement in this embassy rests on identifying him with the 'Chaeremon son of Leonidas' mentioned as a petitioner in Claudius' reply (=Tcherikover and Fuks 1957–64: no. 153; Chaeremon's name at p. 39, l. 17): cf. Chaeremon Test. 5 van der Horst. For discussion of the letter see e.g. Jones (1926); Barclay (1996), 55–60.

Chaeremon fr. 1 van der Horst) is remarkably restrained, especially when it is compared with the accounts of his predecessors. To be sure, his story contains many of the elements to be found in Apion (with whose narrative it shares its general structure), in Manetho, and in Lysimachus: the Jews, he implies, derived from 'polluted people' (*τῶν τοὺς μολυσμοὺς ἐχόντων*) expelled from Egypt under the leadership of the priests Tisithen (identified with Moses) and Peteseph (identified with Joseph). But, uniquely among surviving anti-Semitic historians, Chaeremon does not claim that the presence of these 'polluted' people had been a cause of difficulties for Egypt in the first place, nor does he give his authorial support for the suggestion that the gods would be appeased by their expulsion. Rather the opposite on both counts. According to Chaeremon, it was not the polluted who had caused offence to the gods (as it was in Lysimachus), but the king, Amenophis, himself (*AA* 1. 289). And it was not the gods who suggested their expulsion (as again in Lysimachus, through the medium of an oracle), but the priest Phritobautes (ibid.)—who was clearly not an entirely accurate interpreter of their will, since, far from curing the problems suffered by the king, the expulsion led directly to final disaster for him. Supported by a large body of allies, the exiles returned to Egypt in force, and Amenophis was compelled to flee the country in his turn (*AA* 1. 292).

Josephus does not pick up any of these points: he does not stress, as he might have done to his own advantage in a different polemical context, that Chaeremon refused to accede to the extremes of his predecessors in attacking the moral character of the Jews and their forebears, even *despite* his political opposition to the demands of the Alexandrian community. So why does Josephus attack Chaeremon at all? Because the clear implication of Chaeremon's account is that Jewish culture—perhaps the Jewish race as well—had its roots firmly in Egypt. Moses and Joseph (Tisithen and Peteseph) are explicitly claimed for the Egyptians, and it seems that we are supposed to think that the Egyptians expelled from the land under their leadership formed the basic stock of the Jewish race. Josephus, to be sure, claims that Chaeremon's account leaves it unclear whether the Jews are supposed to be traced back to these Egyptians, or to the mysterious allies who joined them in their struggle (*AA* 1. 291 with 297–302); and he suggests that Chaeremon left it an open question whether these allies were foreigners or Egyptians themselves. Indeed, he says that this unclarity is the 'most amazing' feature of Chaeremon's account (*θαυμασιώτατον*: *AA* 1. 302). But it is Josephus, not Chaeremon, who is fudging the issue. Perhaps Chaeremon did leave the matter unclear: but he would not have to prove that the Jews as a whole were descended from Egyptians in order to suggest the derivation of their theology from Egypt. Presumably Chaeremon might have supposed that his readers would understand the decisive influence on the cultural development of the Jewish people to have been the nationality of their original leaders: Moses and Joseph, clearly identified by him as Egyptians (and priests to boot). And presumably he would have been right to suppose this as well, which is why Josephus spends the time that he does in attacking him.

The focus of pagan antisemitism had shifted, then, by the first century AD. Building on the accusations of misanthropy and cultural isolation on which Hecataeus, Manetho, and Lysimachus had variously relied, but framing their attack in the theoretical terms provided by the work of the later Stoics, Greek historians started to attack Jewish theology by subordinating it to (supposedly) more ancient and purer traditions of thought whose preservation of primitive wisdom allowed them to serve as canons of philosophical validity. If they could show that Jewish theology was an evolution of Egyptian tradition, then its philosophical standing would be undermined just in so far as it differed from its conservative ancestor. The Alexandrian Jews would be left with no intellectual basis for maintaining their ancestral customs against pressure to conform to Graeco-Egyptian norms. But the Jews themselves were ready to answer in kind; and in the next chapter we shall see how their counter-polemic traced exactly the same theoretical development.

5

Antiquity in Jewish Apologetic

1. *Jewish Historians in the Third and Second Centuries BC*

In Chapter 4 I argued that the first century BC saw the introduction of a new motif into the repertoire of anti-Semitic history, an argument from the supposed youth of the Jewish theological tradition to its philosophical inferiority: this, I suggested, provides evidence for the shift in attitude towards ancient cultural traditions as such introduced by the theories of the later Stoa. But the way in which Jews responded to the onslaught of intellectual anti-Semitism provides evidence for this development that is just as interesting and informative. It might be the case that the Jews came to the debate with a distinctive cultural and literary heritage of their own; but at the same time those, at least, who wrote in Greek against the Greeks were naturally familiar with the cultural assumptions and literary forms of their adversaries. They knew, of course, the significance of the arguments moved against them. This means that it is also possible to garner from their own accounts of themselves and their position in Egypt evidence for the way in which Greek thinking on the philosophical question of cultural authority developed.

The Jews, as I say, came to the debate from a different background; but their own understanding of their cultural tradition might have allowed them to describe their theological heritage in terms much closer on the surface of things to the kind of theoretical position adopted by later Greek thinkers such as Apion. It was only in the later Midrashic tradition that Jews started to make a concerted attempt to claim, for example, that the practices codified in the Mosaic Law had already been current among the Patriarchs;[1]

[1] But see already, for example, *The Book of Jubilees*, presumably written at some

nevertheless, they believed long before this that the ancestors of Moses held a privileged relationship with and understanding of God—that in one important sense, the Mosaic religion they had inherited only expressed through certain forms and practices a much older theological tradition which lay at its philosophical core. What is more, the fact that this longer tradition could be traced to a period of human antiquity (to Noah and again, if necessary, to Adam) from which *all* nations must derive their origins shows that pagan theology must strictly be viewed as a result of a *later divergence* from it. The Jewish understanding of God preserved the purest and most ancient theology: the best that might be said of any other religion was that it was a divergent development from it.

If the Jews were, philosophically speaking, in a position to argue along these lines, it is striking that the response of Jewish intellectuals to Greek anti-Semitic propaganda did not, in the first place, contain any hint that they did. As we shall see, the Jews did develop early on the argument that the Gentiles at large and the Greeks in particular owed much to the Jews for their own philosophical and cultural development;[2] but they did not even do this in order to prove the *antiquity* of the Jews, or assert the corruption and youth of the Greeks measured against the standard they provided.[3] And the reason for this must be that such an argument would have been meaningless or worse to a Greek audience at this stage. For the Greeks themselves, as I showed, had not yet come to the belief that cultural traditions could be judged in terms of any philosophical wisdom they might be supposed to have preserved from primitive antiquity, and would not have recognized a response to their criticisms of the Jews that relied on such a belief. When the Greeks criticized the philosophical standing of the Jews, it was (as we have seen in Hecataeus) because they believed them to have isolated themselves from the philosophical *progress*

time in the 2nd cent. BC (cf. Schürer, iii. 308–18, esp. 311). In this work several Jewish festivals are traced back to pre-Mosaic roots—as early as Noah in the case of Pentecost (6. 17–22; and cf. Schürer, iii. 310 with n. 4 for further examples).

[2] e.g. Eupolemus, 723 fr. 1 Jacoby: Moses was the first sage (σοφός), and he invented the art of writing, which was taken from the Jews by the Phoenicians, and thence by the Greeks. Artapanus and Aristobulus make more generous claims, discussed further below.

[3] The fact that later (particularly Christian) authors were able to use them to this end (cf. e.g. Eusebius, *Ecclesiastical History*, 6. 13. 7) is, of course, no counter-evidence to this.

made among the Gentile nations, not because they thought them to be cut off from the primitive roots of philosophy. But for the most part their attacks on Jewish culture did not even touch on any philosophical wisdom it might or might not have contained: the disdain of Manetho, Lysimachus, and their like for Jewish culture was based rather on its supposedly misanthropic and subversive foundation; their arguments were intended to lead their audience to deduce from historical precedent to the political danger still posed by the Jews in their city. This, then, was the accusation that the Jews had to address[4]—and an assertion of their cultural antiquity would be powerless against it. It is, then, no surprise after all that it is the integrity and wisdom of the Jewish race, the beneficial contribution of its members to the history of civilization, that characterizes the Graeco-Judaic literature of the second century—and not at all the demonstration of Jewish antiquity. Oracles were 'discovered' which attested to the historical importance of the Jews and the special favour shown to them by God;[5] a whole industry existed for the forgery of pagan literature, from individual verses[6] to complete monographs devoted to the Jews,[7] all designed to show

[4] This is not to say that the various works to be mentioned below were intended primarily for a Gentile audience—no doubt some were and some were not. But cf. Speyer (1971: 157), according to whom the 'younger books of the Old Testament', along with Esther, Judith, Tobit, *III Maccabees*, and even the Septuagint translation, were composed with an eye on the possibility of a non-Jewish audience.

[5] See on the forged *Sibylline Oracles* Speyer (1971), 165–6; Collins (1974); Barclay (1996), 216–28. Despite their purported antiquity, it was rather to 'exert religious persuasion' (Schürer, iii. 617–18; cf. Barclay 1996: 221) than to demonstrate the antiquity of the Jewish race that they were written. See in particular the fragment (from *Oracles* book 2 or 3: cf. Schürer, iii. 638–40) preserved at Theophilus, *To Autolycus*, 2. 36 (on monotheism); or again *Oracles* 3. 213–47 (with Schürer, iii. 632–9: on the social and political customs of the Jews).

[6] Zeegers-Vander Vorst (1972: 187–9) argues that there were actually Jewish 'anthologies' of (largely forged) quotations from Classical authors compiled for this purpose. For the whole question of Jewish forgeries see Speyer (1971), esp. 150–68; and cf. Schürer, iii. 656–71. For a collection of forged Greek verse in English translation see Charlesworth (1983–5), ii. 821–30.

[7] One of the most important of such forgeries is ps.-Aristeas' *Letter to Philocrates* (translated e.g. at Charlesworth 1983–5: ii. 7–34), which purports to describe the circumstances of the making of the Septuagint: Schürer (iii. 677), characterizing its purpose, calls it a 'panegyric on Jewish Law, Jewish wisdom, and the Jewish name in general'. Much has been made of the 'allegorical' exegesis to be found in ps.-Aristeas, but this plays no part in, and is not associated with, the antiquity of Judaism, and so is largely irrelevant for the present study. It is in any case probable that the allegorical sections of the *Letter* were no part of the original work: see Février (1924), esp. 22–30 and 55–68, arguing largely on the grounds that they are not included in Josephus' paraphrase of the letter. They are not the only sections

that the wisest Greek writers concurred with Jewish monotheism, and that the intellectual and cultural antecedents of someone like Manetho had written with deep interest in and respect for the Jewish people in general as well as for the wisdom and virtue of Jewish individuals. Allusions to the *antiquity* of the Jewish race are conspicuously, almost unnaturally, absent from these works. Consider, for example, the work *On the Jews* ascribed to the fourth-century-BC historian Hecataeus, whose *Egyptian Studies* I examined in the previous chapter. *On the Jews* is philo-Semitic in tone, much more so than the references to the Jewish race in the *Egyptian Studies* might have led one to expect; and this is the primary reason for thinking that it might be a later Jewish forgery.[8] But if so, it is remarkable that its real author had nothing to say about the earlier roots of his people: Josephus was able to find in it nothing more than a proof that the Jews were flourishing as a race at the time of Alexander (cf. *AA* 1. 185). Pseudo-Hecataeus (if such he is) confirms the overwhelming impression that the polemical context within which discussion of Jews was conducted in the third and second centuries BC revolved around the relationship between their religious views and their political morality, not around issues of racial or cultural origin.

None of this is to deny all continuity between the apologetic literature of the earlier Hellenistic era and the arguments put forward by later writers, such as Philo and Josephus, who were very concerned indeed with proving the antiquity of their race. One theme which forms an obvious bridge over the divide I am trying to sketch is the claim that the Greeks had actually *borrowed* from Jewish philosophy, that Greek culture at large was indebted

omitted by Josephus (cf. Fraser 1972: ii. 980); but, nevertheless, they are 'quite different from the rest of the work' (so Schürer, iii. 679), and do not seem to play an important part in the argument of the work as a whole. It should also be noted that the dates of ps.-Aristeas are not at all certain: he is normally located in the 2nd cent. BC, but has been placed as late as Caligula (Willrich 1900: 118–26; 1924: 86–91). See further Schürer, iii. 677–87 (esp. 682 n. 285).

[8] So already Herennius Philo in the 2nd cent. AD (Origen, *Against Celsus*, 1. 15). More recent scholarship has taken every shade of opinion on the subject. Among those who consider the work genuine, cf. esp. Lewy (1932); Gager (1969). Elter (1893–5: 248–54) argues that the work was a part of Hecataeus' *Egyptian Studies*. Among those who consider the work spurious see Walter (1964), 189–94; Schaller (1963); Bar-Kochva (1996). Wacholder (1974: 262–73) thinks the work is triply spurious—that is, he distinguishes the hands of *three* forgers in the work. But others steer a middle path, suggesting that the work is essentially authentic, but that it has been subject to pro-Jewish revision: cf. Stern, i. 23–4; Schürer, iii. 671–3.

at a relatively early stage to the prior activity of the Jews. As we shall see, a form of this argument played an important part in later assertions of the superior antiquity of the Jews; and, through its reception into Christian apologetic, had a long and fertile history in this role (see especially Chapter 9). But its earliest manifestations are to be found at a rather earlier period—at a period when, as I am arguing, the question of antiquity was no polemical issue. The reason why this is possible is simple: we should not be misled by the continuity of the theme into supposing that the purpose behind its use remained the same as well. There were Jews in the third and second centuries BC who argued for the dependency of Graeco-Egyptian culture on the Jewish tradition; but there is no evidence at all that they used this supposed fact to argue for the antiquity of their race. Once again, the issue was not the *age* of Judaism but the value of its contribution to intellectual and social life. This is something that is well illustrated in the work of Artapanus, a shadowy figure, probably of the second century BC, the fragments of whose works include some of the most comprehensive claims for the debt owed by pagan culture to the Jews that can be found anywhere at all.[9] In his work *On the Jews*, which included a lively and imaginative retelling of sections of biblical history, he said, for example, that Abraham taught astronomy to the Egyptians (Eusebius, *Preparation for the Gospel*, 9. 18, 420 B), and that Joseph instituted a system for dividing up the land (Eusebius, *Preparation for the Gospel*, 9. 23, 429 C–D; cf. perhaps Genesis, 47. 18–26). Even more extravagant claims are made for Moses (Eusebius, *Preparation for the Gospel*, 9. 27, 431 D–436 D): he was supposed to have introduced into Egypt machines and instruments to facilitate sailing, war, building, and the drawing of water; he was responsible (curiously) for the form taken by Egyptian religion: its rituals, its pantheon of gods, its sanctification of animals; he instituted a theocratic system of government in Egypt, based on a division of the country into 36 districts;[10] he invented writing, in the form of hiero-

[9] Hardly anything is known about Artapanus—beyond the little his fragments (collected at *FGrH* 726) can tell us. Cf. Schwartz (1896); Schürer, iii. 521–5. Freudenthal (1874–5: ii. 143–74, esp. 166–7) makes a rather tendentious identification of Artapanus, ps.-Aristeas, and ps.-Hecataeus.

[10] Compare Diodorus, *Library*, 1. 54. 3, agreeing with Artapanus in giving the number of administrative districts (or 'nomes') into which Egypt was divided as 36 (cf. also Strabo, *Geography*, 17. 1. 3). There is, however, reason to believe that there ought to have been rather more that this: see Gauthier (1935), 83–8.

glyphics, and was for this reason known by the name of 'Hermes' as well ('Hermes' suggesting *interpretation* in the Greek); he was the teacher of Orpheus,[11] and, in a word, founded philosophy (τὴν φιλοσοφίαν ἐξευρεῖν).

These extensive claims for the debt that the Egyptians owed to the Jewish people might have provided a substantial basis for Artapanus to develop a link between the antiquity of Judaism and its philosophical superiority to Egyptian culture. But, although our evidence for the work of Artapanus is very fragmentary, we have enough to see that this could not have been what he did. If he had intended to prove the antiquity and superiority of Jewish culture as such, it would have been important for him to focus on the oral and written traditions that were its primary means of transmission. Yet he rather alienates his history from these traditions: there is no attempt to anchor his list of Jewish benefactions in them, and Artapanus played fast and loose with such aspects of these traditions as he did make use of. What is more, Artapanus never claimed that Egyptian theology represented a *corruption* of Jewish thought—in the way, for example, that Apion would later on claim that Jewish theology was a corruption of Egyptian. Indeed, according to Artapanus, Moses himself was actually the founder of Egyptian religion. It is, in short, clear that Artapanus' motives were rather more straightforward. What he was interested in doing was to counteract the characterization of the Jews as a misanthropic people found in the anti-Semitic literature of the period, and to create Jewish heroes for a Graeco-Egyptian audience. It is not just coincidence that the achievements Artapanus attributed to Moses matched exactly those of the national heroes of Egypt: the Moses of Artapanus, in fact, 'combines in a single life political, military, religious, philosophical, technical and civilizing elements, which in the Egyptian-Hellenistic view were

[11] As background for this particular claim, it should be noted that Orpheus' teacher in the Greek tradition was *Musaeus*, a name easily enough confused with that of Moses. (Cf. Numenius fr. 9 des Places, where Moses' name is given as *Μουσαῖος*, with Freudenthal 1874–5: ii. 173, and Gager 1972: 139.) There was also a tradition that Orpheus had travelled to Egypt and, in particular, that he instituted the Greek mysteries on the basis of what he had learnt there. See Diodorus, *Library*, 1. 23. 2, 69. 4, 92. 3, 96. 4–6. (For Orpheus more generally as founder of the mysteries cf. Plato, *Protagoras*, 316 D; Lactantius, *Divine Institutes*, 1. 22; Augustine, *City of God*, 18. 14; etc.) Aristobulus is at around this time able to claim that Orpheus' notion of the divine relied on the Jewish notion (ap. Eusebius, *Preparation for the Gospel*, 13. 12, 664 C–665 D).

shared by the deities Isis, Osiris, Thot-Hermes and the national hero Sesostris'.[12] And, in creating a hero, Artapanus created a Jewish response to their critics. If, for example, the Egyptians accused Moses of sedition (as Manetho did), Artapanus will show that he was actually a great military leader and civil administrator; if they reviled him for attacking their religion (as both Manetho and Lysimachus had done), Artapanus will say that he was the one who established it; if they argued that he and his followers were fit only for the ghetto of Auaris (as, again, Manetho), Artapanus will reply that he founded Heliopolis. The virtue of the Jewish race is evident in the history of their deeds—not in the age of their tradition.

Much the same can be said about the one other second-century-BC Jewish writer from whose works substantial claims for the debt of the Greeks to his culture survive—the philosopher Aristobulus. Again, there is very little known about the man (some scholars have questioned his very existence);[13] but we know that he claimed that Jewish Scripture had inspired the works of Pythagoras, Orpheus, Aratus, Homer, Hesiod, and Linus, as well as Plato and, above all, Aristotle and the Peripatetics.[14] A fragment of his exegesis survives in support of the last of these claims (from Eusebius, *Preparation for the Gospel*, 7. 14, 324 A–B):

The same thing can also be referred [μεταφέροιτο δ' ἄν] to wisdom, for all light comes from it. So some of the Peripatetics have said it is like a lamp: for those who follow it consistently will be untroubled through the whole of life. But one of our ancestors, Solomon, put it more wisely and more

[12] M. Braun (1938), 26 (but see all of 26–31). Cf. also Willrich (1900), 111–15; Lévy (1907); Runnalls (1983), esp. 145; Collins (1983), 32–8; also Rajak (1978), 115, and further for Sesostris in particular as an Egyptian model for heroic achievement, M. Braun (1938), 41–3; Murray (1970).

[13] Aristobulus is reported as having written a work addressed to Ptolemy VI Philometor, and Eusebius tells us that his floruit is to be located during his reign (*Preparation for the Gospel*, 7. 13, 323 D), specifically in 176 BC (*Chronicle*, 2. 124). Cf. Schürer, iii. 579–80. Eusebius' witness has been questioned, and a later date proposed for Aristobulus: cf. e.g. Gercke (1896), 919; and, *contra*, Walter (1964), 13–26. Since Clement of Alexandria is the earliest writer to preserve any fragment of Aristobulus, the authenticity of all of them has been doubted. For a discussion of the whole issue, and a systematic defence of their authenticity, see Walter (1964), 35–123.

[14] Cf. Eusebius, *Preparation for the Gospel*, 13. 12, 663 D–668 B (cf. 9. 6, 410 D–411 A=Clement, *Stromata*, 1. 22. 150), quoting from the first book of Aristobulus, *To Philometor*. For the debt of the Lyceum in particular to Moses and the prophets, see Clement, *Stromata*, 5. 14. 97. 7.

beautifully when he said that wisdom existed before the heavens and the earth. This is consistent with the foregoing.

Aristobulus was clearly committed to the interesting claim that the Jewish theological tradition as preserved in Hebrew Scripture contained deep philosophical wisdom from an earlier age of inspired thinkers such as Moses and Solomon; and the claims of Greek borrowing make it clear that this wisdom is taken to be older—and better—than any pagan philosophy. And, coupled with his mode of exegesis, all of this does, to be sure, look very much closer to later Stoic claims regarding the validity of philosophy preserved in an ancient tradition than anything we have so far seen—and to that extent closer to the argument for the authority of a tradition on the basis of its antiquity which, I am suggesting, was not developed for a full century after the death of Aristobulus. The trouble is that the evidence runs out long before we can extract from the fragments of Aristobulus either a more general theory that the Jewish tradition was in reception of a perfect philosophy (let alone that its perfection was accounted for by its antiquity), or that all pagan lines of thought were derivative offshoots from it. In the first place, we do not know the extent of the 'Peripatetic' philosophy that Aristobulus found in Scripture. Aristobulus does not (despite the claims sometimes made for him in secondary literature) seem to have employed the kind of allegorical exegesis that would allow him to convert historical narrative into wholesale philosophical exposition. To be sure, he employed a distinction between a 'philosophical' (translating φυσικῶς) and a 'naïve' way of reading Scripture (μυθῶδες, i.e. a reading that 'made a myth' out of it, took it at the bare level of its narrative: Eusebius, *Preparation for the Gospel*, 8. 10, 376 A–378 B, esp. 376 B); but the one example we have to illustrate this looks much less exciting than anything attempted later by Philo, for example. Discussing the problem that Scripture talks of God in anthropomorphic terms (he moves or stands still; he has a face, hands, and so on), Aristobulus said, simply, that these descriptions cannot be taken literally. The 'hand' of God, he said, referred to his power (as when we talk of a powerful king ruling with a 'mighty hand'); when God is 'stationary', this refers to the stability of the world; and so on. None of this justifies us in supposing that Aristobulus imported the kind of assumptions that we find later behind the use of the term 'allegory' in Philo or the Stoics: for example, a presumed intention on the part of the writer to conceal knowledge, or a specific technical approach to understanding what wisdom has been concealed. The example we are given looks more like an example of metaphor than of allegory—something implied already by the opening word of the passage quoted above (μεταφέροιτο), but supported as well by Aristobulus' own account of his exegetical distinction, which closely echoes the Peripatetic definition and account of metaphor.[15]

But there is a more substantial indication that Aristobulus did not conceive of his project in terms that prefigured the work of the later Stoics, and that is the fact that, whatever Aristobulus thought about the debt of Greek philosophy to Judaic Scripture, there is no suggestion that he had anything to say about traditional Greek or Egyptian *theology*. There is no evidence that he engaged with it on any terms whatsoever, either to accept the validity of some of its insights (as Philo would later do), or to reject it as philosophically void (as Josephus was to suggest). This is important, because if Aristobulus felt that traditional pagan theologies were irrelevant to his purposes, then it shows that he was not primarily interested in demonstrating the superior antiquity of Judaic philosophy to the Gentile tradition at large. All that Aristobulus was trying to do was to refute the assumption made by the opponents of the Jews at this time, that the Jewish theological tradition had nothing philosophical in it to explain why a person might reasonably adhere to it in preference to local religious custom. Aristobulus

[15] Cf. Aristobulus ap. Eusebius, *Preparation for the Gospel*, 8. 10, 376 B: 'Often our lawgiver, Moses, says what he wants by talking about other matters—I mean superficially talking about other matters: [in fact] he is relating the dispositions of nature and the construction of great things.' With this compare e.g. Aristotle, *Poetics*, $1457^{b}6$–9; and, for the appropriateness of metaphor to 'great things', cf. $1458^{a}31$–4: 'The strange word, like the metaphor, the ornamental equivalent, and the other forms mentioned, will save the language from seeming mean and prosaic.' The contrast with Philo emerges clearly from a consideration of *his* discussion of the anthropomorphic descriptions of God. At *On Dreams*, 1. 234–7, for example, Philo explains this manner of describing God not as *metaphor*, as an appropriately dignified way of referring to the divine, but rather as the only means of communicating something of the nature of God to those who are not able to conceive of him except anthropomorphically. This is allegory as it is understood in a philosophical context: allegory here is not employed as a literary trope when the subject-matter seems to deserve it, it is rather a way of structuring a philosophical exposition so that, although the full truth is set out, no one is exposed to more of it than he is capable of understanding. Cf. also Goulet (1994), 380: 'Aristobule ne voit dans ces expressions que des "métaphores" identiques à celles qu'emploie le langage relevé (μεγαλεῖον).'

proves the philosophical significance of his religion by showing that it was recognized—and used—by the greatest Greek philosophical authorities. We might well be expected to conclude that a similar level of wisdom was indiscernible through the Greeks' own theological tradition; but no thesis is offered to explain this, and the question of its relative antiquity never raises its head. Once again, the issue in Aristobulus is of the Jews' contribution to the development of Western civilization—not the age of their religion.

2. *Josephus and the Antiquity of the Jews*

Jewish accounts of their own race and culture in Hellenistic Egypt were, of course, shaped by many and varied literary influences, were written for various purposes, and aimed at various audiences. Nevertheless, the kind of picture which the Jews presented of their race, and the forms of argument and historical evidence to which they appealed in order to show, to their critics or to themselves, that they were a people and a culture worthy of respect, would, as I said earlier, naturally be shaped by a consciousness of how someone might attack their position. So, if I was right in identifying a shift in the way in which the Greeks discussed the Jews by the first century AD, it ought to be possible to see a corresponding shift in Graeco-Jewish literature—not, again, because all Graeco-Jewish literature has an apologetic function, but simply because the Jews would be bound to assimilate any shift in the underlying assumption about what constituted a positive presentation of a people (of their people in particular). And the two Jewish authors whose works survive to represent this period, by far the best preserved of Jewish authors writing for a Greek audience in the early first century AD, do seem to reflect this shift: the historian and apologist Josephus, and the philosopher Philo of Alexandria. In what follows I shall look at Josephus first, since, although he is much the younger of the two (he was born in ad 37/8, when Philo must have been in his fifties),[16] his works enter into debate with Gentile writers in a way that Philo's generally do not—and also because the evidence his work provides for anti-Semitic thinkers whose positions would otherwise be largely unknown has already placed his work at the forefront of my discussion so far.

[16] Josephus has left us an autobiography, the *Life of Flavius Josephus*; and further information about himself in his work *The Jewish War*. Cf. further Schürer, i. 43–63, and Barclay (1996), 346–68.

We have seen already in Chapter 4 that the answer Josephus provides in *Against Apion* to critics of his race is based on an assertion of the Jews' antiquity. The point is brought home in his own summary of the work, at *AA* 2. 288–9:

I have shown that our race goes back to antiquity, whereas our accusers assert that it is quite young. I have produced numerous ancient witnesses who mention us in their works, whereas they confidently assert there is none. They further maintained that our ancestors were Egyptians: but it has been shown that they migrated to Egypt from elsewhere.

The suggestion that the slanders of the Greeks can be summarized in the claim that the Jewish race is 'quite young', and that 'the ancestors of the Jews were Egyptian', comes as something of a surprise. As far as Josephus himself is concerned, the *only* writer to have made such a claim was Apion; and if Chaeremon had also believed something similar, Josephus' argument against him was precisely that he (somewhat like Lysimachus before him) had left it unclear (*AA* 1. 298; 301–2). Josephus' *Against Apion* cannot be taken (merely) as an attempt to correct errors made by pagan writers in their characterization of the Jews; the work *crucially* involves a demonstration that the Jews are not culturally dependent on another nation. It is clear that Josephus is well aware of the capital that, in his own age, could be made of the suggestion that the Jewish race—and, by implication, Jewish culture—did not have autonomous roots. If Judaism was an offspring of Egyptian theology, any claim that it might have had to be taken seriously by philosophers would be nipped, as it were, in the bud.

Josephus understood well the position adopted by Apion and his successors; but, if he challenged their conclusions, he did not question their approach. Rather the opposite; and in constructing his own version of the history of philosophy he made full use of the model suggested by the work of the later Stoics. He argued, as Artapanus and Aristobulus had done before him, that the Greeks and Egyptians owed their progress in philosophy to the Jews—that, for example, Plato, Pythagoras, and 'the wisest of the Greeks' quite generally, borrowed from Judaic Scripture.[17] But for Josephus, this

[17] Cf. esp. *AA* 1. 162 for Pythagoras' use of Jewish philosophy, and 2. 168 for the Greek adoption of Moses' conception of God. Plato's political ideas also seem to be a weak form of Moses' (cf. *AA* 2. 224, where the 'truth about God' which Plato did not dare expose fully clearly refers to the laws by which God intends men to live). Elsewhere, Abraham is said to have taken mathematics and astronomy out of

served as a proof of the Jews' relative antiquity as much as it served as a demonstration of their historical contribution to civilized life. Unlike Artapanus and Aristobulus, Josephus did not restrict himself to considering the debt of the Classical Greek philosophers to Judaism; he wanted to show more broadly that nothing in pagan tradition preserved any glimmer of independent philosophical thought at all. To argue that the Jews benefited the development of Western philosophy would be one thing: but Josephus went further to reverse the argument of Apion, and asserted that no pagan tradition independent of the tradition inherited through Judaism even hinted at a connection with an older philosophy. At *AA* 2. 255–6, for example, Josephus explicitly rejects the validity of any attempt to show (e.g. by allegorical exegesis) that Greek mythology contained an ancient philosophical core—clinching the argument by suggesting that Plato (who, remember, was influenced by Jewish thought himself) exiled Homer from his ideal republic on precisely the ground that his works lacked philosophical content:

> The genuine philosophers among the Greeks were well aware of all that I have said—and they were not ignorant of the affected and specious appeals to allegorical interpretation [τὰς ψυχρὰς προφάσεις τῶν ἀλληγοριῶν].[18] That was why they rightly despised them, and agreed with us in forming a true and befitting conception of God. From this standpoint Plato declares that no poet ought to be admitted to the republic, and even politely dismisses Homer.

It is important to note that Josephus does *not* think that allegorical exegesis is of its nature 'affected' or 'specious'. This is clear, because elsewhere he says that *Judaic* scripture *does* contain allegory.[19] Josephus' claim, then, is the exact counterpart of the criticism that Porphyry would later make of the Christian writer Origen

Chaldaea and introduced the disciplines to the Egyptians; from thence they were received by Greece (*Jewish Antiquities*, 1. 166–8; cf. 1. 143–6 for the common racial origins of the Chaldaeans with the Jews).

[18] The word ψυχρός, literally 'frigid', is used in ancient literary criticism to refer to a particular style of oratory (e.g. Demetrius, *On Style*, 114–27), and perhaps suggests here both affectation and (mere) rhetoric on the part of the Greek allegorical exegetes.

[19] So *Jewish Antiquities*, 1. 24: 'Everything, indeed, is here set forth in keeping with the nature of the universe. Some things the lawgiver shrewdly hints at, others he sets forth in solemn allegory. But where straightforward speech was expedient, there he makes his meaning absolutely plain [πάντα γὰρ τῇ τῶν ὅλων φύσει σύμφωνον ἔχει τὴν διάθεσιν, τὰ μὲν αἰνιττομένου τοῦ νομοθέτου δεξιῶς, τὰ δ' ἀλληγοροῦντος μετὰ σεμνότητος, ὅσα δ' ἐξ εὐθείας λέγεσθαι συνέφερε ταῦτα ῥητῶς ἐμφανίζοντος].'

(*Against the Christians*, fr. 39 Harnack). Just as in Porphyry's eyes the Judaeo-Christian tradition lacked the authoritative basis in antiquity for allegorical exegesis to be appropriate for it, so Josephus thought that the Greek theological tradition lacked the authoritative basis in antiquity for it to be possible that allegorical exegesis would provide any results that had objective philosophical validity.

But one of the passages in Josephus most suggestive of his assimilation of the Stoics' way of thinking about cultural antiquity comes, not in *Against Apion*, but in the *Jewish Antiquities*, in the course of an explanation of the longevity ascribed to some of the earlier biblical characters. What he says is this (*Jewish Antiquities*, 1. 105–6):

> And do not let anyone compare the lifespan of the ancients with the brevity of life nowadays and conclude that what is said about them must be false, or infer that, because no one lives that long nowadays, they could not have reached such an age. After all, they were beloved of God—they were the sons of God himself. Their diet too was more conducive to longevity, so it is only reasonable to suppose that they lived for so long. Again, it is reasonable to suppose that God accorded them a longer life because of their virtue, and because of the usefulness of their discoveries in astronomy and geometry—for they could not have predicted anything with certainty had they not lived for 600 years at least, that being the period of the Great Year.

It is hard to read this without being reminded of the later Stoics' explanation for the philosophical achievements of primitive man. Their account, as I discussed it in Chapter 3, can be rendered schematically as follows:

(1) Primitive man was closest to man's divinely ordained origins (cf. esp. Cornutus, *Introduction*, 20).
(2) Primitive man was intellectually superior to men as they are now (S.E. *M.* 9. 28). This has the consequence that:
(3) (at least some) primitive men practised technical philosophy and so arrived at a correct understanding of virtue, theology, and physics (especially astronomy).

Josephus' argument in the passage quoted can be similarly outlined as follows:

(1) The early Patriarchs were 'sons of God' (ὑπ' αὐτοῦ τοῦ θεοῦ γενόμενοι: cf. Seneca's *a dis recentes*), were especially virtuous and loved by God. This led God to bring it about that:

(2) the early patriarchs lived very much longer than we do now, so that:
(3) these men were able to develop the science of astronomy.

Naturally, there are differences between the Stoics' account and that of Josephus—but none that cannot be explained in general terms by differences between a relatively orthodox Jew and a Stoic, and none, in any case, that undermine the core similarity between their respective arguments for the unique philosophical opportunities held by early man. There is, for example, a difference in the historical stage at which man developed philosophy: the first men according to the Stoics; the Patriarchs according to Josephus. But this is readily explained by the reluctance of the Stoics to involve the direct intervention of god after his original formation of the natural world-order: for them, as we saw in Chapter 3, the direct provision of philosophy was essential for the first generation of men, but further intervention would be unnecessary, and perhaps (philosophically speaking) even unwelcome thereafter.[20] Josephus, on the other hand, has more room in his system of belief to allow the intervention of God at any point in history God deems appropriate. So what if for him the origins of philosophy do not lie with the *first* men, in any case? The important point is only that the ancestors of the Jews were the first to develop it. There is also the question of the scope of philosophy attained by these men: virtue, theology, and physics according to the Stoics; astronomy and geometry according to Josephus. But again, virtue and theology are parts of technical philosophy for the Stoics in a way that they are not for Josephus: one can be virtuous as a Jew without being a philosopher, and one can know enough of God through his revelation of himself without being a theologian. If Josephus wants to make the point that the Jews were the first to develop a technical philosophy, he does best to concentrate on physics—and astronomy and geometry were in any case precisely the subjects most commonly associated in the pagan world with the most ancient traditions of philosophy.

It was an important part of the Stoics' argument that they could show how the earliest men were in a privileged position to develop philosophy: from this could be deduced the fact that they did develop philosophy, and thence the probability that their wisdom was

[20] Although even this can be qualified by reference again to Cornutus, *Introduction*, 20, 39. 12–40. 4 Lang: here too the gods intervened at a (slightly) later stage to create a generation of especially philosophical men.

preserved in some form in the traditions of the ancient nations. What Josephus needed to do was to provide an argument showing that there were men early in the tradition of which Judaism was in direct reception who had a similar privilege—that they must (therefore) have developed philosophy, and that it was their wisdom that was preserved in Judaic Scripture. And it is the way that he contrives the argument for this that makes the *Antiquities* passage so striking. Josephus could not argue *a priori* that providence must have made men philosophers at any point in human history (he would agree with the Stoics that man needs to be created capable of virtue; but would disagree that philosophy is a necessary condition for this). So what he rather does here is to argue *a posteriori* that the longevity of the Patriarchs relative to later men could only have been meant to serve one purpose: to allow them the discovery of technical philosophy. It is the extraordinary premiss implied in this that, in the end, draws one's attention to this passage: that the development of astronomy required many centuries of study. To some extent, of course, this is obviously true; but it is *not* true that the collection and analysis of data needed to be carried out by one individual (or one generation of men). It is standard, and plausible, to suppose that these observations would be collected over many generations. Josephus' claim is scarcely intelligible except as part of a wider argument for the position that philosophy was first developed among the ancestors of the Jews: that there is *no* privileged basis for pagan traditions, but that all philosophical wisdom must derive from the Patriarchs, whose theology in particular was preserved in its purest form through the Jewish tradition. There is no need to suppose that Josephus has self-consciously adopted the precise premisses and structure of the Stoics' argument; but it is very hard to explain what Josephus is doing here unless he has taken on board the general thrust of their approach. The Stoics set the agenda by modelling the way in which the dissemination of philosophy through the nations could be traced; Josephus shows more precisely that the root of it all lay with the Patriarchs of his own tradition.

3. *Philo of Alexandria*

A generation before Josephus, the philosopher Philo, a Hellenized Jew from one of the leading Jewish families in Alexandria, was producing the extraordinary and extensive allegorical expositions of Judaic Scripture by which we now primarily remember him.[21] The elements of Greek philosophical learning that went into this exposition have been variously analysed as Stoic, Platonic, or both, and his mode of exegesis identified variously as Greek and Judaic in influence.[22] But for present purposes there is a more important question—not what methods of allegorization were used by Philo, but *how he justified the use of any at all*. This is a question that has not been asked: it has been thought enough to suppose that, as a matter of brute fact, Philo believed in the authority of Scripture, was convinced as well by the results of Greek philosophy, and had therefore to show how the latter were contained in the former.[23] But if this is true as a psychological explanation of his motives at some level, the real question still remains: the most devoted believer in a sacred text needs, if he is a philosopher, some means of explaining ('rationalizing', as it might be) his belief in that text.

[21] Although a great deal of Philo's work survives, surprisingly little is known of his life. We know that his brother held the office of Alabarch ('i.e. probably, of customs superintendent on the Arabian side of the Nile': Schürer, iii. 136), was enormously wealthy (Josephus, *Jewish Antiquities*, 18. 159–60; *The Jewish War*, 5. 205), and had connections that reached to the imperial family itself (*Antiquities*, 19. 276–7); his nephew, Tiberius Julius Alexander, at the culmination of his career held the governorship of Egypt (Josephus, *The Jewish War*, 2. 309; cf. generally Turner 1954). Philo himself was selected to represent the Jewish cause in the embassy to the emperor Caligula of AD 39–40 (see Josephus, *Jewish Antiquities*, 18. 257–60; and, for Philo's own account of the embassy in particular, his *Embassy to Gaius*). Since he refers to himself as an 'old man' at the time of this embassy (*Embassy*, 1), it is assumed that he must have been born between 20 and 10 BC. See further Wolfson (1947), and Schürer, iii. 809–89 (which is, apart from anything else, an important navigational tool for the enormous bibliography Philo has attracted).

[22] If a Jewish background is preferred (e.g. Bousset 1915, esp. 43–83), there is then the further question of whether Philo's approach was rooted more specifically in the tradition of the Palestinian or Alexandrian school. The former is maintained by R. P. C. Hanson (1959, esp. 48); the latter e.g. in Frankel (1851), esp. 30–4; Nikiprowetzky (1973). But the paucity of evidence for Jewish exegesis before Philo leaves a certain amount to be taken on trust, and the argument that his work is based on Hellenistic models is not without plausibility. See e.g. Bréhier (1925), 60–1; Pépin (1958), 231–42 (esp. 234); also Dillon (1981) with Lamberton (1986), 52–4, for some overtly pagan examples of exegesis in Philo's work. Wolfson (1947), i. 115–38, esp. 131–8, treads a middle path, suggesting that, while the Jewish tradition allowed (or encouraged) a non-literal reading of Scripture, and perhaps even suggested forms of exposition followed by Philo, the mechanics of his interpretation were essentially Greek.

[23] e.g. Barclay (1996), 169: 'Philo's hermeneutic is founded on an absolutist principle: the text is, and must be shown to be, rational and worthy in its every detail'—and Barclay means that it must be shown to be so *through* the use of allegory, not as a prelude to it.

Philo's philosophical outlook was clearly influenced deeply by the Stoics—whether or not his methods of exegesis were too—so it seems reasonable to suppose that he might have considered, perhaps even adopted, their arguments for the philosophical validity of a tradition; and this is what I now want to consider. Sadly, Philo has left us very little by way of explicit comment on his exegetical methodology, and less still on his beliefs about the respective origins of Jewish and pagan culture. But there remains a great deal that we can deduce from his works, and what there is seems to confirm that he too was working to the philosophical model developed in the light of the work of Posidonius.

One of the ways in which it is possible to tell that Philo was concerned with the question of antiquity and validity in the broad terms set out by the later Stoics is the fact that Philo (like Josephus, but unlike, say, Aristobulus) was interested not just in the borrowing of Greek philosophers from the Jews—although he has plenty to say on this score, naming, for example, Pythagoras, Heraclitus, Aristotle, and Zeno of Citium as philosophers indebted to the Jews[24]—but also in the status of traditional Greek theology. Like Josephus, as I said, and within the same framework of thought; but Philo came to a slightly different conclusion from Josephus. For, while Josephus rejected Greek mythology out of hand as philosophically void, and outside the guarantee of antiquity, Philo was prepared to concede that it had roots in ancient philosophical insight. He was even prepared to allow the validity of allegorical exegesis when applied to it. So, at *On the Creation of the World*, 133:

> The earth is also, it seems, a mother: this is why the first men thought fit to call her 'Demeter', combining the words 'mother' [*mētēr*] and 'earth' [*gē*]. For, as Plato said [cf. *Menexenus*, 238 A], the earth does not imitate a woman, but woman the earth. Poets quite rightly tend to call earth 'Mother of All' and 'Fruit-Bearer' and 'Giver of All'.[25]

To say that the goddess Demeter can be traced back to a philo-

[24] For Heraclitus see *Allegory of the Laws*, 1. 108 (and cf. *Who is the Heir?*, 214); for Pythagoras, Aristotle, and the Peripatetics at large: *Questions and Answers on Genesis*, 3. 16; for Zeno, *That Every Good Man is Free*, 57. Philo also refers to the debt of the great legislators of Greece at *On the Special Laws*, 4. 61. Chadwick (1970) thinks that *On the Eternity of the World*, 18–19, shows that Philo attributes Mosaic influence to Hesiod—which might be the implication, but the passage only says that Moses asserted the fact of the creation of the world *earlier* than Hesiod did.

[25] 'Pandora': cf. also *On the Eternity of the World*, 63: 'It is not by chance that the poets called her "Pandora".'

sophically valid insight on the part of 'the first men', and then to intimate that the poets of Greece preserve a real understanding of the nature of the earth in the epithets they give to the Earth, is to concede great importance to the Greek mythological tradition. Examples of Philo's positive attitude towards Greek mythology can be multiplied, but it is worth mentioning one or two more in particular.[26] In the *Embassy to Gaius*, for example, Philo says that the ornaments provided for the gods in Greek iconography have emblematic significance (see 98–113): this is in stark contrast to Josephus, *AA* 2. 252, where Greek sculptors and painters are criticized for their inventive depiction of the gods.[27] Again, we have seen that Josephus criticizes the allegorization of Greek myths, whose literal immorality is, he thinks, evidence of their worthlessness (*AA* 2. 255). Philo, on the other hand, explicitly rejects such a criticism and, applying much the same reasoning to Greek mythology as he uses in his exposition of Scripture, suggests that the very things that attract our surprise in these myths indicate to us that they are to be taken allegorically. In a passage from *On Providence* (2. 40–1) Philo addresses his nephew Alexander in the following terms:[28]

I pass over the fact that the mythical element in poetry that you [sc. Alexander] were just talking about contains no blasphemy against the gods, but is rather an indication of the allegorical meaning contained therein. Its mysteries must not be laid bare before the uninitiated, but in passing I shall give you a demonstration by way of example of some things that in

[26] For some lists cf. Bréhier (1925), 38; Pépin (1958), 232–7; Lamberton (1986), 51–4. Note that it is, on the whole, only Greek wisdom to which Philo refers. One possible exception comes in *That Every Good Man is Free*, 94, where Alexander of Macedon attempts to introduce to the Greeks an example of Indian wisdom that is like a 'copy and imitation of the original picture' (*καθάπερ ἀπ' ἀρχετύπου γραφῆς ἀπεικόνισμα καὶ μίμημα*)—that is, it seems from the context, the purest possible example of virtue. But there is no attempt in any of this to relate the virtue (or 'wisdom') of the Gymnosophists to an ancient tradition on which it rests. For *That Every Good Man is Free*, 94 in general, and the image of the 'direct copy' in particular, cf. Dörrie (1972), 160–1.

[27] Indeed, Philo's position here is much more akin to that taken by Dio Chrysostom later on: see *Oration* 12.

[28] Philo's work *On Providence* survives only in Armenian: see Aucher (1822) (with Latin translation; cf. Hadas-Lebel 1973 for a French translation of Aucher's Latin). The English translation of the present passage is taken from Lamberton (1986), 50. There is, it might be noted, something rather ironic about Philo's attempt to justify pagan mythology to his nephew: Alexander (for whom see again n. 21) was himself more highly assimilated into pagan culture than his uncle, and 'several inscriptions demonstrate his necessary commitment to Romano-Egyptian polytheism' (Barclay 1996: 105–6, esp. 106).

some people's view are fabricated and fictitious, in so far as it is possible to establish a thesis according to the law, respecting at the same time the rule that it is not allowed that the mysteries be revealed to the uninitiated.[29] If you apply the mythical story of Hephaestus to fire, and the account of Hera to air, and what is said about Hermes to reason, and in the same way that which is said of the others, following in order, in their theology, then in fact you will become a praiser of the poets you have just been condemning, so that you will realize that they alone have glorified the divine in a seemly manner. While you did not accept the principles of the allegories or hidden meanings,[30] then the same happened to you as to boys who out of ignorance pass by paintings on boards of Apelles and are attached to the images stamped on little coins—they admire the laughable and scorn that which deserves general acceptance.

All of this is entirely consistent with the Stoic model for the transmission of ancient wisdom, which can accept (and rather welcomes) the fact that more than one tradition can trace its roots back to primitive antiquity. It might seem surprising that Philo does concede this much—although his work is exegetical, and not apologetic or polemical in the way that much of Josephus' is. But of course none of it stops Philo from thinking that the Jewish tradition is superior to, and purer than, that of the Greeks. In particular, and using an argument whose roots in Stoic theory should be obvious, Philo (as later on the Christians) said that the Greeks came to treat physical entities as gods, and so lapsed from the true faith into polytheism (*On the Decalogue*, 52–8). He argues, in other words, that the Greeks have *diverged* from the purest tradition of thought: they have retained enough to show that they were once closer to the truth (perhaps, that they once shared it), but have distorted it to the extent that it has become much inferior to the Jewish tradition. Indeed, seen in these terms, Philo's concessions to the Greeks actually support his argument: by showing that the Greeks' tradition has come from the same place as the Jewish, their corruption of it only becomes the more obvious.

Philo's exegesis does not exist in a vacuum, then. We do not have direct evidence for the grounds of his own belief that a more ancient theology might as such be more philosophically valid—perhaps he

[29] For the use of initiation imagery in Philo's exegesis of Hebrew Scripture cf. e.g. *On the Cherubim*, 48–9.

[30] For the 'rules' (*κανόνες*) of allegory according to which Philo sees himself as working, cf. e.g. *On the Special Laws*, 1. 287.

adopted something like the Stoics' theory to explain that. What he certainly did was to adopt the growing understanding among intellectuals of his time, an understanding which had its roots in the work of the later Stoics, that the antiquity of a tradition can be used to demonstrate its validity. It is, for him, because Scripture can be shown on historical grounds to be older than any Greek philosophical literature, older even than any pagan mythological tradition (which at best might be a derivation and corruption of it), that Philo can argue for its preservation of a superior theology, and so justify his programme of allegorical exegesis. But of course there is one significant asymmetry between Philo's use of the argument and the original developed by the Stoics. For the Stoics supposed that fragments only of an ancient wisdom could be reconstructed from the traditions available to them: Philo, on the other hand, believed that he had full access through Scripture to the ancient and privileged fountain-heads of his, the Jewish tradition. So Philo, perhaps for the first time in this context, did not have to negotiate the possibility of later accretion, and was able to engage in a thoroughgoing interpretation of complete allegorical texts. In this, as I say, he differed from the Stoics; but a century after Philo there would be Greek thinkers too who thought that a full account of the primitive wisdom was available in their own tradition. And even if, in their case, it had been made available through a perfect reconstruction rather than an untrammelled transmission, the discovery constituted a revolution in the way that philosophy in the West was to be done.

PART II

Ancient Tradition: Post-Hellenistic Philosophy

6

The Authority of Plato and Primitive Wisdom

The development of Platonism as a historical phenomenon has been a very controversial area of discussion: the where and the when of it cannot be neatly pinned down, because, as far as we know, Platonism had no single founder. (Platonism in any case did not begin as a 'school' in the institutional sense familiar from Hellenistic philosophy.) Its origins have been located in the increasingly Dogmatic stance taken by the later Academics—notably by the two last heads of the Academy, Philo of Larissa[1] and Antiochus of Ascalon;[2] they have been traced to the Stoa, a school which had always set the standards of Dogmatism, and which in its later periods (especially in the philosophy of Panaetius and Posidonius) looked back to Plato and remodelled itself to some extent in the light of his beliefs;[3]

[1] Cf. e.g. Tarrant (1980); (1985), 13. For Philo's philosophical development see esp. Görler (1994); Brittain (1996).

[2] Cf. e.g. Theiler (1930), 51 (and cf. 39–40); Donini (1982), 73. Dillon (1996: 433; cf. 105, 114) refers to him as a 'precursor' of Platonism. For the once-popular theory which placed Antiochus at the head of a Platonist tradition leading specifically through Arius Didymus and Gaius to the so-called 'School of Gaius' see e.g. Theiler (1930), 37; Witt (1937), 21–113; Moreschini (1978), 57, 61 n. 28. This particular theory is now fairly discredited (see most recently Göransson 1995); but for the doxographical (quite apart from the theoretical) impediments to a theory that makes Antiochus the 'founder' of Platonism in any more general sense either see Dörrie (1944), 22, 25; Glucker (1978), 379; Tarrant (1980), 110–11; and even Dillon (1996), 105–6; and cf. already Diels (1879), 71–2.

[3] e.g. Dillon (1996), 112; Tarrant (1985), 13 (and cf. Witt 1937: 21–113; Dörrie 1976: 24–7). It should be noted that, whatever might be distinctive in Posidonius' use of Plato, he was by no means the first Stoic to show an interest in him. Cf. Kidd (1971), 213: 'It is indeed true that Posidonius had a strong admiration for Plato and Aristotle, but so, of course, did other Stoics; Chrysippus, Antipater and Panaetius, for example; and, according to Posidonius, Zeno and Cleanthes.' Antipater in particular said that 'according to Plato too virtue is sufficient for happiness'; and he

and they have been seen in various trends of thought (including, for example, neo-Pythagoreanism) which appear to have arisen in Alexandria in the first century BC. The names of Eudorus and Philo of Alexandria are prominent here,[4] and Thrasyllus and Ammonius should, perhaps, be considered in a similar context.[5] And it must be true that all of these philosophers were important for fostering an interest in Plato during the Hellenistic period—and at least some of them certainly had an influence on the doctrinal development of Platonism later on (Ammonius, for example, was the teacher of the Platonist Plutarch). But many are the thyrsus-bearers, few the devotees: precisely because so many different people had for some time been using Plato for their own purposes, none of this can, in the

showed in addition that 'many more of his doctrines were in agreement with the Stoics'. See *SVF* iii, Antipater fr. 56 (=Clement, *Stromata*, 5. 14. 97. 6). Finally, cf. Reydams-Schils, arguing that much of our evidence for Posidonius has 'passed through a screen of Platonism' (1997: 456) and exaggerates the degree of Platonic doctrine in his work in any case.

[4] For Philo cf. Zeller (1892), iii/2. 470; Dörrie (1967), 48; (1976), 39, 40–2; Berchman (1984), 23–53; cf. also Runia (1995). For Eudorus see Dörrie (1944); (1976), 45; Dillon (1996), 115–35; O'Meara (1989), 9.

[5] Thrasyllus and Ammonius come closer to being Platonists in the stricter sense than any of the other thinkers mentioned. In their cases, we do not know of their being self-consciously affiliated with any other school; Ammonius was the teacher of Plutarch; and the doctrines of Thrasyllus were associated with those of the Platonists Numenius, Cronius, and Moderatus by Porphyry (*Life of Plotinus*, 20. 71–6 and 21. 1–9=T19a and b Tarrant; cf. also the scholion to Juvenal, *Satires*, 6. 576=T1a Tarrant, which says that Thrasyllus 'latterly gave himself to the Platonic sect'). But, although their close connection with the indisputable Platonists who followed them in the next generation perhaps suggests that we should see *their* work (rather than the work of the so-called Middle Platonists such as Atticus, Plutarch, and Numenius) as properly 'transitional', the limited evidence we have for their views does not really justify the designation 'Platonist'—as will become clear from the account of the term that I develop in this chapter. It is worth noting that mathematics featured centrally in the work of both Thrasyllus and Ammonius (for Ammonius see esp. Plutarch, *On the E at Delphi*, 391 E), but that Plutarch's own Platonism involved an explicit rejection of such a role for it. See *On the E at Delphi*, 387 F (Plutarch speaking): 'I was then devoting myself to mathematics passionately, although I was soon, on joining the Academy, to honour in all things the maxim "Nothing in excess".' Glucker reads Ammonius as a ('Middle') Platonist (1978: 124–34), and suggests (at 257–80) that this passage points to Plutarch's personal adoption of Academic Scepticism later in life. It seems to me, however, that the passage might well point us towards Plutarch's developing *Platonism* in reaction (partly) to the more narrowly mathematical philosophy of Ammonius. Since Plutarch believed (presumably while he was a Platonist) in 'the unity of the Academy since Plato' (*Lamprias*, 63), 'becoming a member of the Academy' might mean, for him in retrospect, precisely becoming a Platonist. On Ammonius see also Dillon (1996), 189–92; also Donini (1986), 97–110 (arguing that Ammonius' epistemology was more 'Academic' than Glucker allowed). For Thrasyllus see Tarrant (1993) (testimonia at 215–49).

end, tell us anything about the rise of *Platonism*—that is, Platonism *as distinct from* Academic philosophy, or Stoicism, for example. It is perhaps tempting to set about investigating the origins of Platonism by looking for specific doctrinal precedents, because it is easy in any case to see the history of philosophy as a history of ideas: to trace specific doctrines and chronicle their invention, suppression, re-emergence, grouping, and regrouping in different forms.[6] But this is an endless (and to that extent pointless) task, *unless* it is bounded by some understanding of how these doctrines were used by the people who invented, rejected, revived, and organized them. It is, for example, just misleading to call Posidonius a Platonist, because the 'Platonic' elements of his philosophy were contained in a framework that was self-consciously Stoic; and it is likewise misleading to refer to Philo, Antiochus, or Eudorus as 'Platonists' because *their* use of Plato (and, in the case of Eudorus, of Pythagoras too) was contained in a context that was self-consciously Academic, and always referred to as such in antiquity.[7] The evidence we have gives us no licence to refer to them as 'Platonists'; indeed, it makes a historical nonsense of the term to do so.[8]

[6] Cf. Napolitano (1985), esp. 29; Dillon (1996), 115, referring to the 'amalgam of doctrine to which we give the name of Middle Platonism'.

[7] A useful contrast can be made here with Plutarch, who provides a *Platonist* context for arguments which are ostensibly *Academic* in form: see esp. Boys-Stones (1997). For the description of Eudorus as an Academic in antiquity see Stobaeus (who discusses Eudorus' ethical division after the ethics of Philo of Larissa, and confirms the association by calling them both 'Academic philosophers': *Eclogue*, ii. 42. 7 Wachsmuth); Simplicius (whose interest was in Eudorus' logic and metaphysics: *Commentary on Aristotle's* Categories, 187. 10 Kalbfleisch); the anonymous commentator on the *Phaenomena* of Aratus (97. 2 Maas). Dillon himself is not consistent in maintaining Eudorus' 'Platonist' credentials: elsewhere he assimilates Eudorus' philosophy to that of Antiochus (although he calls it 'Antiochian Platonism' at 1996: 115); and later on, in the same mould, refers to his philosophy as a 'Stoic-influenced Pythagoreanism' (135). Tarrant argues more cogently for a link between Eudorus and Philo of Larissa (1983: 180–4). In the same article he draws attention to a dispute between Plutarch and Eudorus, which he formulates as follows: 'Plutarch claims that we should ask "What is it likely that Plato was trying to say?", not "What is likely to be the case?".' However, Tarrant goes on to say that this 'strongly suggests that they are Academics of similar persuasion engaging in an esoteric dispute' (181–2); but it seems to me that he has in fact explained very clearly why, despite the doctrinal similarities of the two thinkers, the dispute between Plutarch and Eudorus is precisely and characteristically a dispute between a *Platonist* on the one hand and an *Academic* on the other.

[8] For the history of the term *Platonicus* see Glucker (1978), 206–25. 'It is', he says at 206, 'only when we reach the second century that we meet with a number of philosophers described in contemporary sources—or in sources derived from them—as *Platonici*.'

So what is Platonism? The failure of attempts to explain it as an outgrowth of the Hellenistic schools might suggest that it is not in terms of Hellenistic school philosophy that we should be approaching the question. The related failure to explain it in terms of its doxography suggests likewise that we should not be looking to define it in terms of its doxography.[9] The particular doctrines held by particular Platonists is (obviously related, but actually) incidental to what they were: I want to argue that they held the doctrines they held *because* they were Platonists rather than vice versa. And Platonism at root seems to me to be this: the belief that Plato's philosophy was Dogmatic and authoritative. Everything else follows from that.

If my definition seems somewhat trivial, that is only because of a tendency among commentators not to take the force or originality of the Platonists' location of authority in Plato very seriously. David Sedley (1989) has stressed the fact that the authority of the founder (or assumed founder) of a school was in some sense axiomatic for Hellenistic philosophers too: that, despite the diversity of opinion within, for example, the Stoa, there was scarcely a Stoic who would not have believed, or at least claimed, that his doctrines were consistent with those of Zeno; that arguments within the school would be expressed as arguments over the interpretation of Zeno, never as disagreements with him. If it were right to apply this analysis to Platonism, or if, more generally, it were right that Platonists argued for the authority of Plato and the conformity of their beliefs with his writing *post hoc*, then my definition of Platonism *would* be unhelpfully trivial—no more informative than the claim that 'Epicureans' belonged to the school founded by Epicurus. But there are difficulties in applying Sedley's analysis of the Hellenistic view of school loyalty to the later question of Platonism. For a start, such an analysis would beg the question: it would tell us, in effect, that Platonists believed in the authority of Plato because they were part of movement which claimed Plato for their founder. But this does not tell us what we wanted to know, which is *why* such a movement arose in the first place, or how its existence was justified by those associated with it. It might, of course, be the case that Platonism was a simple evolution of the Academy and not, as such, a distinct

[9] And cf. e.g. Donini (1994), 5056, on the fluid doxography of pre-Plotinian Platonism quite generally. For the failure in particular of attempts to explain Plutarch's philosophical outlook in terms of Hellenistic sources cf. Froidefond (1987), esp. 230.

movement at all: in this case the assumption of Plato's authority would be inherited with the tradition of the school. But this is at best tendentious as a historical account of Platonism, and in any case falls foul of a second objection. For the claim that the Platonist notion of authority is much the same as the notion which operated within the Hellenistic schools simply does not *look* right: it *looks* as if Platonists meant something more substantial when they appealed to the authority of Plato than was meant by the Stoics, for example, when they appealed to the precedent of Zeno. Stoics did not argue *from* the pronouncements of Zeno. They could (when necessary, though they by no means always did) assert the *consistency* of their views with those of Zeno; but even here there is no evidence that they did so as an argument for their truth.[10] To invoke Zeno in support of a doctrine seems merely to have been about the right of the doctrine to be considered a legitimate Stoic view, rather than (at least directly) its right to be considered *true*. This contrasts with Platonist practice: Platonists were able to commit themselves to the truth of a proposition *on the grounds that* Plato had said it, and, it might be, even before they themselves understood *why* it was true. Platonist philosophy involved *imprimis* puzzling out what Plato meant as a means of advancing towards knowledge: and the real uncertainties that might be thrown up by this exegetical process (as, for example, in Plutarch's *Platonic Questions*) show that the process was quite honest in its conception, not a disingenuous appropriation of Plato for doctrines worked out in spite of him. One might usefully consider this new kind of approach to Plato's authority as a basis for the extensive commentary tradition that grows up with the movement as well.[11] Nothing really similar exists within

[10] Cf. examples at Sedley (1989), 98 n. 2—though very little here even goes far beyond what might be required of a principle of charity in reading Zeno. I hesitate to say that the deference shown towards the school's founder is simply, for example, a matter of rhetoric, or of school etiquette; but to consider things in these terms might help explain why Seneca is able to argue against Zeno more openly (Sedley 1989: 119): he is a Stoic, but not *by virtue of being a member of the Stoa*. He is not bound by the conventions of the Hellenistic school.

[11] Donini (1994) has suggested that Platonists used commentary on Plato's works 'per arrivare a una sistemazione unitaria del Platonismo' (5068, referring here to Plutarch in particular), and Sedley (1997) has suggested in addition that Plato's texts stood in particular need of linguistic elucidation (cf. on this also Dörrie 1976: 20–4). But while these suggestions may illuminate aspects of the tradition, they do not really explain the spirit in which it is developed: Donini assumes an *a priori* belief in the authority of Plato without suggesting a credible philosophical basis for it; and Sedley's suggestion has rather little to say about early Platonist works

the work or presentation of the Hellenistic schools of philosophy—even among Epicureans, whose ostensible respect for their 'divine' founder brings them closest to the language of the Platonists; and certainly not among Stoics or Academics.[12] 'Authority' can mean many different things, as we have already to some extent seen in this study: it can, for example, mean the right to be taken seriously (and by extension the right of the person following the authority to be taken seriously himself); but it can also mean something stronger: the unquestioned possession of the truth. On the face of it, one of the things that seems to distinguish Platonist from Hellenistic philosophy is precisely the Platonists' attribution of the latter kind of authority to Plato.[13]

There needs to be more to it than appearances, of course—otherwise the differences I have highlighted might be explained by shifts in rhetoric as easily as by changes in philosophical approach. If Platonism really did attribute the stronger notion of authority to Plato, and if it really does make sense (non-trivially) to define Platonism in terms of this attribution, then it had better be grounded in argument. I hope to show that it was, that Platonism (wherever its exact historical origins) crucially involved an *argument* for the

like, for example, Plutarch's *Platonic Questions*, or his exegetical discussion *On the Procreation of the Soul in the* Timaeus, neither of which presupposes difficulties in the understanding of Plato's Greek.

[12] The Epicurean ascription of authority to Epicurus is not so *obviously* different from the Platonist ascription of authority to Plato as the Stoic ascription of authority to Zeno (*pace* Sedley 1989, who perhaps overstates his case): cf. e.g. Lucretius, *On the Nature of Things*, e.g. 3. 15, for the 'divine intellect' (*divina mens*) of Epicurus, and 6. 6 for his total grasp of the truth (claims unparalleled in Stoicism). Nevertheless, a radical difference does exist between both the Epicureans and Stoics on the one hand and the Platonists on the other (again, *pace* Sedley 1989: 117), and its nature will become clearer in the course of this chapter. In brief, the Epicureans based their claims on the remarkable genius of Epicurus himself, and the obvious truth of his discoveries: the proofs which support Epicurus' status are proofs for the truth of his doctrines. The Platonists, on the other hand, believed that the *source* of Plato's doctrines must make them actually infallible—and we can know this even before we have proved, or even perhaps understood, what he thought.

[13] It is worth emphasizing that this is not an exhortation to philosophy by the *ipse dixit* of Plato—as illustrated in a story related (and approved) by Olympiodorus (*Commentary on the* Gorgias, 41. 9) concerning the Platonist Ammonius. If someone tried to win his point by announcing that 'Plato said it' (*Πλάτων ἔφη*), Ammonius would reply *first* (significantly) that Plato did *not* say it; but *second* that, even if he had, a proof was needed as well. Neither Ammonius nor Olympiodorus challenges Plato's authority in fact: but his authority provides the *starting-point* for philosophy (which involves working towards an understanding of *why* he was right), not its termination.

unique claim that Plato had on our philosophical attention—an argument, what is more, that (quite unlike the arguments of any Hellenistic philosopher) worked independently of the particular doctrines ascribed to Plato in any one Platonist's interpretation of him. But there are, strictly speaking, two questions here: first, how the strong sense of authority which I have argued is characteristic of Platonism came to be attributed to Plato over and above the belief that his philosophy was true; and secondly, how Platonists came to believe that Plato's philosophy was true in the first place, in a sense that justified the further argument that it was actually authoritative. Roughly speaking, these questions correspond, respectively, to the questions of *what*, exactly, is characteristic of Platonist philosophy, and *why*, philosophically speaking, the movement arose at all (how, to put the question another way, the pursuit of philosophy in this characteristic mould could be justified against the background of contemporary alternatives). The latter question is the subject of Chapter 7; but for the remainder of this chapter I shall deal with the issues raised by the former, and examine the account given by Platonists, not so much of the truth of Plato's philosophy, but rather of its *authority*. For this account was, as we shall see, developed through the Platonist adoption of the Stoic theory of ancient wisdom which has been the subject of this study so far: it is this wisdom which the Platonists argued formed the basis for Plato's philosophy.

1. *Platonism and Primitive Wisdom*

At some point in the second century AD the Platonist philosopher Celsus published an anti-Christian treatise called *The True Doctrine* (ὁ ἀληθὴς λόγος)—the earliest philosophical response (as far as our evidence goes) to the new religious movement which was at that time starting to come to the attention of, and even to draw support from, members of the Western intelligentsia. The work does not survive; but we have a wealth of information about it from the lengthy response (*Against Celsus*) written a century later by Origen.[14] I shall be returning to Origen's response to Celsus in later chapters; but for now it is Celsus' argument that interests me in so

[14] For a translation of the whole work, with introduction and notes, see Chadwick (1965); for an attempt at reconstructing Celsus' treatise cf. Hoffmann (1987); and for a discussion of Celsus' philosophical position see esp. Frede (1994). Origen, in the earlier parts of the *Against Celsus* (cf. e.g. 1. 8), seems to have assumed that

far as it reflects on his position as a Platonist, because Celsus gives us the clearest evidence we have for the wholehearted adoption into Platonist thought of the Stoic theory of ancient wisdom and its preservation. For Celsus' argument against Christianity—that is to say, his *primary* argument (it is supplemented by many and various indictments)—is precisely that *Christianity is vitiated by the youth of its foundations.* In particular, Celsus argued that Christianity was a *deviant* form of Judaism, and that the Jewish race and their religion were in turn corrupted scions of Egypt.[15] The argument here is, quite clearly, an extension of the argument offered against the Jews by the anti-Semitic historians of the later Hellenistic period: as they stigmatized Jewish tradition as a corruption of something much older and purer, so Celsus could argue that Christianity was even worse: a corruption of a corruption of a source maintained in its purest form in the traditional (pagan) theologies of the ancient nations.

The simple conclusion of this simple observation is what is most important in this. If Celsus was able to criticize the Christians in exactly the terms used by later Hellenistic authors in their attacks on the Jews, then the most natural assumption is that he held the same view of the transmission of primitive wisdom as well—that is, that Celsus adopted precisely the theory of the later Stoics. Like them, he must have believed that the truth which philosophy was intended to recover had been available to men at the earliest period of human history, that it was preserved in the traditions of the oldest nations, and that, therefore, every branch of thought which had distanced itself from these ancient traditions must be intellectually inferior to them. But we do not have to speculate about this: we have it in Celsus' own words (from Origen, *Against Celsus*, 1. 14):

Thinking that the same doctrine unites the thought of many nations, Celsus

Celsus was an Epicurean, and he has been identified with the Epicurean friend of Lucian (for whom see e.g. Lucian, *Alexander*, 1): so especially Keim (1873: 275–93). But in later parts of the work Origen himself realized that Celsus' doctrines are inconsistent with Epicureanism (cf. already 4. 54) and much more like Platonism (e.g. 4. 83). For a discussion of the issue see Zeller (1892), iii/2. 231–4, Chadwick (1965), pp. xxiv–xxvi; also Frede (1997), 223–7, and especially (1994), 5191–2: 'now that we are more familiar with the philosophy of the Early Empire and in particular with the Platonism of this period, Celsus' true affiliation can no longer be a matter of controversy. He undoubtedly is a Platonist.'

[15] See Origen, *Against Celsus*, 3. 5, and, further on the nature of his argument and Origen's response, my chs. 8 and 9.

names all those nations which take this dogma as their starting-point . . . Listen to what Celsus says: 'An ancient doctrine [ἀρχαῖος λόγος] has been handed down, which has always been maintained by the wisest nations and cities and wise men.' And he would not allow that the Jews constituted one of the 'wisest nations' on a par with the Egyptians, Assyrians, Indians, Persians, Odrysians, Samothracians, and Eleusinians.

As in the case of the Stoics, it is important to stress that this is not mere rhetoric: Celsus' argument was not a matter of appealing to atavistic sensibilities by garbing pagan philosophy in a cloak of venerable antiquity. The argument was *central* to Celsus' account—indeed, its importance to him is proved by the very title of his work: *The True Doctrine* is an obvious allusion to the 'ancient doctrine' mentioned in the passage just quoted.[16] Celsus' diatribe was, it seems, not just an attack on the Christians, but functioned at the same time as a positive affirmation of the validity of pagan theology as proved through its connection with primitive thought—precisely on the model of the argument offered by the Stoics.

Celsus is not unique in his adoption of this theory. It is true that his work is, in many ways, atypical of the evidence we have for Platonism at this early period—to the extent, indeed, that scholars have sometimes doubted whether Celsus was a Platonist at all.[17] And one might suppose that the overtly polemical nature of *The True Doctrine* makes it a weak basis from which to derive generalizations about Platonist belief more widely. It might, for example, be supposed that Celsus' appeal to an 'ancient wisdom' preserved among pagan cultural traditions is to be read as an *ad hominem* response to the Christians' claim to antiquity through their appropriation of the Hebrew tradition. But in fact things stand almost exactly the other way round. I shall show in Chapter 8 that it was the Christians' appropriation of the Hebrew tradition as a means of proving their own antiquity which was the response, and a response in particular to attacks such as that mounted by Celsus. And in any case, we have direct evidence from Celsus' contemporaries that the theory he adopted found much wider acceptance among Platonists of his period.

Consider, for example, Plutarch—in some ways a benchmark in our evidence for second-century Platonism. In a lost work *On the*

[16] Cf. Wifstrand (1941–2), 396–400. At 399 Wifstrand suggests that the phrase ἀληθὴς λόγος to represent an ancient theological tradition derives from Plato, *Meno*, 81 A; cf. also Frede (1997), 230.

[17] See again n. 14.

Festival of Images at Plataea Plutarch discussed 'ancient natural philosophy' in terms which seem unambiguously related both to the 'true doctrine' of Celsus and to the later Stoics' account of the development and transmission of primitive philosophy. This is Plutarch, fr. 157. 16–25 Sandbach (=Eusebius, *Preparation for the Gospel*, 3. 1. 1, 83 c):

> Ancient natural philosophy [ἡ παλαιὰ φυσιολογία], among both Greeks and barbarians, took the form of an account of nature hidden in mythology, veiled for the most part in riddles and hints, or of a theology such as is found in mystery ceremonies in which what is spoken is less clear to the masses than what is unsaid, and what is unsaid gives cause for more speculation than what is said. This is evident from the Orphic poems and the accounts given by the Phrygians and Egyptians. But nothing does more to reveal what was in the mind of the ancients than the rites of initiation and the ritual acts that are performed in religious services with symbolic intent.

The parallels, not just with Celsus, but perhaps especially with the Stoic Cornutus, go very deep in this passage. Compare, for example, Cornutus, *Introduction to Greek Theology*, 35, 75. 18–76. 5 Lang—a passage I discussed in Chapter 3. There also we saw the claim that mythical material which 'appears to be about the gods' might hide a deeper account of nature, and that, in particular, 'the ancients were no ordinary men, but capable of understanding the nature of the cosmos and inclined to use symbols and riddles in their philosophical discussions of it'. The theory of mythology expressed here by Plutarch is undeniably Stoic in its source.

But if Plutarch's theory of mythology is essentially adopted from the Stoics, so too, as a natural corollary, is the exegesis he applies to it. In fr. 157 Plutarch goes on to give allegorical accounts of the rites of Hera and Dionysus, of a myth concerning Hera, and of the identification (which presumably formed part of local Boeotian cultic belief)[18] of Leto and Hera, which stand very much in the Stoic exegetical tradition. To be sure, not everyone agrees that Plutarch himself assents to the approach for which he here provides evidence: Decharme, for example, has argued that Plutarch's identifications of Zeus with fire and Hera with 'wet and windy nature' (fr. 157. 115–18) are incompatible with his belief in the transcendence of the divine, and concluded that the whole fragment as we have it

[18] See Hardie (1992), 4769, against Decharme (1898), 115.

might therefore represent the views, not of Plutarch, but of an interlocutor in his work.[19] But his argument is very weak: whatever Plutarch's view of the divine, it is in no way inconsistent for him to interpret mythological stories about the gods as allegories of natural philosophy. The transcendent divinity coexists with the natural world; and there is no reason at all to believe that the 'gods' as they occur in a mythology which is taken to be allegorical must represent aspects of the one rather than the other. In any case, we have unambiguous evidence elsewhere that Plutarch did read myth in the way implied by this fragment. In his work *On the Face in the Moon* (at 938 F) Plutarch suggests that the moon was known as Artemis 'because she is a virgin and sterile, but is helpful and useful to other women [in childbirth]'. This passage is an interesting parallel to the fragment from *The Festival of Images*, not least because Plutarch's identification of Artemis with the moon, and his suggestion that the identification has a serious philosophical contribution to make, are explicitly drawn from 'ancient report' (παλαιὰ φήμη).[20]

There is more that can be said in support of Plutarch's adoption of the Stoic theory of ancient wisdom as well. Particularly significant is fr. 190. 6–9 Sandbach, in which Plutarch criticizes the Ionians for introducing idolatry to Greece:[21]

> Plutarch, censuring them [i.e. the Ionians] by the ancient philosophy [ἡ παλαιὰ φιλοσοφία] that was approved among Greeks and foreign nations, declared that certain of them introduced the erroneous use of images.

[19] See Decharme (1898). Decharme cites *Oracles at Delphi*, 400 D, as a proof-text for his case: here Plutarch rejects the suggestion that Apollo is to be identified with the sun. However, this passage seems to be contradicted by Plutarch himself at fr. 194 (c) Sandbach; and cf. further Babut (1969), 380–1; and Hardie (1992), 4766–70, pointing to other Plutarchean texts where gods of mythology are identified with heavenly bodies (*Table-talk*, 3. 10, 658 F–659 A, and *On the Face in the Moon*, 938 F). Hardie himself (1992: 4770) sees a parallel between the kind of interpretation we are offered in fr. 157 and suggestions Plutarch makes in his speech at *The E at Delphi*, 388 E–390 C, which are rejected by Ammonius later in that dialogue. But the parallel is not strong: Ammonius' reason for rejecting Plutarch's arguments in *The E at Delphi* would not, for example, have any relevance to the exegesis of fr. 157. And it seems to me that much stronger and more obvious parallels can be drawn between fr. 157 and the indubitably Plutarchean exegesis in *Isis and Osiris*.

[20] This particular phrase was, and presumably not coincidentally, used by Proclus as a way of referring to the 'ancient philosophy' transmitted through the nations (as, for example, at *Platonic Theology*, 1. 7, 30. 23; 5. 22, 82. 15 Saffrey and Westerink).

[21] The excerpt quoted from this fragment below = John Malalas, *Chronographia*, 56. 3–5 Dindorff, summarized at George Cedrenus, *Compendium of Histories*, 82. 19–83. 4 Bekker.

This fragment does not just confirm Plutarch's belief in an 'ancient philosophy', comparable with Celsus' 'true doctrine' and like it preserved in the traditions of various nations, but it also shows that Plutarch (again like Celsus, and indeed the Stoics) believed that this 'ancient philosophy' was actually *authoritative*. Plutarch can use it as a standard by which he can *criticize* the divergence of the Ionians—just as the anti-Semitic historians of the later Hellenistic period were able to criticize the Jews *because* they (supposedly) strayed from Egyptian tradition, and just as Celsus was able, in addition, to criticize the Christians for diverging (*because* they diverged) from the 'true doctrine' of the nations.

Someone resistant to the claim that Plutarch's approach to mythology is indistinguishable from that of the Stoics might still object that for Plutarch to say that there exists an *ancient* philosophy is not yet for him to commit himself to the position that that philosophy is *primitive*—an essential premiss for the Stoics' guarantee of the authority of the wisdom preserved in mythology. Plutarch (the objection would go) might well have respect for wisdom sanctioned by antiquity; but this need not be anything stronger than, or theoretically different from, for example, Aristotle's respect for the ancient wisdom of the Egyptians. It would, as it were, be lent credence by its staying power, not validated by its origins. But another fragment from the *Festival of Images at Plataea* comes to the rescue. Here (fr. 158 Sandbach = Eusebius, *Preparation for the Gospel*, 3. 8. 1, 99 B–C) Plutarch discusses his own opinions about the appropriate manufacture of cultic statues:[22]

[22] It should be noted immediately that Plutarch is not here contradicting his criticism of the Ionians in fr. 190: presumably the idea here is that simple wooden statues have a symbolic value in the allegorical ritual handed down in the tradition. The Ionians, on the other hand, were criticized in fr. 190 for introducing the *worship* of statues as if they were gods themselves. Indeed, it is tempting to take fr. 190 much more closely with fr. 158, and suggest that the practice of making statues in precious metals was linked in Plutarch's mind with the degeneration into idolatry of Greek religion. But whatever the merits of the suggestion, one deceptive piece of evidence in its favour should be dismissed, and that is Sandbach's claim that the phrase 'erroneous use of images' (πλάνην ἀγαλμάτων: he translates it 'imposture of images') 'comes from' Sophocles (cf. 1025 Nauck). Since the Sophocles fragment involves a criticism of the manufacture of statues of gods in stone, gold, ivory, or wood, this might appear to provide a solid thematic link between the two Plutarch fragments. However, although the phrase πλάνην ἀγαλμάτων might be taken (tendentiously) to be an allusion, it is certainly not a quotation from the Sophocles fragment: Sandbach may have been misled by the fact that Cedrenus quotes this fragment (whose first appearance is in Clement: see *Protrepticus*, 7. 74. 2; *Stromata*, 5. 14. 113) immediately before summarizing Malalas' report of Plutarch. And in any case, the

The manufacture of wooden images seems to be an early and ancient practice, if wood was the material of the first statue sent in honour of Apollo by Erysichthon to Delos for the festivals there, and also of the statue of Polias set up by the aboriginals, a statue which the Athenians preserve to this day. They did not choose to hack a stone into a hard, awkward, lifeless representation of a god; gold and silver they thought of as pigments due to disease in corrupt, infertile earth, or as disfiguring excrescences, swelling up like weals where it had come under the lash of fire; as for ivory, they did on occasion use it lightheartedly to lend variety to their sculpture.

From this it emerges that ritual practice, of the kind which, as we saw in fr. 157, Plutarch considered to be a symbolic vehicle for the ancient philosophy, is not just *ancient*, it is actually *primitive*. It is here explicitly the practices of the *aboriginals* (αὐτόχθονες: perhaps even earth-born men) which lend legitimacy to cultic tradition. In other words, we can be confident that Plutarch believed just what the later Stoics believed about the preservation of wisdom in mythology, and he believed it for the same reasons too. Note in this passage that gold and silver are described as 'pigments of a corrupt, infertile earth', and as 'disfiguring excrescences, like weals' in the earth. Clearly implied in this description is a tale of the decline of human morality with the rise of civilization. The discovery and use of metal was often an important staging-post in such accounts:[23] it symbolizes here (because at the time its increasing use actually contributed to) the rise of avarice and, ultimately, the decline of morality and philosophy quite generally. Plutarch's reference to primitive men and his location of them in a period of moral purity *explains* the authority of wisdom derived from them—exactly as it was explained by the Stoics.[24]

Plutarch, then, like Celsus, and both, like the Stoics, believed that the cultic practice and traditional theology of the Greek and ancient barbarian nations have their roots in an authoritative phi-

Sophocles fragment itself is probably a Jewish or Christian forgery (cf. Charlesworth 1983–5: ii. 825–6): Cedrenus may be inviting us to cross-reference it, but Plutarch himself could not have done so.

[23] Cf. e.g. Posidonius at Seneca, *Epistle* 90. 12; fr. 240a EK; and fr. 239 EK for the theory, alluded to by Plutarch in the passage just quoted, that metals were discovered in the aftermath of a devastating forest fire which drew them to the surface. (Contrast the rather seductive picture of the same phenomenon in a progressivist, Epicurean account: Lucretius, *On the Nature of Things*, 5. 1241–61.)

[24] And compare Plutarch, *Roman Questions*, 12, 266 E–F: 'Why do they consider Saturn father of truth? Is it . . . because the age of Cronus related in myth is likely, if it was most just, to have participated most in the truth?'

losophy which derives as such from the earliest generations of men; and the evidence of Plutarch and Celsus together provided very reasonable grounds for generalizing the attribution of the theory to Platonists of the period as a whole. And if we do not find such direct evidence for a theory concerning the transmission of wisdom from primitive antiquity in the fragments of other Platonists of the time,[25] we can in any case deduce the extent of its permeation from the widespread evidence we do have for the adoption of Stoic *methodology* in the reconstruction of philosophy from the traditions of the ancient nations—for the adoption, that is, of their method of allegorical exegesis. As I mentioned in Chapter 3, Porphyry's list of the great Platonist exegetes before him is headed, not by a Platonist, but by the Stoics Chaeremon and Cornutus—and I suggested there that the reason for this is that these two writers were influential exponents of the science of comparative mythology developed in the Stoa and adopted by the Platonists. It was certainly to Chaeremon that Porphyry looked for the allegorical interpretation of Egyptian mythology and practice—from the story of Isis and Osiris to the rituals associated with the life of Egyptian priests.[26] There is good reason to believe that Porphyry's account of the symbolism behind Egyptian hieroglyphics (*Life of Pythagoras*, 12) derived from Chaeremon as well.[27] But there is plenty more in Porphyry's work which suggests his adoption of the Stoics' theoretical model for

[25] In fact there is very little discussion in surviving Platonist literature of the state of the first men, and even passages in Plato which broach the subject tend to be treated by Platonists as moral rather than historical allegories. But cf. perhaps Proclus, *Platonic Theology*, 5. 7, 27. 2–4 Saffrey and Westerink.

[26] For Isis and Osiris see Chaeremon fr. 5 van der Horst = Porphyry, *Letter to Anebo*, 2. 12–13; for Egyptian priests, Chaeremon fr. 10 = Porphyry, *On Abstinence*, 4. 6–8. A number of other interpretative passages in Porphyry may derive from Chaeremon: Porphyry, 360F Smith = Chaeremon fr. 17D van der Horst; *On Abstinence*, 4. 9 = fr. 21D van der Horst.

[27] Compare Porphyry, *Life of Pythagoras*, 12, with Chaeremon, fr. 20D van der Horst (with his nn. 1 and 2; also Vergote 1939 as cited there). Note also that at *Stromata*, 5. 5. 31, in the chapter following the passage from which this fragment is drawn, Clement speaks of the sphinxes hung in front of Egyptian temples to indicate the enigmatic and symbolic nature of their theology—a claim which is first found in Chaeremon, fr. 2 van der Horst. The question of whether Porphyry is relying directly on Chaeremon is complicated by the fact that the source for sections 10–14 at least of the *Life of Pythagoras* is generally taken to be Antonius Diogenes' *Wonders from Ultima Thule* (described by Photius at *Library*, 166): see e.g. Jäger (1919), 34–40, and Reyhl (1969), 21–3. But a general dependency on Diogenes for these sections would not preclude a specific reference to Chaeremon in the matter of hieroglyphics.

the reconstruction of ancient wisdom from a process of comparative mythology. He claimed, for example, that the gods of the Greeks, Romans, Egyptians, Syrians, and Thracians are the same gods (*Against the Christians*, fr. 76 Harnack)—a statement which obviously invites comparison with Celsus' claim to be in reception, through Plato, of a unified and ancient pagan theological tradition. Porphyry also tackled the associated question of which nations were entitled by their possession of a sufficiently well-preserved ancient wisdom to inclusion on the list. He concluded that the Greeks (i.e., presumably, the later Greeks) had strayed from the 'path towards the gods' (fr. 324F Smith);[28] but that pre-eminent among nations that had not were the Egyptians, Phoenicians, Chaldeans, Lydians, and (in this detail, at least, *pace* Celsus) the Hebrews (see frr. 323F, 324F Smith).[29]

The same approach can be found among Platonists earlier than Porphyry as well. In his biography of his teacher Plotinus, Porphyry tells us that, at a certain point in his philosophical education, Plotinus felt the need to augment his researches with a study of Persian and Indian philosophy (Porphyry, *Life of Plotinus*, 3. 13–17)—suggesting that Plotinus thought that higher philosophical achievement would require a wider knowledge of ancient theologies (something in which he might have been encouraged by his teacher at the time, the Platonist Ammonius Saccas). Earlier still, the 'Stoic' method of exegesis was also encouraged by Numenius (one of the thinkers associated with the exegetical methodology of

[28] Compare Iamblichus, *On the Mysteries of Egypt*, 7. 5, 259. 9–18 Parthey: the Greeks are lovers of novelty, and so have strayed from a truth to which the barbarians remained faithful. It is fairly clear that neither Porphyry nor Iamblichus believed that *Greek theology* lacked ancient roots: they must believe that the practice of the Greeks themselves was at fault. Perhaps they concurred with Plutarch fr. 190: Plutarch criticized the Ionians, not for using statues in their ritual (that was a very ancient practice), but rather for introducing the worship of statues (see again n. 22). It may in this context be relevant to note that, in the line after Plutarch fr. 190, John Malalas reports that Plutarch was praised by Porphyry (*Chronographia*, 56. 10–11 Dindorff: cf. Porphyry, 199T Smith): the implication might be just that his criticism of the worship of statues was one of the things he praised.

[29] Porphyry's inclusion of the Hebrews in his list of ancient nations was not wholly idiosyncratic: cf. Numenius fr. 1a des Places. But neither was Celsus' omission of them: cf. perhaps Plutarch, *Isis and Osiris*, 363 D. Note, by the way, that Porphyry's argument with the Christians is still very much the same in kind as Celsus'—that the Christians had diverged from the ancient tradition, this time as represented directly by the Jews. See *Life of Plotinus*, 16. 1–9 (also 345F, 345aF, 345cF Smith for the interesting claim that it was the Christians, not Jesus himself, who had erred).

Cornutus and Chaeremon by Porphyry), who argued that theological study should be anchored around the doctrines of Plato and Pythagoras, but should include a comparative study of the Brahmans, Jews, Magi, and Egyptians (fr. 1a des Places). And before him, in the work of Plutarch again we find a very extensive allegorical account of an Egyptian myth—the myth of Isis and Osiris—which is organized on just the kind of basis that we saw being used in Cornutus. Plutarch argued, for example, that Osiris and Dionysus are the same god on the grounds that the traditional rites associated with each of them are so similar (364 E–365 B), and he engaged in a much wider comparative survey, employing Egyptian, Persian, Chaldean, and Greek theology, to support the theory of cosmic dualism which, he says, is at the root of the Isis and Osiris myth (see 369 B–371 C). Of course it is important for this kind of study that one can establish the antiquity of the traditions employed, and there is a nice example of Plutarch's concern with this issue in his work *On Herodotus' Malice*. One of the malicious claims identified by Plutarch in Herodotus is the assertion that Greek theology was younger than Egyptian religion and that, while Egyptian gods were real deities, those of the Greeks were merely the memories of men who had died (857 C–F; cf. Herodotus 2. 4, 50). This interpretation of Greek religion was vigorously attacked by Plutarch;[30] and one might explain his concern over the issue by appealing, for example, to his sense of national pride, or even to his obligations to the religion of which he was, after all, a priest. But there is a serious philosophical level to his interest as well. If wisdom was to be sought by a comparative study of theology, it was naturally important to know that the Greeks supplied usable material.

2. *From Stoicism to Platonism*

I have argued that the Stoic theory of ancient wisdom and its preservation in mythology was adopted wholesale into Platonism from its inception in the late first century AD. But at the beginning of this chapter I suggested that the adoption of this theory was something rather deeper than an example of doxographical influence: that it could be used to *explain* in some way the Dogmatic authority of Plato for the Platonists, and could thereby play a role in the very

[30] And for a general attack on Euhemeristic interpretations of the ancient religions see *Isis and Osiris*, 360 A–B.

definition of Platonism. None of the evidence I have so far surveyed suggests how this was so: precisely because (as I have argued) the theory of ancient wisdom was adopted so completely from the Stoics, it might seem that there is very little room to use it as means of explaining the peculiar nature of Platonism. However, without altering the theory they inherited from the Stoics, the Platonists added a single premiss which made all the difference in the world. Platonists believed, with the Stoics, that fragments of ancient wisdom *could* be recovered by an exegesis of ancient traditions; but they believed in addition that the ancient wisdom *had been* reconstructed in its entirety by Plato. Plato's philosophy, they thought, was effectively a textbook of the ancient wisdom, reconstructed, compiled, and explained.[31] And, since the ancient wisdom (as we saw in Chapter 3) was validated by its origins, Plato's philosophy was likewise bound to be true.

It might be objected that the Platonists are actually rather unlikely to have believed that Plato had reconstructed the ancient wisdom of the nations. After all, if this were true, and the ancient wisdom was readily available in the texts of Plato, then they would presumably not have felt the need to engage in their own comparative reconstructions of it. But in fact it will quickly be seen that the opposite is the case: the Platonists' own pursuit of a reconstruction is itself good evidence that they believed that Plato had achieved it. In the first place, there is certainly no contradiction here, because an independent reconstruction of elements of ancient wisdom could function as part of a *demonstration* of Plato's achievement. And it is in any case false to suppose that the availability of the truth in the writings of Plato obviates the need for study by his followers, for the simple reason that to read something is not yet to understand it. Just as the Platonists' belief in the authority of Plato in no way conflicts with their need to write commentaries for the elucidation of his philosophy—indeed, it is rather presupposed by it—so the fact that Plato had arrived at his thought by a reconstruction of the primitive truth does not preclude the need for the Platonists to look down this path as well. Quite the opposite: if the Platonists did believe that Plato's thought derived from the ancient traditions, then

[31] One possible proof-text in Plato's own work could have been *Statesman*, 272 C, alluding to the possibility of a 'common treasure-house of wisdom' among the men of the Cronian age. Plato suggests that we have some evidence for its existence: stories (presumably traditional mythological stories) which he supposes to have originated in the symposiastic discussions of this age.

the soundest way of coming to an understanding of Plato's philosophy would be to look at the sources from which he derived it. So (again) Numenius fr. 1a des Places:

> On this point [the nature of the godhead] it will be necessary, having stated and drawn conclusions from Plato's evidence, to go back to Pythagoras, and tie it in with his doctrines; then to call in the respected nations, comparing such of their mystery rites, doctrines, and institutions as the Brahmans, the Jews, the Magi, and the Egyptians have laid down, and as are conducted in conformity with Plato.

Plato is the starting-point of enquiry: but to understand Plato properly is, at least in part, precisely to understand *that* his philosophy is the essence of ancient wisdom. The fact that the Platonists engaged in the study of traditional theologies is actually *explained* by their belief that Plato had perfected the study himself. One might note in addition that, if the Platonists thought that the Stoics had provided the means to reconstruct a privileged philosophy from traditional theology (and I have shown that they certainly did), then it would make no sense for them to think of Plato as authoritative *unless* he had done the same, and done it successfully, himself. The Platonists would not be 'Platonists'—they would not think it important to recover the thought of Plato—if the reconstruction of primitive philosophy provided a route to the truth that was safer. The only reason that they could have had to believe in the primary authority of Plato was a belief that Plato himself provided an account of the truth preserved in these traditions.

There is evidence of another kind on the matter as well, in the Platonists' own accounts of Plato's philosophical education. For although, on occasion, they attributed Plato's insight into the truth to divine 'inspiration', we should not suppose that they meant by this that he had no need of education or research of his own. Indeed, it seems that Plato's 'divine inspiration' rather constituted his ability to carry out this research than a substitute for it. Just as the interpreters of Plato (that is to say, the best of them) were lauded for their 'divine inspiration' by those who came after them—although the whole point is that their wisdom was drawn out of Plato—so Plato in his turn was 'inspired' in his own understanding of the sources available to him.[32] This is not only consistent with,

[32] For Plato as 'divine' or divinely inspired cf. e.g. Apuleius, *On the Doctrine of Plato*, 1. 2; Celsus ap. Origen, *Against Celsus*, 7. 28 (cf. 41). Among Platonic inter-

it also helps to explain, one of the most characteristic features of Platonist biographies of Plato, namely their ascription to him of extensive foreign travels, apparently in search of ancient wisdom. Plato's connection with Pythagoras (or at least with Pythagoreans) was established at an early stage, presumably on the basis of Plato's own writings;[33] but the Platonists sent him out much more widely than his dialogues would suggest to the ordinary reader. In addition to his time with the Pythagoreans, for example, they described how he was taught by Egyptians and Persian Zoroastrians and Magi. In the sixth century Olympiodorus even went to the trouble of explaining how political circumstances at the timemeant that he must have encountered the latter in Phoenicia.[34] Clearly we are supposed to understand that it is from these ancient peoples (as well, of course, as from the Greeks) that the raw material for Plato's philosophy was gathered.[35] Plato's genius, in other words, did not lie for his interpreters in the novelty of his system: it lay precisely in the unparalleled success of his reconstruction of what Celsus was calling the 'true doctrine'. That is why later on, in a parenthetical

preters, divine inspiration is attributed to e.g. Plotinus (Porphyry, *Life of Plotinus*, 23. 18–21; but for his rejection of originality cf. 16. 1–12; also Plotinus himself at *Enneads*, 5. 1. 8. 10–14); Syrianus (Proclus, *Platonic Theology*, 4. 23, 69. 8–12 Saffrey and Westerink); Ammonius (Hierocles ap. Photius, *Library*, 214, 172ᵃ2–9). Proclus generalizes the principle that theological enquiry must start from the gods and be kindled in the soul by them (*Platonic Theology*, 1. 1, 7. 11–21 Saffrey and Westerink), but explicitly links such inspiration with the interpretation of Plato (e.g. *Platonic Theology*, 1. 1, 8. 7–10 Saffrey and Westerink). Cf. generally Bieler (1935–6), i. 17 (with reference to Porphyry, *On Abstinence*, 2. 45), 73–6; Dodds (1960).

[33] Cicero, *Republic*, 1. 16 (cf. also, for his wider travels, *Tusculan Disputations*, 4. 44; *On Ends*, 5. 50, 87); Quintilian, *Institutes of Oratory*, 1. 12. 15. Eudorus speaks of Socrates and Plato agreeing with Pythagoras on the nature of virtue: Stobaeus, *Eclogue*, ii. 49. 8–12 Wachsmuth.

[34] See variously: Plutarch, *On Isis and Osiris*, 354 D–E; D.L. 3. 6; Apuleius, *On the Doctrine of Plato*, 1. 3 (including an account of a thwarted attempt to visit India); Anon., *Prolegomena*, 4; Olympiodorus, *Commentary on the* Alcibiades, 2. 138–4 Westerink (cf. Porphyry, who argued that no genuine work by Zoroaster would contradict Plato: *Life of Plotinus*, 16). Cf. D.L. 3.6 and Anon., *Prolegomena*, 4, for Plato's contact with the most important of the 'Presocratic' schools. And finally, given his acquaintance with Pythagoras, we can take it that Plato benefited indirectly from the wide circle of ancient traditions with which Pythagoras himself had come into contact as well: see further below. On this topic in general see Dörrie and Baltes (1990), 166–91.

[35] Frede (1997: 220; cf. 1994: 5198–9) argues that Plato was, for the Platonists in general and Celsus in particular, 'not the discoverer of the truth, but rather the last ancient who still had a grasp on the full truth' (and cf. 230, with reference to Origen, *Against Celsus*, 6. 10). It is certainly correct that Plato's philosophy is not *new*; but this does not mean that it had been transmitted unsullied down to Plato.

exclamation of praise for Plato, Proclus was able to say, in terms which in any other context might have seemed ironical or paradoxical: 'I am amazed at Plato's inspired intellect, its ability to make clear [to those who follow in his steps] *the very same things*' as Orpheus, the 'theologians', and the 'barbarians' (*Platonic Theology*, 5. 10, 33. 21–34. 2 Saffrey and Westerink).[36]

Plato, then, was thought to have reconstructed the ancient, primitive, and (thereby) privileged wisdom of mankind. But it should be noted that Plato was not the only thinker reckoned to have achieved an understanding of the ancient wisdom: he was, in fact, only one, and not the first, of a number of thinkers who stood at the head of the Classical tradition of Greek philosophy, and whose philosophy was thought to be based on an understanding of the 'true doctrine'. This should be immediately evident from Proclus' mention of Orpheus in the passage just cited;[37] but the same goes for Pythagoras as well. The Platonists' respect for Pythagoras was by no means restricted to so-called 'neo-Pythagoreans' such as Moderatus of Gades and Numenius. He was adopted much more generally by Platonists, who wrote biographies of Pythagoras which incorporated many elements paralleled in their descriptions of Plato's life. Most importantly, perhaps, Pythagoras too was widely supposed to have travelled to barbarian lands in search of the ancient streams of wisdom preserved in their traditions. That he had had contact with the Egyptians was an early belief (cf. Isocrates, *Busiris*, 28; cf. Cicero, *On Ends*, 5. 87, where he also visits the Persian Magi); but Porphyry said that he had visited the Phoenicians and Chaldeans as well (*Life of Pythagoras*, 6–7; cf. 11, where the list includes the Egyptians, Arabs, Chaldeans, and Hebrews); Iamblichus has him go to Phoenicia, Egypt, and Babylon (where he met the Magi: *On the Pythagorean Life*, 4. 19). Apuleius said that he was taught by Zoroaster himself (*Florida*, 15; cf. perhaps Plutarch, *On the Generation of the Soul*, 1012 E). And the same conclusions can be drawn about his philosophy: it was an inspired reconstruction of the primitive wisdom, and that is why the Platonists took it so seriously.

The list of Greek thinkers who reconstructed the ancient wisdom does not stop with Pythagoras either: Celsus mentions Linus,

[36] This expression of admiration for what we might think of as Plato's lack of originality is not unique, either: cf. also *Platonic Theology*, 1. 7, 30. 22–4; 5. 35, 127. 8–11 Saffrey and Westerink.

[37] And cf. again ch. 5 n. 11 for Orpheus' acquaintance with Egyptian religion, and the foundation of the Greek mysteries by him.

Musaeus, Pherecydes, Zoroaster, Homer, and Heraclitus along with Pythagoras, Orpheus, and Plato as men who had all understood the 'true doctrine' (Origen, *Against Celsus*, 1. 16 with 6. 42).[38] In comparison with the Stoics one of the most striking members of the list is Homer: the Platonists argued that he too had achieved this remarkable insight, and, where the Stoics had believed that Homer was very much 'merely' a poet who unwittingly transmitted fragments of ancient wisdom, the Platonists in some sense reverted to the earlier, Presocratic view of Homer's place in the history of philosophy, believing him to have been a philosopher of high achievement—but this time because they saw in his poems deliberate allegorical expositions of the highest philosophical truths (that is, the same philosophical truths as Pythagoras and Plato had also recovered).[39] When the Platonists wrote commentaries on Homer which argued for profound and thoroughgoing philosophical content to his works, they were not looking for scraps of the primitive tradition accidentally trapped in the poetry, they were looking for Homer's deliberate reconstruction of that tradition.[40] Again, they did not think that he had some kind of direct access to the truth

[38] The absence of the majority of thinkers we would designate 'Presocratics' is interesting: Heraclitus is the one exception on Celsus' list. The 'physicists' are mentioned at the anonymous *Prolegomena*, 8—and criticized for their materialism and lack of understanding of causality. Parmenides (with one of whose pupils Plato was supposed to have studied: *Prolegomena*, 4; cf. D.L. 3. 6) is likewise criticized for thinking that 'Being' is the first principle of things that are (Plato went on to show that the One precedes Being). The idea seems to be—although how far this can be generalized is not clear—that these thinkers were not on the whole actually wrong, but that their philosophy was not complete in the way that Plato's was. It is as if they were early—but not entirely successful—attempts to translate the ancient wisdom into a 'philosophical' genre. The Presocratics retain this rather ambiguous status throughout Platonist writing: for the opinion of Plotinus in particular see Gelzer (1982).

[39] The anonymous *Prolegomena* talks (at 7) of a 'poetical sect' (ποιητικὴ αἵρεσις) including Orpheus, Homer, Musaeus, and Hesiod, as one of the main philosophical schools before Plato.

[40] For an allegorical account of Homer's poetry see most famously Porphyry's *Cave of the Nymphs* (with Edwards 1990 for its debt to Numenius); cf. the fragments of his work *On the Styx* (372F–380F Smith). Porphyry wrote a number of works on Homer as a philosopher, including one *On the Philosophy of Homer* (371T Smith). The first book of his lost *History of Philosophy* seems to have included a discussion of Homer (cf. esp. 201F and 204F Smith). We have the title of another lost work, *On the Usefulness of Homer for Kings* (370T Smith), and significant fragments from Porphyry's exegetical work on the poetry of Homer, including his *Homeric Questions* (see the editions of Schrader and Sodano, the portions included by the latter being translated in Schlunk 1993; also fragments 381F–406F Smith). See further Pépin (1966).

through inspiration (and the fact that this was an explanation given by certain thinkers associated with the Second Sophistic, including Platonizing thinkers such as Maximus of Tyre, should not beguile us into thinking that they did).[41] Platonists adopted biographies of Homer which emphasized his connection to ancient nations, just as they had done for Plato and Pythagoras: Plutarch, for example, says that Homer was educated by Egyptians (*On Isis and Osiris*, 364 C–D), and Clement of Alexandria, presumably drawing on pagan texts, actually claims that Homer *was* Egyptian himself (as 'most people claim': *Stromata*, 1. 15. 66. 1; cf. later Calcidius, *Commentary on Plato's* Timaeus, 126).[42] It might be possible to view in this context Lucian's suggestion (*True History*, 2. 20) that Homer was Babylonian as a whimsical reflection of the debate over the relative antiquity of the Egyptian and Babylonian philosophical traditions.

Plato, it is clear, was one among a whole body of particularly able men whose work established the Classical Greek intellectual tradition, and did it, not by invention or unaided individual perception of the truth, but rather by uncovering a true philosophy through understanding and explicating the ancient traditions of wisdom in the world. So why were the Platonists 'Platonists'—and not, for example, 'Orphics' or 'Homerists'? In one sense (as they themselves would have seen it), they might have been any of these things—and some of them, indeed (Numenius among them), concentrated on Pythagoras in particular to the extent that they were actually known as 'Pythagoreans' as well.[43] But the point, presumably, is that Plato

[41] Cf. Maximus of Tyre, *Dissertation* 38. 1 Trapp with Kindstrand (1973), esp. 163–8 (and cf. 115–24 and 194–8 for the divine inspiration of Homer in Dio of Prusa and Aelius Aristides respectively).

[42] The suggestion that Homer had some connection with Egypt is not, however, original to the Platonists: cf. e.g. Diodorus (*Library*, 1. 69. 4, 96. 2, 97. 7–9); and perhaps already Herodotus (*Histories*, 2. 50 with 53: the connection hinted at by the fact that Greek theology was derived from Egypt, but given its original form in Greece by Homer and Hesiod). For the claim that Homer was an Egyptian cf. also Heliodorus, *Aethiopica*, 3. 13. 3–14. 4.

[43] The matter is largely a question of degree: most Platonists considered that the obscurity of Pythagoras made him, in practical terms, of secondary use. Numenius obviously thought that more primary use could be made of him—although even he argued that Plato had contributed something further in showing how the thought of Pythagoras could be reconciled with that of Socrates (cf. fr. 24. 57–9, 73–9 des Places, with my discussion of Numenius in ch. 7). At a further extreme, a thinker might be a Pythagorean first and foremost (possibly including Moderatus of Gades, but see O'Meara 1989: 11 with n. 8)—not because he believes that Plato's philosophy is necessarily *inferior* to that of Pythagoras, but rather because he believes that

developed a more transparent genre of exposition peculiar to philosophy as such: the 'theologians', such as Orpheus, exploited the mystical symbolism of religious ceremony to communicate the ancient wisdom; symbolism of a kind is likewise the vehicle for the wisdom of the Pythagoreans, whose 'sayings' (*ἀκούσματα*) were part of the means they used to preserve this wisdom for the elect; Homer, again, employed the techniques of poetry, and expressed the 'true doctrine' in complex allegorical narratives. Plato, however, is easier to approach: the means he found to express this wisdom was by far the clearest of all. And if Plato is the clearest of all (cf. perhaps Proclus, *Platonic Theology*, 1. 4, 20. 1–25 Saffrey and Westerink), then presumably he provides the safest route for later interpreters to pursue the wisdom they all held in common. The anonymous *Prolegomena* to Plato's works, written by a pupil of Olympiodorus, certainly regards Plato's superiority with respect to the philosophers who preceded him largely as a matter of his clarity, and his provision of well-worked-out proofs;[44] and note again Proclus' admiration in the passage quoted above from *Platonic Theology*, 5. 10: although his point there is that Plato and Orpheus held the same beliefs about god, it is Plato's clarity of exposition, his ability to lead others to the truth, that is the immediate object of his praise. The commentary tradition, of course, can view itself as extending the process thus begun in Plato of securing the ancient wisdom by leaving as little room for doubt as possible over what it actually contained.[45]

The Stoics' theory of a primitive, privileged wisdom which was transmitted through the theological traditions of the nations was a crucially important step towards the development of a philosophy based on its reconstruction. But the Stoics viewed such reconstruction as essentially auxiliary to the main approach required in philosophy: they marched forwards towards the truth, glancing back

Plato can add nothing to the account of the primitive wisdom already available in Pythagoras (cf. Porphyry, *Life of Pythagoras*, 53).

[44] See *Prolegomena*, 7–8: Plato's arguments are more apodeictic and more decently presented than those of the poets; they are more apodeictic and divine than those of the 'physicists' (the philosophers we would normally call the 'Presocratics'); and they are clearer and more apodeictic than those of the Pythagoreans.

[45] Cf. Proclus, *Platonic Theology*, 1. 2, 9. 20–1 Saffrey and Westerink: 'In everything, we shall prefer the clear, articulated, and simple to their opposites [*ἐν ἅπασι δὲ τὸ σαφὲς καὶ διηρθρωμένον καὶ ἁπλοῦν προθήσομεν τῶν ἐναντίων*].' Compare perhaps Barnes (1992), 267–74, on the Aristotelian commentators.

at mythology only to check (and to prove) that they were heading in the right direction. The Platonists stopped and turned round: they believed that the unique philosophical tradition of Greece had been established on the basis of the achievement of a series of brilliant thinkers in the Classical and pre-Classical period who had succeeded in reconstructing the primitive truth in its entirety, and that, in consequence, the shortest road to the truth would be the one that led back there through them. This not only gave them a methodology of their own (to seek for the truth in Plato), it also gave them a justification for their belief in the unique validity of their enterprise.

7

Divergence and Disagreement: The Platonist Alternative to Scepticism

As the dominant school of the later empire, and through the profound influence it had on the development of Christian theology, Platonism was to have a defining effect on the course of later Western philosophy. And everything that might be said about the nature of its effect must ultimately refer back to the revolutionary new model for philosophical research introduced through the Platonists' ascription of authority to Plato under the definition set out in the previous chapter. The suggestion that the purpose of philosophy was to understand a truth that was already available (rather than to work towards finding that truth afresh), the primary focus on antiquity which this encouraged, the doctrinal systems themselves as they emerged from this process, must all be seen in terms of the unprecedented notion of authority ascribed by the Platonists to Plato. But the arguments outlined in the previous chapter still only tell half of the story. For, while they offer an explanation for the absolute authority of Plato, they can only properly succeed in explaining it to someone who thinks that Plato is *right* in the first place. The belief in their founder's authority was, in the way that they meant it, distinctive of the Platonist movement, but only someone impressed by the truth of Plato's philosophy would find it necessary to wonder *how* he arrived at the truth, or be attracted by the explanation the Platonists offered. So, while my account thus far says something important about what Platonism *was*, it has not yet said anything of why it arose—why, against the background of a long philosophical tradition that had always taken Plato seriously, one group of people suddenly came to argue that his philosophy contained such a thoroughgoing account of the truth that its origins could only be accounted for in a way that made it actually authoritative.

There is a simple way of answering this question: at some point, somebody read Plato in a particular way and became convinced by the doctrines he saw there, became convinced that Plato had an answer (and a true answer) for everything; this *Ur*-Platonist took up Plato's cause and argued for his reading of Plato and the validity of the doctrines that emerged from it so successfully that others soon joined him; he, or they together, realized that such a complete and perfect system of philosophy could only be explained under the terms I have set out in the previous chapter, and their conviction that Plato was always right became transmuted into the belief that he was authoritative—that he was not only always, but was also necessarily, right. In this way, Platonism was born.

With suitable refinements, a story like this might be true—but it would be disappointing if it were the whole truth, if the origins of Platonism could be reduced to an essentially biographical incident like this. It would be as if we explained the origins of Stoicism by attributing a vision of the new system to Zeno of Citium and said nothing of his dissatisfaction and engagement with earlier systems of thought. For Plato had always been read, had always, as I say, been taken seriously: the question, then, of *why* Platonism arose as a movement is more importantly considered in terms of the *justification* someone could offer for developing a way of reading his works so that they all came out to be true. The point has a particular urgency for Platonism, which would find it less than usually adequate to rely on the 'obvious' truth of Platonic doctrine. For by reverting to the texts of Plato, Platonists were ostensibly rejecting some four hundred years of subsequent philosophical research. A person might find the doctrines of Plato attractive, but in order to prepare such a person to *believe* what he found in Plato, to revise his assumption that Plato's philosophy had been superseded by schools in the later tradition, to ensure that he was not tempted to dismiss Plato's doctrines as *merely* plausible precursors to different but at least equally plausible systems of thought developed later on in their light, the Platonists *first* had to provide him with reasons for thinking that it made sense to pursue the truth through an examination of Plato. Only if he could be led to *expect* that Plato's philosophy might be superior to systems of thought that came later could his attraction to Plato's doctrines be expected to solidify into a belief that they were right. In this chapter I shall suggest that the Platonists offered a justification of their philosophy which argued for just such an expectation. In particular, I shall argue that we misunderstand a great deal about Platonism, its success and its influence, if we think that its theoretical genesis lay in a moment of insight even that Plato was right. The belief that Plato's philosophy was universally true is obviously of crucial importance (there would be no Platonism without it); but it is itself something that belongs in the later stages of the philosophical tale, as the result and confirmation of an original expectation that Plato alone could show us the way to the truth.

1. *The Argument from Disagreement*

The Platonists naturally could—and did—argue that the doctrines they adduced from Plato ought to command our assent in some manner: they asserted, for example, their superior ability to make sense of the evidence available to us when compared with the attempts of alternative schools. No doubt too, many people were convinced by such arguments and turned to a study of Plato because of them. But equally, many people would fail to be convinced by them at all. Furthermore, for every argument the Platonists adduced in support of one of their own doctrines, they would be met with counter-arguments from the schools of their opponents—counter-arguments whose weakness might not be apparent to anyone viewing the debate from outside. Indeed, to generalize the point, and quite apart from any objections that could be levelled against individual doctrines, the revived system of Dogmatic Platonism only contributed to the apparently irreconcilable diversity of opinion among Dogmatic philosophers which formed one of the starting-points for the Sceptics' doubts over whether the truth had been or could be discovered at all—the Argument from Disagreement (διαφωνία).[1]

The Argument from Disagreement asks us to abstract ourselves

[1] For the use of this argument in the Academy, and by Carneades in particular, see e.g. Cicero, *Academica*, 2. 117–47. It occurs in Pyrrhonism as the first of the five 'Modes of Agrippa' (see S.E. *PH* 1. 165), and in the course of Sextus' description of the second of the 'Ten Modes' (S.E. *PH* 1. 88–9, where Sextus also scorns attempts to answer the argument by appealing to a majority view—something which, as I suggest below, Antiochus might have tried). It should be noted that my account of the argument in what follows is shaped more by a desire to provide a context for

from any opinions we might happen to hold, and to consider from that point of view what reasons we might have for preferring the claims made by one side of any Dogmatic argument to those made by all of its opponents. It suggests that we shall find that there are none. It is a strictly separate argument that the reasons Dogmatists give for believing their own system at one point tend to be reasons that rely on the truth of their system at points elsewhere—in short, that they all beg the question, so that no doctrinal assertion could ever amount to an objective reason to suppose that the system in which it is contained is true. The Argument from Disagreement works from this position (which, as it stands, could be effective even against truth claims made by a Dogmatic consensus) to say that, given a plurality of opposing systems, there are no reasons *even* for thinking that one school is more *capable* of finding the truth than any other, or more *likely* to find it than any other (whether or not it has in fact found it or will in fact find it). It might be the case that, on surveying the field, one of the schools seems more promising to me than another; but even if it does, I am forced to admit that there are many people for whom this is not so, who are inclined towards a different school. Unless I can prove to myself that my own inclinations can be justified—that is, that they are based on good objective reasons which are not peculiar to my own disposition and which do not already presuppose the truth of doctrinal claims made by the school itself—then it is only rational to conclude that my inclination betrays a lack of true objectivity, and to curb my assent here as well. The Argument from Disagreement as such says that the very existence of debate among serious and intelligent philosophers provides reason enough to doubt that any Dogmatic school is preferable in fact to any other, however their doctrines might strike me.

This is what the Platonists wished to deny—and their denial of it comes to the heart of why (as I argued in the previous chapter) it is so important to view Platonism rather as a methodology than as a collection of doctrines. The force of the Argument from Disagreement derives from its assumption that the *only* reason one might have for becoming, say, a Stoic rather than an Epicurean

exploring the justification offered by the Platonists for their Dogmatism than it is to expound the use of the argument by the Sceptics. For a closer and less partial reading of the argument as it appears in Sextus Empiricus at least, see Barnes (1990), 1–35.

is that one comes to believe in the truth (or superior likelihood) of Stoic doctrine. Any doubt that could be raised over the justification for such a belief—whether through attacks made directly on the doctrine itself or through the demonstration offered by the Argument from Disagreement that they struck many other equally intelligent people as false—would remove in addition the justification for pursuing philosophy in the Stoa at all. Until you can be sure of the doctrines, there is no reason for joining the school. But the Platonists suggested that there might be *other* reasons for inclining towards one school rather than another—reasons, that is, which did not (in the first place at least) rely on attraction to its doctrinal position. They aimed to provide, even for someone who had surveyed all the doctrinal options and been led to suspension of judgement over the truth of them all, objective reasons for becoming a Platonist rather than, say, a Stoic. An initial belief in the truth of Plato's doctrines, they claimed, was only one reason to become a Platonist: it was not, however, one they relied on—realizing that to do so would be to concede the Sceptics' position. Divorcing their philosophical methodology from the particular doctrinal consequences of it, they were able to say that, as long as the latter could not actually be shown to be false, a study of Plato would still be the only reasonable course open to the seeker of truth.

There is more than one way in which a philosophy could attempt a strategy like this, and argue for adherence to its own school's approach independently of particular doctrines it espouses. One might, for example, consider in this light the Stoics' claim that theirs was the only *consistent* philosophical account of the world, that it should be obvious to a truly 'objective observer' that other philosophies fell prey to self-contradiction, and that theirs was in consequence the only school which offered a viable account of the world. Such an approach is attempted in Cicero, *Academica*, 2. 23, for example—a passage which refers to Antiochus' system in particular, but whose premisses are all shared in common with the Stoics, from whom he might be supposed to have derived the argument (along with so much of his system itself).[2] In this passage, then, the system is shown to be capable of giving an adequate account of the world on the grounds of its internal consistency; it is

[2] Cf. Cicero, *On Ends*, 3. 74, where the Stoics claim *in propria persona* that their doctrinal system has a distinctive level of consistency shared only with Nature herself.

shown to be the *only* system that could do this, on the grounds of its *unique* consistency (dispelling equipollence from its disagreement with alternative models); and finally, since the possibility of knowledge is included as one of the elements which contributes to the consistency of the system, it leaves us no room for doubt (even before we have assented to particular Stoic doctrines) that the system is the only one which offered any hope of leading us to knowledge about the world.

But the immediate trouble with this response to the Sceptics is that the Stoics were not alone in claiming that alternative systems to their own were contradictory—indeed, they were accused of self-contradiction in their turn (as we shall see further on). This tends to undermine the claim that the consistency (never mind the unique consistency) of Stoicism was *objectively* clear. Rather than extricating the objective onlooker from *aporia*, this approach only throws him back into an impossible position of judgement. The Stoic answer, in short, turns out to be another way of *asserting* the superiority of the Stoical way, but hardly a means of converting the Sceptic to follow it.

A second, bolder strategy, then, might be to deny the extent of serious philosophical disagreement in the first place, and so remove the basis for the Argument from Disagreement to work on. This is something that might have lain behind another, more distinctive, of Antiochus' arguments. For Antiochus argued that Plato, the Old Academy, the Stoa, and Lyceum all held what were, in essence, exactly the same beliefs—something which, he said, was only obscured by the fact that they differed in their use of terminology (e.g. *On Ends*, 5. 88–92). The seed of this theory seems to have been sown in his earlier days as a Carneadean Sceptic (*Academica*, 2. 63, 69) since Carneades, and before him Arcesilaus, had long ago started to accuse the Stoa precisely of maintaining Peripatetic ethical theory under the guise of a new terminology (*On Ends*, 3. 41; Arcesilaus at *Academica*, 2. 16). But Antiochus' extended syncretism, and in particular the claim that *Plato* and the Stoics agreed, was presumably not something he could have maintained as an Academic Sceptic at least: members of the New Academy (whatever accusations might be moved against them) never felt for themselves that they had betrayed its founder. So Antiochus' theory that most of the Dogmatic schools agreed in essence must be specifically linked to the Dogmatic phase of his own thought, and the point of it might have been just this: that despite the exaggerated claims of the Sceptics, the only major Dogmatic school that stood outside of the philosophical consensus was that of the Epicureans; and the weight of the consensus created without them could be used to isolate and marginalize their position to the extent that it might not even count as a 'serious' alternative at all.[3] None of this would furnish a proof that Antiochus' consensus was actually *right* (it does not even claim to prove that the development of a consensus was inevitable).[4] But at least it would capture the rhetorical advantage, and provide the objective observer with some sort of reason to think that doctrines which commanded such general assent would be more worth investigating than their supposedly unpopular alternatives.

Sadly, however, Antiochus' claims of agreement were themselves tendentious and essentially subjective: they, at least, were *not* agreed upon, certainly not, for example, by the Stoics. It is by no means *objectively* clear in the first place that the level of agreement on which he rested his claims actually existed at all.

The Platonists, I shall argue, took a third approach to this question—one whose strength in comparison with the Stoics and Antiochus was precisely that it relied on premisses already conceded by their opponents. For the Platonists *agreed* that philosophy was, as a matter of fact, riven with irreconcilable diversity, but went on to argue that a Sceptical conclusion was not at all the only or even the most reasonable response to it. As we shall see, they provided an alternative model for explaining the diversity which, they argued, provided objective justification for seeking the truth through an examination of Plato in particular.

[3] Epicurean hedonism was in any case easily enough caricatured in a light that made it unacceptable from the start: cf. e.g. Cicero, *Academica*, 2. 140; but compare, more interestingly, the Stoics' strategy of isolating the Epicurean position as discussed at Algra (1997), 109–18.

[4] Although compare Antiochus' use of the *divisio Carneadea* (e.g. Cicero, *On Ends*, 5. 16–22), by which he presumably hoped to show that the number of *possible* positions that could be adopted in ethics was strictly limited. (Antiochus' pupil Varro listed the number of possible ethical sects as 288; but argued that they were based on only three *essentially* different positions: see Augustine, *City of God*, 19. 1–2.) This, anyway, had been Chrysippus' intention when he developed his ethical *divisio* (Cicero, *Academica*, 2. 138). On the subject of these various *divisiones* and their use, see Algra (1997). That Antiochus worked specifically with *Carneades*' division rather than that of Chrysippus does, by the way, suggest that he wished to make some form of response to the Sceptics by it.

2. *Plato in the Platonist History of Philosophy*

From the perspective of later centuries, Plato held a unique position in the history of philosophy, as the latest philosopher whose works formed in some sense a common reference-point for the various schools that took their rise in the later tradition. Of course, Plato had his opponents while he lived: both survivals of earlier strains of thought against which the dialogues struggled, and alternative movements whose genesis, like his, lay in the interpretation of Socrates. Yet, viewed in terms of direct historical influence, and from the perspective of later Hellenistic hindsight, the contribution of Plato's immediate opponents could be thought of as minimal indeed. The schools that *mattered* in post-Platonic philosophy were not felt to be, for example, the Cynics or Cyrenaics (though the Cynical movement, at least, continued to find its adherents); they were (in order of foundation) the Academy, the Lyceum, the Garden, and the Stoa. This is important because, if the objective observer of philosophical debate was to be led to suspension of judgement by the very fact of the Dogmatists' inability to agree, it would not be because disagreement between Dogmatists had *sometimes* existed, or even because they had failed to bring *everyone* to agreement in the present. The quondam existence of long-defunct alternatives would not register difficulty at all;[5] and Dogmatism can happily coexist with eccentrics or sophists whose very isolation might argue that they had failed to understand the mainstream positions, or were simply unwilling to do so. The numbers alone involved in the Hellenistic schools ensured that they would have to be taken seriously; but by the same token, the relatively insignificant following achieved by movements outside of these schools and their marginal position in the debate might well lead an objective observer to suppose that they could be discounted as in effect an irrelevance. The Cynics themselves, to take the most persistent of the 'marginal' Socratic movements, far from contributing to the mainstream debates of the day, refused altogether to engage with many of the arguments (in logic and physics) which were central to the Dogmatic claims of the Stoics and Epicureans. If the Sceptics were going to make their argument rhetorically effective, to make Dogmatic philosophers feel uncomfortable about their Dog-

[5] Compare Cicero's perfunctory treatment of the 'long-abandoned' systems of Pyrrho, Herillus, and Aristo (esp. *On Ends*, 2. 43, 5. 23; *On Duties*, 1. 6).

matism, and to keep the objective observer in justifiable suspension of judgement, they would have to be able to show that there was significant disagreement among *these four schools*, the schools which shaped the developing debate and to which the vast majority of philosophers were variously attracted. Dogmatism can accommodate marginal dissent; it is disagreement in quarters popular enough for one to expect to find there a share of the most intelligent thinkers that ought to give pause for thought. Antiochus, at any rate, must have thought this if it is right that his revisionist conflation of the Old Academy, the Stoa, and the Lyceum was meant to act as any kind of reply to the Sceptics.

Looking, then, at a history of philosophy which includes only those movements which *matter* from the point of view of the question in hand, it becomes clear that Plato is effectively the *sole* reference-point for all subsequent philosophy. None of his opponents inspired schools or movements which survived to form part of the 'serious' debate of the Hellenistic era;[6] fully three of the four schools that mattered, however, could trace their development directly back to Plato. Plato himself founded the Academy, of course; and the Lyceum was established by his most famous pupil, Aristotle. It does seem to be true that the earlier Stoa viewed itself as part of an attempt to rescue Socrates' heritage *from* Plato's metaphysical absurdities, and as such that they bypassed Plato in tracing their lineage back through Crates and the Cynics;[7] but an alternative historical construction was possible, since Zeno, the founder of Stoicism, had been a pupil, not just of the Cynic Crates, but also of Plato's successor Polemo (D.L. 7. 1). Stoicism, in other words, could be viewed as a descendant of Plato as well, and certainly by the time that the Platonists were writing, this is precisely the view taken by the Stoics themselves. The Stoics had become increasingly embarrassed by their Cynical roots, and at a relatively early stage had embraced the Platonic patrimony which Zeno's link

[6] I should stress that I am not endorsing the view that the rival Socratic schools to Plato—which include the Megarians and Cyrenaics as well as the Cynics—had little influence in Hellenistic thought. The Cynics and Cyrenaics presumably were influential for Zeno and Epicurus respectively, whatever their later followers thought; the Megarians were tremendously important in the development of logic and, through logic, had an influence in other areas of philosophy as well. But what matters, of course, is how they were *perceived*, by the Platonists and the people to whom the Platonists wished to appeal.

[7] Cf. e.g. Long (1988), 161–2.

with Polemo allowed them.[8] In fact the only Hellenistic school that could not trace its development back to Plato was the Garden of Epicurus; and it, for all its debt to Democritus (even, it was possible to argue, through the Cyrenaics to Socrates),[9] was essentially a *new* foundation, and not in any case a *continuation* of any of Plato's forebears or opponents. This at least, just as importantly, is how it was viewed by the Epicureans themselves.[10]

This skeletal history of philosophy, and the unique place conceded to Plato within it by all of the Platonists' significant rivals, was what gave the Platonists their chance. What it allowed them to say was that the rise of disagreement in the Hellenistic age *must* be viewed (perhaps even trivially described) as a consequence of the development or conscious rejection of Plato, by most or all of the various schools. Again, none of the Platonists' opponents would seriously object to this claim. Indeed, they might welcome it, since it seems fatal to the Platonists themselves: it seems to argue general agreement that Plato had after all been in need of improvement. But, if we take it that all of these later schools were seriously engaged in attempting to discover the truth, and that all of them could boast powerful intellects to help, what such a response fails to do is to explain the real crux of the issue: why so much disagreement existed among them. The objective observer knows one thing at least, which is that no more than *one* of these schools can be right, so that *most* and possibly *all* must be wrong. So how do we explain that at least most and possibly all serious philosophers had failed so badly? There are only three possible explanations, offering justification for two possible responses from the objective observer.

One explanation is that *nobody* in this debate, not even Plato, had the truth. Since everyone was wrong, the scope for continuing debate was naturally very wide.

[8] Cf. ch. 6 n. 3. The Stoics also tried to distance themselves from the apparently Cynical doctrines to be found in some of Zeno's writings (his *Republic* in particular) by claiming, for example, that such writings were juvenilia, dating from before his association with Polemo, *and which did not, therefore, properly represent Stoicism*: cf. D.L. 7. 4 and esp. Philodemus, *On the Stoics*, col. IX. 2. 1–2 Dorandi. These claims presumably tell us much more about the attitude of Zeno's successors than the historical facts of the case: Philodemus already doubted that they were right (cf. *On the Stoics*, col. XIV, 4. 4–5 Dorandi), and cf. more recently Erskine (1990), 9–15.

[9] Cf. Cicero, *On Ends*, 1. 26, with *On the Orator*, 3. 62.

[10] Cf. e.g. Lucretius, *On the Nature of Things*, 1. 62–79, for the originality of Epicurus (note the repeated *primum . . . primusque . . . primus*). For the rather negative view of Socrates in the Garden see Kleve (1983) with Long (1988), 155–6.

The second explanation is that Plato was wrong and one of the post-Platonic schools was right (or at least, heading in the right direction). But in this case (via the Argument from Disagreement), no objective criteria could be used to discern their improvements as such among the burgeoning disagreement of their era. From the objective point of view, this is as useless as if they were actually wrong.

These two explanations, then, underpin the Sceptics' position: the existence of disagreement argues either that nobody has the truth, or that the truth is indiscernible, and in any case that we have no reason to incline to one school rather than another. However, there is something that both of these possibilities still fail to do, and that is to offer an explanation for the *diachronic* spread of the disagreement identified—to explain why, in particular, the serious disagreement identified arose only *after* Plato. If Plato himself had been obviously wrong, why did he have no serious opponents in his own day, opponents whose philosophy proved equally fruitful starting-points for later traditions of thought? The need to explain this as well is what opens up the third possibility. For the evidence adduced by the Argument from Disagreement is also compatible with the hypothesis that *Plato* was right, and that those later schools which turned away from his thought were simply too hasty in doing so. Indeed, it is not only compatible with this hypothesis, but more fully explained by it: on the hypothesis that Plato was right, we would understand *both* why no serious philosophical tradition existed in the Hellenistic age that traced its origins back through a route that bypassed Plato *and* why disagreement arose after Plato's death—because, of course, if Plato *did* have the truth, then it *would* naturally follow that the schools founded in reaction to his philosophy would find themselves causing serious trouble.[11]

The crack this opens is small but highly significant, for it allows the Platonists to say that a proper description of the disagreement to which the Sceptics appealed, one which takes the historical dimen-

[11] For a clearer statement of the principle that those who err from the truth fall into debate with each other cf. e.g. Iamblichus, *On the Mysteries*, 9. 4, 277. 8–13 Parthey; Proclus, *Commentary on the* First Alcibiades, 310. 3–311. 7 Segonds. The latter is a commentary on *Alcibiades I*, 111 A–E, which gives a Platonic basis for the principle (Socrates: 'Don't people with knowledge agree with each other and not differ?' Alcibiades: 'Yes.' 'And where they differ about something, would you say that they know it?' 'No.'). Cf. the very similar remarks of Socrates at *Phaedrus*, 237 C.

sion into account, leads us to a rather different conclusion from that offered by the Sceptics themselves. Properly described, the conclusion to the Argument from Disagreement is the following alternative: *either* Plato was right, *or* Plato was wrong and it is impossible to know whether any of the Hellenistic schools was right. And, while this offers us no argument that Plato was in fact right, what it does is to argue that *Plato's being right is the one hope we might have of finding the truth*. Furthermore, the superior explanatory power of the hypothesis that he was right gives us a real reason to test that hypothesis further. Working from the Argument from Disagreement, the Platonists were able to offer to someone genuinely in search of the truth—and even the Sceptics claimed to be in search of the truth (cf. e.g. S.E. *PH* 1. 7)—a reason to seek it in Plato. It is not an argument yet for the truth of particular doctrines, but it is an argument for a method of pursuing philosophy—the distinctively Platonist method, indeed, in terms of which I suggested in the last chapter the movement ought to be viewed.

The Platonists, naturally, had more to say to maintain the momentum behind this move, to show that it does (as a matter of fact) lead to a belief in the truth and thence the authority of Plato; I shall return to this later on. There are also details in the history of philosophy so far outlined that will need filling in. For the Platonists' suggestion does not argue that *all* of the Dogmatic Hellenistic schools are wrong—only that none could on its own merits be perceived to be right from an objective point of view. But, if the Platonists succeed in leading us to a belief in Plato's authority, we could go on to consider whether any of the Hellenistic schools were right simply by asking whether any remained faithful to Plato. This question will turn out to be of great practical importance when it comes to working out *what* Plato believed, since one's interpretation of Plato will be affected according to whether, for example, one comes to believe that Aristotle had remained faithful to him—as Platonists such as Plutarch and Apuleius, not to mention Plotinus and the later Platonist tradition, largely supposed; or whether one believes that Aristotle too had diverged from his Master. Atticus certainly thought that he had;[12] and even those early Platonists who

[12] See the fragments (1–9 des Places) of his work *Against Those Who Undertake to Interpret Plato's Doctrines through Those of Aristotle*, discussed further below; and cf. Calvenus Taurus, who wrote a work *On the Difference between the Doctrines of Plato and Aristotle* (*Suda*, s.v. *Ταῦρος*). There is, of course, a question of degree in all

were generally well disposed towards Aristotle were prepared to argue that in the matter of ethics at least Plato was more faithfully represented by the Stoa.[13] Again, the question of the fidelity of the New Academy to the teaching of Plato was to remain a difficult issue: Numenius, to take the most extreme example, argued vehemently that Arcesilaus had seceded from Plato; but others, notably Plutarch, found ways of reconciling his intentions with those of the school's founder.[14] However, even these questions are of rather less *theoretical* importance. The argument as I have outlined it is focused on *Plato*, and can only give us a reason to take *him* more seriously because of *his* unique historical position; the validity of individual Hellenistic schools is a question that is strictly posterior.

I have argued that the Platonists appealed to the history of philosophy to provide us with justification for hoping, at least, to find the truth through a study of Plato, and for understanding the nature of post-Platonic philosophy in the light of the hypothesis that Plato was in possession of the truth. If I am right about this, then it explains some of the more prevalent and characteristic themes in the rhetoric and polemic of Platonism. For the Platonists were

of this, and it is no contradiction to think that Aristotle remained essentially true to Plato, while making innovations of his own. Plutarch, for example, generally accepts the 'Platonist' credentials of Aristotle, but still has disagreements with him (as at *On the Neglect of Oracles*, 424 A–C; cf. *On the E at Delphi*, 389 F). Later on, Porphyry wrote one work *On the Unity of the Platonic and Aristotelian School*, and another *On the Disagreement of Plato and Aristotle* (239T and 238T Smith, respectively). As late as the 6th cent. we find some ambivalence in the anonymous *Prolegomena to Plato's Philosophy*: this work starts with a quotation from 'the divine Aristotle', but devotes part of sect. 9 to the inferiority of Peripatetic thought. For the general principle, compare perhaps Numenius' comments on the immediate successors of Plato: they, he said, diverged from Plato's philosophy, but do not deserve great censure since they 'preserved the ethos of his teaching' (fr. 24. 5–10 des Places).

[13] Cf. Atticus, of course (e.g. fr. 2. 9–17 des Places); but also Alcinous, *Didaskalikos*, 180. 39–41 Hermann (and cf. D.L. 3. 78).

[14] The ancient catalogue of Plutarch's works contains the title of a work *On the Unity of the Academy since Plato* (*Lamprias*, 63: *περὶ τοῦ Μίαν εἶναι τὴν ἀπὸ τοῦ Πλάτωνος Ἀκαδήμειαν*). On Plutarch's own approach to the reconciliation of the Academy and Platonism see esp. Brittain (1996), 208–20 (218–20 for Arcesilaus); and cf. Boys-Stones (1997). For other approaches to this questions see e.g. the *Anonymous Commentary on Plato's* Theaetetus, 70. 12–26, suggesting that Academic Scepticism was formulated *ad hominem* (against, that is, the Stoics). Another theory, that the Academy positively maintained a secret Dogmatic tradition behind its Sceptical arguments, is attributed to one Diocles of Cnidus, possibly as early as the 3rd cent. BC. See Numenius fr. 25. 75–82 des Places (cf. 27. 56–9) with Flammand (1994); and further S.E. *PH* 1. 234; Augustine, *Against the Academics*, 3. 37–43, and *Epistle* 118, with Brittain (1996), 233–7.

unusually concerned to point out, not just the self-contradictions and obvious absurdities of their opponents' philosophies (though naturally they did this as well), but also the disagreements they provoked *with each other*; and the key to understanding these themes would seem to be the most characteristic and (from a philosophical point of view) seemingly irrelevant theme of all: the relative *youth* of their foundation. Taking these themes together, it does seem that the Platonists wish us to understand that the proliferation in debate between post-Platonic schools, and their individual philosophical shortcomings, are meant to support the hypothesis of Plato's having been right—to the extent that they can be understood as somehow *bound* to result if that hypothesis holds. A good case in point is Plutarch, from whom a number of polemical writings against Dogmatic schools of the Hellenistic era survive. Consider, for example, the opening lines of his anti-Epicurean treatise *Against Colotes* (the pupil of Epicurus). For at the beginning of this work, which attacks a philosophy which prided itself on its novelty, Plutarch places a dedication to a friend (presumably a Platonist friend) who was a 'lover of beauty and antiquity' (*φιλόκαλον καὶ φιλάρχαιον*), and who considered it 'a most royal occupation to recall and have in hand, so far as circumstances allow, the teachings of the ancients' (*τοὺς λόγους τῶν παλαιῶν*: *Against Colotes*, 1, 1107 E). Plutarch is not one to spell out what his audience might have been expected to deduce for themselves, but this preface to the catalogue of doctrinal difficulties and absurdities within Epicurus' philosophy must be intended to provide us with gentle direction towards the conclusion that these difficulties are somehow the *result* of the novelty of the system itself.

The very same moral seems to be repeated in the two of Plutarch's major anti-Stoical works that survive: *On Stoic Self-contradictions*, and *On Common Conceptions* (which catalogues Stoic doctrines that offend against our natural sense of what seems true). Neither of these works is overtly historical in tone, but both are shaped and directed by the attempt to explain the difficulties in Stoicism in terms of the Stoics' innovations with respect to Plato in particular. I have argued elsewhere (Boys-Stones 1997) that the contradictions listed by Plutarch in the philosophy of the Stoics are contradictions that occur at just those points where he thinks that the Stoics have diverged from Plato. In doing this, he supports a conclusion that it is simply not possible to differ from Plato and maintain a consistent philosophy. Or at least, that it *may* be possible to remain consistent, but only then at the expense of patent absurdity: this, of course, is the moral of the *Common Conceptions*.[15] In both of these cases it is the assumption of Plato's being right that somehow explains the absurdities demonstrable in the later system of the Stoa. If Plato had been wrong, the Stoics' divergences *might* have led to improvement; but if Plato was right, their divergences were *bound* to result in the kinds of difficulty identified. Using language which, we shall see, was common throughout Platonist polemic, Plutarch argues that it only makes sense that the Stoa exists at all if we assume that it was the product, not of serious objections to Plato, but of a childish or sophistic attempt to gain some share of glory in a field he had effectively conquered (*παιδιὰν καὶ εὑρησιλογίαν ἕνεκα δόξης*: *On Stoic Self-contradictions*, 1, 1033 B).

Plutarch wrote a work *On the Self-contradictions of the Epicureans* as well (*Lamprias*, 129), and, although this is sadly now lost, it makes sense to suppose that it had a similar theme to its Stoic counterpart: that Plutarch showed in that work that the Epicureans contradicted themselves in every point of doctrine where their new system stood in opposition to Plato—leaving us to realize that it must be *because* it stood in opposition to Plato that its difficulties arose.[16] And Plutarch was by no means the only Platonist to argue in these terms. His near contemporary Atticus, for example, wrote a work attacking Aristotle—and by extension *Against Those Who Undertake to Interpret Plato's Doctrines through Those of Aristotle* (*Πρὸς τοὺς διὰ τῶν Ἀριστοτέλους τὰ Πλάτωνος ὑπισχνουμένους*). And in the fragments we have of this work we can see that he too argued not *just* that Aristotle was wrong, but more precisely that we can understand his being wrong in terms of his innovation (fr. 5. 9–15 des Places):

> It seems that Aristotle hoped that he would appear somewhat superior in intellect if he produced a superfluous material substance, so he counted a fifth on top of the four there obviously are. The act of a very generous and liberal character; but he did not see that a student of nature is supposed to examine nature, not legislate for it.

The 'invention' of a quintessence brought Aristotle, not (here at

[15] Compare also Plutarch, *That the Stoics Talk More Paradoxically than the Poets* (*Lamprias*, 79), of which a synopsis survives (1057 C–1058 E).

[16] There was likewise a companion piece to the work mentioned in n. 15, namely *Lamprias*, 143, *That the Epicureans Talk More Paradoxically than the Poets*.

least) into self-contradiction, but, just as bad, into conflict with what was *obviously* true (a point spelt out in the continuation of the passage just quoted, at fr. 5. 15–38, where Aristotle's absurdity on this point is further discussed and contrasted with Plato's position). Once again, there is no way of explaining Aristotle's philosophy except to suppose that he wilfully introduced innovation through conceit, or a love of contention (see fr. 5. 9–15 as just quoted; also 6. 72–3: φιλονικῶν; and cf. 7. 34–9: ἐφιλονίκησε). It is certainly the case that if Plato was not right in the first place, Aristotle's innovations did nothing to improve the situation.

But perhaps the most striking discussion of this theme is to be found in the work of another second-century Platonist, Numenius of Apamea, *On the Academics' Dissension from Plato*—a work whose surviving fragments engage extensively with the divergences of Aristotle and the Stoics as well as with those of the Sceptical Academy.[17] For Numenius too, the philosophical deficiencies of the Hellenistic schools quite generally could be explained by their divergence from Plato (always on the hypothesis that Plato had been right).

Numenius argues for the general principle, that divergence from the truth leads to philosophical difficulty, in a particularly striking manner—paradoxically taking the Epicureans as paragons of how philosophy ought to be done. At a time when 'Epicureanism' was a term of reproach common to the Platonists, Stoics, and Aristotelians (Antiochus was right about that much at least), Numenius actually found something here to *praise* in the school. This is certainly not because he was more favourably disposed towards their doctrines than anyone else outside of their own school, but was rather because he thought that the Epicureans shared with the Platonists an understanding of the dangers of *innovation* (καινοτομία)—something, said Numenius, which they outlawed, prizing agreement with each other (ὁμοδοξία) and invariance from the teachings of their founder (see all of fr. 24. 22–36 des Places). Wrongly, as it happens, they believed in the 'divine' authority of Epicurus; but quite correctly they deduced from this supposed fact that no deviation from Epicurus could be an improvement. Numenius

[17] The fragments of this work are nos. 24–8 des Places, drawn from Eusebius, *Preparation for the Gospel*, 14. 4. 16–9. 4 (727 A–739 D). For the life and philosophy of Numenius more generally see esp. Frede (1987) (1040–50 for the *Academics' Dissension*).

presumably thought that Epicurus' own teachings were innovative (that is, with respect to Plato): his praise for the fidelity of Epicurus' school surprises not least because his audience would realize that. But this element of surprise is intended to highlight the basic theoretical point: if your source is correct, then no deviation from it will be an improvement. And the purpose of this iconoclastic passage of praise for the Epicureans in the context of Numenius' book on the Academy must have been just this: that the Academics (and the Stoics and Aristotle) were *worse* than the later Epicureans to the extent that they did innovate, and innovated on the teaching of *Plato*. Epicurus, at least, was wrong—or in any case implicated as one of the causes of Hellenistic disagreement which made the truth indiscernible among the schools of the time altogether. To change his philosophy could not have made matters very much worse than they were already. But the innovations on Plato *led* to the increasing disagreement in the first place; and we can best understand this disastrous result on the hypothesis that Plato had been right all along. Much like Plutarch and Atticus, and presumably for the same reason, Numenius stresses the *obvious* difficulties suffered by post-Platonic schools, in particular their self-contradictions and the inevitable proliferation of disagreement between them. Stoicism, for example, suffered factionalism (or 'civil war': ἐστασίασται) from its very inception, right up to the present day (fr. 24. 37–8 des Places); Arcesilaus is compared to a self-maiming Hydra, with a philosophy whose very tool was self-contradiction (cf. fr. 25. 49–50); and Lacydes, Arcesilaus' successor as head of the Academy, is made to confess that there is an inevitable contradiction between his philosophy and life as it actually is (fr. 26. 96–8).[18] The explanation for this explosion of difficulties was not that the truth could not be discovered (as the Sceptics suggested: but note that the Sceptics themselves are now part of the very problem of diversity Numenius identifies in philosophy). The reason is rather that the schools had hobbled their attempts to discover the truth by setting off from the very place where it was to be found. As Plutarch and Atticus, so Numenius explained the disastrous rejection of Plato by the love of contention (φιλονεικία: see fr. 25. 62–3 on Arcesilaus) or by the love of honour (φιλοτιμία: of Arcesilaus and Zeno at fr.

[18] Cf. Plutarch, who points to the disagreement between the Stoics' lives and doctrines as being one component of their self-contradictory philosophy: see *On Stoic Self-contradictions*, 1–4, 1033 A–1034 A, with Boys-Stones (1997), 47–9.

25. 10–11; in a qualified sense, at fr. 24. 14, even of the immediate successors of Plato: Speusippus, Xenocrates, and Polemo). If Epicurus' successors ironically exemplify one of the key philosophical virtues, Plato himself provides Numenius' model for how philosophy really ought to be done: according to Numenius, Plato had followed a constructive path in philosophy, drawing together the truths that were already agreed upon, especially as represented in the thought of Socrates and Pythagoras (fr. 24. 57–9, 73–9; cf. 24. 18–22). The innovations of his successors, however, had torn his philosophy apart (fr. 24. 67–73):[19]

> As at the beginning we proposed to separate [Plato] from Aristotle and Zeno, so now we shall separate him from the Academy, god willing, and, separating him, allow him now to be himself, a Pythagorean. As it is, he is pulled about and treated more wildly than some Pentheus, and suffers limb by limb; but taken entire, his entirety never changes or counter-changes.[20]

This, then, Numenius' most vivid and famous image, sets the programme for the whole of his argument: it offers an explanation for why philosophy after Plato erupted into violent and persistent disagreement among schools which, individually, were self-contradictory and absurd. The image of Pentheus, torn limb from limb at the hands of the Maenads, acts, of course, as a striking metaphor for the blind and selfish motivations of the founders of the Hellenistic schools; but it goes deeper than this as well in explaining the entrenched difficulties in which the objective observer

[19] This act of philosophical thuggery is prefigured in the treatment of Socrates by his immediate successors (Numenius names Aristippus, Antisthenes, the Megarians, and Eretrians): see fr. 24. 47–56 des Places (immediately before the image of Pentheus, discussed here, is invoked). Numenius implies that it was only Plato's grasp of what Socrates really meant (cf. esp. 24. 57–9) that prevented things getting out of hand at this stage.

[20] . . . *ὡς νῦν μανικώτερον ἢ Πενθεῖ τινι προσῆκε διελκόμενος πάσχει μὲν κατὰ μέλη, ὅλος* [des Places; Gaisford prints *ὅλως*] *δ' ἐξ ὅλου ἑαυτοῦ μετατίθεταί τε καὶ ἀντιμετατίθεται οὐδαμῶς*. The Greek is compact, and more difficult as Numenius sustains his Pentheus simile through deliberate ambiguity, but the point is clear enough (see discussion below in the text). Numenius here presents his work as a means of collecting the limbs back together and restoring Plato whole. (Why not go directly to Plato, as e.g. at Numenius fr. 1a des Places? One reason may be precisely that, by working backwards through the Hellenistic schools, one acquires in addition the demonstration that Plato was right through seeing how these schools all fell into trouble *in so far as they differed from Plato*.) Atticus described Plato's own approach to philosophy in similar terms to Numenius' approach here (and using the same mythological image: see fr. 1. 19–23). Cf. also, at roughly the same period, and using the same image again, Clement on pagan philosophy (see ch. 9 with n. 26).

would find them, in arguing that they cannot be right, and in supporting the hypothesis that Plato embodied the truth. What needed to be explained is why the Hellenistic schools were engaged in increasing debate with each other; and the key to explaining it lay for Numenius in the superficial similarities shared by parts (but only parts) of their respective philosophies with Plato. The correct conclusion, of course, is not that Plato's philosophy contained inconsistency at its core, such that disagreements between the various Hellenistic schools merely spelt out those contradictions. Rather, as Numenius here maintains, the disagreements are much better explained on the assumption that Plato's philosophy in its original state *was* consistent—was, indeed, true. In this case, we can easily understand why the later philosophies based severally on various of its 'limbs' were bound to fall into disagreement. To possess one of Pentheus' legs is, after all, not to possess *Pentheus* at all, of whose death it only serves as a reminder. Indeed, one might well suppose (in Aristotelian terms) that to possess just Pentheus' leg is a sure way of not possessing *even* his leg, since detached from the living body of Pentheus the thing might be considered a 'leg' only homonymously, failing to fulfil for its new owner the function it had for Pentheus. In short: if Plato embodied the truth, then a philosophy based on only part of his system must of necessity *not be true* at all.

This, then, is what the jury has to decide. That the Hellenistic schools are guilty (to extend Numenius' metaphor) of the murder of Plato is beyond doubt: the question is whether they are implicated by that act in the murder of the truth: whether, then, Plato embodied the truth. The forensic evidence provided is incompatible with a tale of philosophical progress—there is no evidence that the murder of Plato brought anyone closer to the truth. Nor is the evidence contradictory (such as to lead to a hung jury and suspension of judgement on the issue). The evidence, while not demonstrative, is uniformly consistent with the hypothesis that Plato did embody the truth; that the Hellenistic schools in murdering Plato had murdered the truth, and set off from the very place of the murder in the hopeless attempt to find it alive somewhere else. The case against them is not, as I say, proven; but the court has every reason to call for Plato's body to be reconstituted and examined; and as long as nothing in the restored Plato can be found to raise questions over his identification with the truth, the chances of acquitting the Hellenistic schools become increasingly slim.

There are themes in all of this which recall arguments found already in the Hellenistic Academy: but, again, one should be wary of using similarity of theme as sufficient evidence for unity of purpose. The Academy, for example, had been interested in philosophical history and the fragmentation of the Dogmatic schools—but for different, specifically Sceptical, ends of its own.[21] There had been a debate between Antiochus and Philo over the question of whether the New (Sceptical) Academy had remained faithful to Plato or not, and the works of Plutarch (who believed that it had: see *Lamprias*, 63: *On the Unity of the Academy since Plato*) and Numenius (who believed, as we have seen, that it had not) have tended to be read as a simple extension of this debate.[22] Antiochus and Philo traded insults of just the kind which were employed by Platonists later on: Antiochus seems to have ascribed the rise of the New Academy to Arcesilaus' stubborn refusal to accept what was obviously true, or to his desire for victory in debate (to judge by the defensive remarks at *Academica*, 1. 44); Philo in his turn insinuated that Antiochus' own secession from the New Academy was inspired in part by the hope that his followers would become known as 'Antiocheans' (*Academica*, 2. 70). But if Antiochus and Philo traced their beliefs back to Plato, there is nothing in what either of them says to suggest that their arguments for the continuity of the Academy were part of an argument for the authority

[21] Cf. Cicero, *On the Orator*, 3. 62–8 (and also *Tusculan Disputations*, 5. 11). The discussion here looks like a historicized version of the *divisio Carneadea*, being a way for Crassus (spokesman for the Academy) to articulate a synoptic overview of the possibilities offered by the full range of philosophical schools. When I say that the process is *Sceptical*, I do not mean that it is necessarily *negative* in its conclusions. It should lead one to suspension of judgement with regard to the possibility of *knowledge* as such, but following Carneades himself, it might allow one to survey the field of possible philosophical beliefs to identify which seems most plausible (under whichever definition of 'plausible' one might adopt: see Frede 1984 for the disagreement of Carneades' pupils over this question). Carneades and his successors, however, focused on the subjective plausibility of doctrines as such as it might emerge from an investigation of them (see esp. Allen 1994, and further n. 28), and did not, as the Platonists crucially did, consider the historical course of philosophy as providing objective, extra-doctrinal support for the likelihood that a particular philosopher was right.

[22] So e.g. Dillon (1988), 106: 'Philo stated a position, but it was Antiochus's violent reaction to this that really started the controversy, one carried on by the author of the *Anonymous Theaetetus Commentary* . . . Plutarch . . . and Numenius.'

of Plato.[23] Philo's theory of the unity of the Academy, for example, was much more about the status of *his* beliefs than about the status of Plato's: Philo wanted to explain why his apparently innovative beliefs were consistent with the tradition of the Academy, not to provide reasons to go back to Plato as a basis for further doctrinal investigation. Nor is there any indication of such a claim in Antiochus' much-trumpeted reversion to the Old Academy. Antiochus undoubtedly thought of Plato as the greatest philosopher (*princeps philosophorum*: cf. Cicero, *On Ends*, 5. 7), and the founder of the Dogmatic consensus he identified; but it is the consensus that interests him and not Plato's role in its foundation as such.[24] He stresses his affinity with Peripatetics and Old Academic philosophers such as Polemo (Cicero, *Academica*, 2. 131) more often than with Plato himself,[25] and could even suggest that Plato had been in need of reform.[26] If it is right to read Antiochus' syncretic account of school history as a philosophical argument at all, it is an argument *from* the consensus established by Plato, not *to* the authority of Plato. Yet the Platonists' development of this argument is certainly meant as part of a strategy of support for the truth of Plato himself. The Platonists show, in effect, that the history of philosophy since Plato gives the objective observer of the Dogmatic schools *more reason* for believing that knowledge might be found through a study of Plato than for believing that it could be found among his Dogmatic successors. In doing so, they undermine the conclusion of the Argument from Disagreement, which works from the objective equipoise of the Dogmatists' *doctrines* to the conclusion that the only reasonable course is to suspend judgement about *where the truth might be found* altogether.

The historical argument I have so far examined in Platonism is far from the end of the story, of course: it gives, to repeat, not a proof that Plato is right, but an objective reason to pursue a certain approach in seeking the truth, namely to investigate the doctrines of Plato. It is quite within the bounds of possibility that such an approach would prove barren, that turning back to Plato we could soon see that his doctrines *could* not be right (however consistent

[23] Cf. Glucker (1997), 59, describing the debate as a matter of the 'right to the "trade-mark" "Academic"'.

[24] Cf. Dörrie (1976), 14–15.

[25] And cf. Cicero, *On Ends*, 5. 14, with Barnes (1989), 78.

[26] Cf. *Academica*, 1. 35–42, and esp. 43: 'I think it true, as our friend Antiochus used to hold, that [Stoicism] should rather be viewed as a reform (*correctio*) of the Old Academy than as a new system.'

they might be), that his successors were therefore justified in moving away from his thought (however unsuccessful they proved). But as long as it remained possible for Platonists to defend Plato's works, as long as they could interpret those works in a way which produced doctrines defensible in their own right, and *at least* as good at explaining the world as those of the Hellenistic schools, a virtuous circle was established in which the hypothesis of Plato's identification with the truth gained increasing plausibility—tending in the end towards certainty. The Platonists approached Plato in the first place with the expectation that the truth might be found there; what they certainly found were doctrines which could be made to hold their own against later Dogmatic developments; it thereby became harder to understand why those developments took place at all (they ought either to be conclusive, which they clearly are not, or more reasonable attempts than Plato's, which they turn out not to be either); and this in turn supported the initial hypothesis, that Plato was right and the divergences unphilosophical. This in its own turn would make it worth looking harder into Plato's dialogues for more and more satisfactory answers—and so on. We started (to revert to forensic imagery) with the fact of a fight between schools with Plato's blood on their clothes, and the hypothesis best able to explain this fighting was that Plato had embodied the truth for which they had murdered him in the first place: that the blood was the blood of the truth. As the investigation into this possibility proceeds, an increasing amount of evidence is turned up which is consistent with this hypothesis. And, while no one piece of evidence is on its own conclusive for the identification of Plato and the truth, the whole makes it increasingly likely. As Quintilian says, discussing the use in court of this kind of argument from 'indications' (*signa*; Greek σημεῖα, literally 'signs'):[27]

> A garment might be stained with blood from a sacrifice or a nose-bleed, so not everyone with a blood-stained garment has committed murder. But while it is not enough in itself, yet it can be produced as evidence when there are other indications as well—for example, if the suspect was the enemy of the murder victim, had threatened him before, had been in the same place. When it is added to these indications, it can make what was previously only suspected seem certain.

The Platonist question is whether the *truth* has been murdered with

[27] *Institutes of Oratory*, 5. 9. 9–10; cf. e.g. Cicero, *On Invention*, 1. 48.

Plato; the main 'indications' we have seen so far are that the murderers of Plato squabble among themselves (as they would in the absence of the truth); that an account of their motives for murdering Plato can be given (including, for example, a desire for glory) which is consistent with their holding the truth in disdain; that nothing in the autopsy of Plato's corpus undermines his identification with the truth. But there is one more indication to consider as well. I have had very little to say in this chapter about the theory of Plato's authority considered in the last. The reason for this is that, as I said, an account of Plato's authority strictly waits on a belief that Plato was right in the first place. But now we are starting to build up justification for such a belief, the account of *how* he might have come to be right itself feeds into the accumulation of 'indications' *that* he was as well. From the demonstration that, if the truth can be found through any school of Greek philosophy at all, it can be found only through a study of Plato, a large range of diverse indications—all suggestive rather than probative in themselves—build up quickly into an ever strengthening framework of support for the belief of the individual who pursues them that Plato was right after all. Every step of the Platonist way gives one more reason to go further down it.

Still, it might be objected, none of this *proves* that Plato was right in any rigorous logical sense—and of course it does not, or we would all be Platonists now. But what it does is to lever away at the pans of the Sceptics' equipoise with ever increasing plausibility tending in the end towards outright belief. It makes it *reasonable* on the available evidence, not in the first place to believe specific doctrines (and just what Plato himself said or meant remained a matter for lengthy debate among Platonists themselves), but in any case to pursue a certain approach, to look for the truth in Plato. Furthermore, the Platonists could claim, it makes it reasonable according to the requirements of their toughest opponents, the Sceptics, and reasonable *a fortiori* (via the Argument from Disagreement) against any Dogmatic contender as well. The accumulation of 'indications' that Plato embodied the truth shifts the onus of proof: now the Platonists are justified in not abandoning their philosophy until a proof can be found that will *undermine* their hypothesis, or at least until a superior (or even equipollent) hypothesis can be found to explain the phenomena. Until then, the only justifiable path even for a genuine 'Sceptic'—someone genuinely in search of the truth—is to start work as a Platonist. And once he has done so, he will find before long (so the Platonists confidently suppose) that *belief* in Plato's philosophy will start to grow.[28]

It might be added, in conclusion, that this argument was remarkably successful: it is perhaps not by chance that ancient Scepticism becomes extinct in our sources at just the time in the third century when Platonism reaches its zenith.[29]

3. *Postscript: The Influence of the Argument*

I have spoken so far of the Platonist philosophers of the later first and second centuries only, since it is here (as far as our evidence goes) that the Platonist history of philosophy, and with it Platonism itself, was established.[30] At this point modern commentary posits a

[28] It is worth noting that the process I have described here in terms of the accumulation of 'indications' drawn from a forensic context could easily be redescribed in the terms developed by Carneades for testing 'plausible' (πιθανός) impressions. For Carneades too, an impression becomes more plausible as it is tested more closely and from different angles, and as no conflicting impressions emerge to undermine its claims on our assent. See esp. S.E. *PH* 1. 227–9 and *M.* 7. 166–89, with Allen (1994). I have already indicated in n. 21 the crucial difference between the approach I am ascribing to the Platonists and the 'probabilism' of Carneades: Carneades sought for subjective plausibility in particular doctrinal positions (and denied that one's sense of their plausibility could ever amount to knowledge); the Platonists, on the other hand, believed they had found objective (extra-doctrinal) reasons that made it plausible that Plato had been right—whatever in fact he had thought. Furthermore, they believed that the procedure of investigating this possibility would bring the investigator sooner or later to *knowledge*. Nevertheless, the comparison does, I hope, add some historical plausibility to my case—not only by providing a philosophical precedent for the general approach in terms of which I have described the Platonists' argument, but also by providing one drawn from a school in which the Platonists were particularly interested as forming some kind of line of continuity (in name if not in purpose) between themselves and their Master.

[29] The last 'mainstream' ancient Sceptic whose name is recorded is one Saturninus, a pupil of Sextus Empiricus (D.L. 9. 116): he must therefore have died during the lifetime of Plotinus.

[30] The only evidence for strictly Platonist activity which might point to an earlier date for the genesis of the movement is the *Anonymous Commentary on Plato's* Theaetetus (which contains references to other Platonic commentaries written by its author as well). At least, attempts have been made to date this work as early as the 1st cent. BC: cf. severally Tarrant (1983); Bastianini and Sedley (1995), 254 (and cf. Sedley 1997: 117–18). But none of these attempts is conclusive; indeed, Tarrant (who identifies Anon. with the *Academic* Eudorus despite Anon.'s own anti-Academic stance, revealed especially in coll. 54. 38–55. 13) is certainly mistaken in his reasoning: see Mansfeld (1991), 543–4; Bastianini and Sedley (1995), 251–4. For a critique of Sedley's own (rather more suggestive) argument see Brittain (1996), 226–32. Cf. also Opsomer (1998), 35–6, for some lexical considerations in favour of a later dating. It is tempting to think that the efforts made to date Anon. earlier than the

new beginning to Platonism in the work of Plotinus and his followers, what it calls 'Neoplatonism'. The distinction does make some sense: Plotinus' work is of undoubted significance in its own right, and, historically speaking, he did much to establish a more unified Platonist school of thought and a doctrinal programme for it to follow. But it is crucial to understand that Plotinus' *approach* to philosophy, and that of his successors, their philosophical methodology, was just the same as that of the Platonists I have already discussed: ancient Platonists are united and defined as such *both* by the claims (discussed in the previous chapter) for Plato's sources and methods, *and also* by their view of later philosophy and their justification for seeking the truth through an examination of Plato's works. In the work of Plotinus himself we find exactly the respect for the 'ancients' that we saw in the earlier Platonists, and, although the term 'ancient' might by this stage be applied to Plato (e.g. *Enneads*, 3. 7. 1. 13–16, 7. 10–17; 5. 1. 8. 10–14) as well as to the older traditions on which he drew, it certainly does embrace them as well (e.g. *Enneads*, 3. 5. 8. 17–23, 6. 19. 25–41).[31] Indeed, Plato's own status as an authoritative figure seems to rest on his consistency with these traditions—as at *Enneads*, 3. 5. 2. 1–6, which asserts the consistency of his views on love with those of the 'theologians'.[32]

evidence securely warrants is driven in part by an attempt to support the closer links between Platonism and the Hellenistic schools posited by much scholarship in this field (although the 'Hellenistic' tradition of philosophy was continued well beyond the end of the Hellenistic age as historically defined, and beyond the boundaries of the Athenian schools—not least by thinkers such as Cornutus and Chaeremon themselves, who lived into the second half of the 1st cent. AD). It will, however, be seen that nothing of ultimate importance for my argument hangs on the question one way or the other: the Stoic theory which forms, as I argue, the basis for the emergence of Platonism must, as we have seen, have been established by the last decades of the 1st cent. BC, making it possible that Platonism first arose as early as this.

[31] The word 'ancient' (παλαιός), in fact, is generally used in two senses by Platonists—absolutely, as it were, and relatively. It refers absolutely to the thinkers of primitive antiquity, but it can also refer to the 'ancient' thinkers in the Greek tradition such as Homer or Plato (cf. Celsus at Origen, *Against Celsus*, 7. 28), who are ancient relative to the Greek tradition of philosophy of which they were the founders. In this latter sense, it is perhaps the nearest equivalent to our use of the word 'Classical'. The similarity of the two groups, such that they can both be called 'ancient', lies in the fact that they both stood at the head of a deteriorating philosophical tradition; but there is a difference between them too, which is that the antiquity of the former group actually goes some way to explaining their privileged grasp of the truth, which it does not in respect of the latter.

[32] This is a theme which finds voluble expression later on in Proclus: cf. his *Platonic Theology* at e.g. 1. 7, 30. 22–4; 3. 3, 11. 17–22; 5. 35, 127. 8–15 Saffrey and Westerink.

But Plotinus too believed that Plato's authority was assured not just by his consistency with the truly ancient traditions,[33] but also by the difficulties met by those who innovated on him—as Aristotle at *Ennead*, 5. 1. 9, for example.[34] Particularly interesting is Plotinus' attack on the 'Gnostics' at *Enneads*, 2. 9. 6.[35] They, it seems, had stolen their doctrines from the ancient Greek tradition (from Plato in particular), but dressed them up in a new language (*καινολογούντων* at 2. 9. 6. 5). However, they misunderstood what Plato had said (2. 9. 6. 19–24), and so degraded his thought and accused *him* (and other 'blessed philosophers') of a lack of understanding (2. 9. 6. 24–8). Their *innovation* thus involved them (as we now know was inevitable) in separation from the truth (2. 9. 6. 10–13): 'Generally, some of their doctrines were taken from Plato, but others—those in which they innovated [*ὅσα καινοτομοῦσιν*] so as to establish a philosophy of their own—these were found outside of the truth.' The motives of the Gnostics' innovation should already be clear enough: they were obviously keen to be thought to have discovered a new and better philosophy. Plotinus says that they spoke in an uncouth and unphilosophical manner (2. 9. 6. 43–52)—by contrast with the Greeks, whose philosophy was presented 'without pomposity' (*ἀτύφως*: 2. 9. 6. 8). All of this, naturally, reinforced Plotinus' own approach to philosophy: it supported his belief that the truth should be sought, not in innovation, or in building on what had gone before, but rather in restoring again the wisdom received by the ancients, and passed on through the work of Plato.

I do not intend to labour the point by pursuing it through the more voluminous works that survive from later Platonism—a process which might lengthen this study considerably without adding anything substantial to its conclusion. But it is worth noting that the arguments (or at least the forms of argument) developed by the Platonists to demonstrate the truth and explain the authority of Plato had an impact and influence that quickly spread out from 'mainstream' Platonism, becoming assimilated in various forms into the many and diverse systems of thought where Platonism itself had any

[33] *Pace* Éon (1970), who has argued the opposite—that Plato's position as an exegete of more ancient traditions somehow serves to qualify his authoritative status in Plotinus' thought.

[34] Compare Éon (1970), 267–8. For Plotinus' view of the decline of philosophy after Plato more generally cf. Charrue (1978), esp. 20–1.

[35] 'Gnostics', at least, is how they are normally described. Cf. on this e.g. Igal (1981), esp. 138–9.

kind of influence. The Platonizing Maximus of Tyre, for example, like many other thinkers of the Second Sophistic, thought that Homer was the supreme voice of Greek philosophical authority, but, interestingly, described Plato's achievement in understanding and preserving the thought of Homer in exactly the terms used in more 'orthodox' Platonist circles to talk of his understanding and preservation of primitive wisdom.[36] A strikingly similar pattern of argument can be found as well in Galen—whose respect for Plato paralleled his respect for Hippocrates. Galen did not take Plato's (or Hippocrates') authority as his *starting-point*, in the way that the Platonists did: both writers had to earn his respect, and he was capable of correcting them where they seemed wrong to him.[37] Nevertheless, he dignified both with the epithet παλαιός ('ancient'),[38] and criticized those of his enemies who disagreed with them in exactly the terms I have been examining (cf. *PHP* 4. 7, 288. 13–14 De Lacy; 4. 4, 258. 19–25 De Lacy). According to Galen, for example, it was only the love of contention and honour (φιλονεικία and φιλοτιμία) that caused the Stoics to disagree with these 'ancients';[39] and the inevitable result for them was wrangling and self-contradiction.[40]

[36] See esp. *Dissertation* 26. 2–3 Trapp: most of Homer's predecessors mistakenly thought of him as a *mere* poet, so that their own philosophy fell into a ruinous state, reduced to a swarm of sophisms in mutual and unedifying combat; Plato was the one person who understood Homer and so preserved his thought unpolluted.

[37] That Galen did not think that either Plato or Hippocrates derived their authority from a previous tradition is shown most clearly by the fact that Galen recognizes no philosophical authority earlier than them—not even Pythagoras. Galen refers occasionally to reports of Pythagorean doctrines as passed on by Posidonius, but he is aware that there are historical difficulties with such claims: none of Pythagoras' own writings survive (he says) and we can only make inferences from his pupils (see *PHP* 5. 6, 334. 30–3 De Lacy). Even where there might be a case for thinking that Pythagoras was the first to formulate a certain important doctrine, Galen still gives the credit to Plato for having *worked it out to completion* (4. 7, 290. 1–55 De Lacy). (And cf. Kidd 1971: 213.)

[38] See again n. 31 for this use of the term. Galen, as it happens, does not have any time for the notion of a more ancient wisdom, as we have seen. So he refers to Plato and Hippocrates, but even to Aristotle and his medical contemporary Diocles of Carystus, as 'ancients' (cf. e.g. *PHP* 4. 7, 288. 32–290. 2 De Lacy; cf. 9. 5, 564. 28–30 De Lacy, for Diocles).

[39] Cf. *PHP* 5. 1. 9, 294. 11–12 De Lacy, for this motive behind Chrysippus' apologists (ὑπὸ φιλονεικίας τῆς πρὸς τοὺς παλαιοὺς). For Chrysippus' pursuit of glory see 2. 1, 102. 12–14 De Lacy: 'All such notions have been boldly advanced by men fired by a love of contention to overthrow all the excellent teachings of the ancients in order to found a newer school of their own [ἀποτετόλμηται γὰρ ἅπαντα τὰ τοιαῦτα πρὸς ἀνθρώπων ἀνατρέψαι φιλονεικούντων ὅσα καλῶς εἴρηται τοῖς παλαιοῖς, ὑπὲρ τοῦ νεωτέραν αἵρεσιν ἰδίαν συστήσασθαι].'

[40] And note that Galen's project in the *PHP*, at least, is to look at the *agreement*

In diverse fields of thought where Platonism had an influence, then, this model of argument seems to have followed. But the area where Platonism exerted what was, perhaps, its greatest historical influence was in the philosophical development of Christianity—a religion whose contact with pagan intellectual life soon put it in need of arguments by which it could establish in this context its own internal coherence and external credibility. In the following chapters (the remainder of the book) I shall show how the Platonist model of argument had a literally defining effect on the way that Christian 'Orthodoxy' in the second century developed its self-image and asserted its philosophical superiority against pagans and heretics alike, by showing that it was the true guardian of a wisdom purer and more ancient than any that the pagans could pretend to.

between Plato and Hippocrates: see *PHP* 1, fr. 1, 64. 5–14 De Lacy; and cf. 5. 6, 334. 33–336. 2 De Lacy). Chrysippus is the butt of Galen's criticism in the *PHP* as Posidonius and (occasionally) the physician Marinus are objects of praise; and just as they are praised for their consistency with Plato (cf. Marinus at 8. 1, 480. 28–9 De Lacy), so Chrysippus is criticized for his arguments with the ancients. And again we find that his argument with ancient doctrine is presented as the *cause* of further wrangling, and in particular self-contradiction, that his philosophy gives rise to. This lapse into self-contradiction is explicitly linked to divergence from 'the ancients' at 4. 3, 246. 36—248. 3 De Lacy (cf. 280. 9–12): '*Because of this* [sc. divergence] Chrysippus contradicts Zeno and himself and many others of the Stoics [*καὶ γὰρ Ζήνωνι κατά γε τοῦτο καὶ ἑαυτῷ καὶ πολλοῖς ἄλλοις μάχεται τῶν Στωϊκῶν*].' Galen regularly accuses Chrysippus of self-contradiction himself (e.g. 140. 17–18; 152. 17–19; 154. 16–18; 156. 21; 248. 14–19; 314. 15–17 De Lacy), and supplements this by reporting self-contradictions identified by Posidonius (258. 19–25; 328. 8–18 De Lacy). Galen even says that he intended to write a book on the matter (4. 4, 250. 3–5 De Lacy).

8

The Invention of Hebraeo-Christian Orthodoxy

In previous chapters I have tried to suggest that our tendency to speak of 'Middle' Platonism as a period of doctrinal transition between the Hellenistic schools on the one hand and the philosophy of Plotinus and his successors (that is, of 'Neoplatonism') on the other is fundamentally misleading: that a concentration on doxographical evolution misses what in many ways is more important, namely the shift in philosophical methodology which characterized the Platonist movement. The influence of this new methodology, and the view of antiquity and tradition it entailed, were far more decisive and influential for the future development of Western philosophy than any particular beliefs formulated within the framework it provided; not least because, as I hope to show, it came to be adopted by the Christian Church as well, and used by it as a means of transporting itself (philosophically speaking) from Jerusalem to Athens.

Christianity in the second century was still very much in the process of formation, and there was within the religion a wide variety of competing views as to where it should go: what, indeed, it was. And for this reason, as soon as it started to make itself visible on the Western philosophical stage, Platonists were able to lose no time in attacking it for the very diversity of opinion evinced by its adherents. They mobilized, in fact, a theme familiar to us from the last chapter to argue that, *because of its lack of internal agreement*, the truth could not be discernible within Christian philosophy even if it happened to lie there. This internal disagreement indicated for the Platonists that Christianity as a whole could be of no more use to the philosopher than were the divergent schools of Hellenistic thought. Indeed, the Platonists were able to make the stronger claim, that Christianity was not likely to be in possession of the truth at all, in so far as their disagreement could be accommodated under precisely the hypothesis originally used to explain the proliferation of Hellenistic schools. According to the Platonists, Christianity had started out, as it were, on the wrong foot, its factionalism the inevitable result of its straying—perhaps not from *Plato* as such, but at least from the purest ancient traditions which preserved elements of the philosophy reconstructed by Plato. Clement of Alexandria reports, for example, that the pagans argued against Christianity 'saying that you should not believe in it because of the disagreement of its sects: for who has the truth where different people teach different doctrines?' (*Stromata*, 7. 15. 89. 2–3); and we know that the Platonist Celsus, a rough contemporary of Clement's, 'reproached the sectarianism of Christianity' in his work *Against the Christians*, criticizing them on the grounds that 'since they have spread to become a multitude they are divided and rent asunder' (ap. Origen, *Against Celsus*, 3. 12).

To answer this attack, the Christians had only one option: they needed to turn the tables on the Platonists and do for Christianity exactly what Platonism had already done for itself. In the first place, and as a minimal defensive measure, they needed to show that Christianity was *not* essentially riven by disagreement, that a genuine Christian tradition *could* be objectively identified such that it would be obvious to the Greeks that the truth, if it lay within Christianity at all, would be discernible there. But this argument on its own could only go part of the way. Internally consistent or not, the Platonists could still maintain that Christianity was a divergence from earlier traditions, with which it created new disagreements, and that, as such, it had no special claims on the attention of the objective observer of its debate with the pagans. In particular, the Platonists argued that Christianity was a divergent branch of Judaism, and occasionally (as we saw in Chapter 6 was the case with Celsus) that Judaism in turn was a divergent offshoot of the Egyptian theological tradition. So the Christians needed further to prove that this wider view of history was wrong, and to do it they argued a double thesis: first (and perhaps most straightforwardly), that the Hebrew tradition was of the greatest possible antiquity; but second, that Christian philosophy was not to be viewed as *different* from Hebrew thought at all. In other words, they argued that

Christian orthodoxy represented a philosophically unified *Hebraeo-Christian tradition* which was the oldest tradition of all—such that all other traditions (including all pagan traditions) were properly viewed as later divergences from *it*. This represented a major advance towards an argument whose conclusion was now that *if the truth could be discerned in any tradition at all*, it could only be in this single, primitive Hebraeo-Christian tradition.

There was, however, one additional difficulty faced by the Christians. For, if the Christians could plausibly argue that pagan theological and cultural traditions were divergent branches of an original 'Christian' truth, they still needed to account for the sudden rise of pagan *philosophy* in the Classical period, as represented, for example, in the work of Plato. Since pagan traditions of thought were supposed now to be divergent branches in the Christians' history of philosophy, they ought only to have been able to continue their course of decline in so far as they developed at all; yet the emergence of Classical philosophy (in particular, for example, the theology of Plato, which came so much closer to the Christian truth than anything in Greek mythology) appeared to represent a reverse that would throw the whole model into confusion. There was a danger here that the objective observer might suppose that the Greeks had started to *improve*; or else that they had founded a new and independent tradition of thought which could not be explained, let alone refuted, within the terms of the Christian history of philosophy. In this latter case, the objective observer would once again have no (objective) basis by which to suppose that one tradition might be superior to the other, and would be forced once again to suspend judgement over the claims of *both* traditions. In order to assert that Christianity remained the *only* justifiable choice for a seeker after the truth, the Christians needed to find a way of explaining Greek philosophy in terms which related it historically to their own tradition, but which showed at the same time that it was doomed to failure. They argued, then, that it had been sparked into existence, one way or another, by contact with the Christian truth—perhaps, for example, through encounters with Hebrew Scripture. And by appealing to the subsequent degeneration of Greek philosophy in the Hellenistic age to show that the same characteristics that had led the Greeks to diverge from the truth in the first place likewise prevented them from perfecting their stolen philosophy, the Christians were able both to explain what seemed good in pagan philosophy, but also (importantly) to show why it could not contain a path to the truth. In the end, even the positive aspects of pagan philosophy served to demonstrate the strength of the Christian tradition from which it derived its origin.

To summarize this, the Christians developed a three-pronged response to their Platonist critics. Their strategy was: (1) to isolate 'heretical' positions from an 'orthodoxy' which represented genuine Christianity; (2) to reinterpret and so to appropriate the Hebrew tradition through which they could assert the primitive antiquity of Christian orthodoxy; and (3) to demonstrate the *essential* corruption of pagan modes of thought, such that what philosophy there was among them must itself have relied on the aid (and presuppose the truth) of the prior, Christian tradition, and must in its own turn tend to corruption. In what follows, I shall examine these three themes in turn—starting with (1) and (2) in this chapter, and completing the story with (3), the 'dependency theme', in the next.

1. *Orthodoxy and Heresy*

The term 'heresy' (Greek: *αἵρεσις*) referred, originally and etymologically, to a 'choice'. In Hellenistic philosophy it was used to refer specifically to *moral* choice, the opposite of avoidance (*φυγή*). But towards the late second century BC it started to take on a new connotation, as the choice one made of a philosophy, one's philosophical persuasion or 'school of thought'.[1] It is important to note that in pagan Greek literature the term never had, and never acquired the negative connotations which became attached to it in Christian circles; it was very much a neutral term (like, indeed, the English phrase 'school of thought'). However, to leave things at this would be to oversimplify the situation. For while it is true that no one would or could reproach a *hairesis* just for *being* a *hairesis*, this was not because of a generally democratic attitude towards philosophical opinion. No Greek philosopher took the line that diversity within philosophy was a good thing: there was, after all, only one truth (at most), and the more *haireseis* proliferated, the further away seemed to be the chances of recovering it. Someone who looked at the matter objectively, then, and who was himself interested in finding the truth, might ask himself whether there was

[1] For a comprehensive discussion of the word *αἵρεσις*, and in particular its use for a 'school of thought', see Glucker (1978), 166–206; cf. also Staden (1982).

an objective philosophical consideration (that is, a consideration which did not itself already imply allegiance to one of these schools of thought) which would lead him to see that one of the *haireseis* was after all the repository of the truth, and the others mere imposters. The ancient Sceptics looked for such a consideration; but, failing to find what they wanted, they were led instead to suspend judgement over the whole matter—both over the question of whether anyone was, as a matter of fact, in possession of the truth, and whether it was attainable at all. They reacted, that is, to the existence of a plurality of *haireseis* by finding a way of doing philosophy without making a choice of allegiance. The Pyrrhonists, at least, insisted that their position did not constitute yet another *hairesis*;[2] it was rather a kind of meta-*hairesis*, the common pursuit of its members being the objective and uncommitted judgement of all *haireseis* and possible *haireseis* which were defined by a positive doctrinal stance.

Sceptics were not the only ones to be concerned by the proliferation of philosophical *haireseis* and to see the need for an objective criterion to judge between them. As we saw in the previous chapter, Platonists of the second century AD were also concerned at the proliferation of schools, and of schools of thought within those schools. However, while the Pyrrhonian reaction was to decamp to a militantly non-sectarian position, the Platonists rather found a hypothesis by which the proliferation of philosophical positions could be explained—and so (for as long as the hypothesis held) explained away. For reasons we saw, they argued that the truth, if available through any existing position, would be available through Plato, and Plato alone. The later proliferation of schools was indeed an indictment of the state of Hellenistic philosophy; but unless the possibility that Plato contained a way to the truth could be shown to be empty, a philosopher who was interested in discovering the truth had a genuine alternative to Scepticism.[3] A distinction in terminology is not made here, between the Platonist 'sect' and the others; but the claim obviously is that the Platonist sect stands

[2] Or at least not in the relevant sense: cf. S.E. *PH* 1. 16–17; also D.L. 1. 20: in so far as they 'follow or seem to follow some principle in respect of appearances', the Pyrrhonists did constitute a *hairesis*; but in so far as they held no positive beliefs, they did not.

[3] For a reflection of this wider argument in a Christian context see Lactantius, *Divine Institutes*, 7. 7, arguing explicitly that the fragmentation of philosophy among the pagan schools *might* lead one to Scepticism (as it led some Greeks), but *ought* rather to encourage one to aim at a reconstitution of the wisdom now dispersed among them.

in a special relation to the rest—not as a meta-sect, as with the Pyrrhonists, but as a kind of *pre*-sectarian sect (since the distinction of different sects only arises at all, according to the argument, in reaction to this original position). And this is precisely the distinction to which the Christians, when they adopted the Platonists' model of argument, were to apply their distinctive terminology of 'orthodoxy' and 'heresy'.

The entrance of the word *hairesis* into Christian literature was marked by a neutrality which is consistent, not only with its use in pagan philosophy, but also, just as importantly, with its use by Jews and of Judaism.[4] The author of the Acts of the Apostles could describe as *haireseis* the Sadducees (Acts 5. 17), the Pharisees (15. 5), and even the Christians (24. 5; cf. 24. 14, 28. 22). Paul himself is reported as associating himself with the Pharisaical *hairesis* at Acts 26. 5. For Luke and for Paul, the word *hairesis* clearly need be no more negative than it was for pagans of the period.[5] However, it was no more positive either.[6] If a *hairesis* was not by definition a bad thing, it is clear none the less that Paul viewed the proliferation of *haireseis* within Christianity as a very real danger—a danger as all disagreement might be.[7] So for example Galatians 5. 19–21:[8]

The works of the flesh are evident: such things are fornication, impurity, lewdness, idolatry, witchcraft, enmity, strife, rivalry, anger, intrigue, dis-

[4] Cf. Glucker (1978), 184–7 with references to Josephus.

[5] *Pace* Staden (1982: 96), who implies something too strong when he says, of Acts, 24. 5 and 24. 14 in particular, that they 'belong to the earliest text in which *hairesis* seems consistently used to designate a "sect", "faith" or "school" that opposes one's own'. Cf. also Desjardins (1991), 74.

[6] In qualification of Bauer, who ascribes to Paul 'eine Duldsamkeit . . . die kaum einen Ketzer kennt' (1964: 236, quoted approvingly at Lüdemann 1996: 12).

[7] And cf. the first epistle of Clement of Rome (I Clement 45–6, 54), where dissension in the ranks of Christianity is attacked (although not labelled with the term 'heresy' as such).

[8] Cf. also 1 Corinthians, 11. 19: 'For there must be also αἱρέσεις among you, that they which are approved may be made manifest among you'—compare Clement's use of this text at *Stromata*, 7. 15. 90. 5, discussed below. Cf. also 2 Peter 2: 1, where there is a prophecy of 'damnable sects' (αἱρέσεις ἀπωλείας: does this imply that *all* sects are 'damnable'? or only those prophesied?). It might be possible to link all of this with the early Christians' ostensible disdain for pagan philosophy, the 'wisdom of this world': the suggestion might be that αἱρέσεις will only come about where people are discussing the kind of 'philosophical' issues which are not, strictly speaking, the point of Christianity at all. Note the association in Titus 3: 9–10: 'Avoid foolish questions, genealogies, strife, and legal contentions: for they are unhelpful and pointless. Reject a man who causes faction [αἱρετικὸν ἄνθρωπον] after the first and second admonition.'

sension, *factions* [αἱρέσεις], hatred, drunkenness, revelry, and things like this . . .

That Paul links *haireseis as such* with 'rivalry, anger, intrigue' and so on is important—perhaps decisive for the peculiar development of the word within later Christianity. But while Paul might retrospectively provide important Scriptural authority to support the transformation of *hairesis* into 'heresy', the philosophical roots of the transformation itself seem to lie in the adoption of the Platonist model of argument by Greek intellectuals of the Western Church towards the end of the century. As thinkers in close contact with the Platonist movement, and faced most directly from them with the accusation of factionalism (and therefore of philosophical decadence), they started to argue that there was, in fact, only *one* genuine Christian tradition—that is to say, the *original* Christian tradition, of which other 'Christian' schools of thought should be regarded as later divergences. And to mark this distinction, and as part of the rhetoric associated with this line of argument, they started to restrict the term 'heresy' to the latter group. The idea, it seems, was to emphasize the fact that Christianity was not, *essentially*, factional—indeed, that it was essentially *not* factional. Even to call the 'orthodox' interpretation of Christianity a *hairesis* would be to give a false impression: since it predated the rise of the schismatic schools it was itself a 'pre-sectarian' sect. Perhaps, then, not really a sect at all, since it only makes sense to talk of a sect where disagreement already exists. It was the later, divergent positions that were the 'heresies' *par excellence*.[9]

The plausibility of maintaining this distinction (between orthodoxy and heresy), and so of starting to answer the Platonists' claim that Christianity was philosophically decadent because philosophically divided, does rely on one's being able to identify objectively, and so bracket off, the 'heresies'. And the Platonist model provided just the tools needed to do it. Exactly as the Platonists rescued the possibility of Dogmatic philosophy through the hypothesis that later Greek schools were rebellious rejections of the truth as embodied in Plato, so Christians began to assert that, if there was truth to be discovered in Christianity at all, it could be found only in its

[9] But it should be noted that, if αἵρεσις comes to have the ordinary sense of a 'heresy' for Christians, it still remains possible (where the meaning is unambiguous) to refer to the orthodoxy as a 'sect'. Cf. Clement, *Stromata*, 7. 15. 92. 4: 'the truly excellent sect' (ἡ τῷ ὄντι ἀρίστη αἵρεσις, to contrast with the other kind under discussion).

original expression. Using much the same language as the Platonists to express much the same foundational hypothesis, they stressed in the first place the *youth* of the heresies—arguing, in particular, that they were born *out of* (and away from) the 'orthodox' position. In the third century, Origen put the matter like this:[10]

> *All heretics come first to belief*, and afterwards depart from the road of faith and the truth of our doctrines, as the apostle John also says in his epistle [1 John 2. 19]: 'They went forth from us, but they were not of us; for, if they had been of us, they would no doubt have remained with us.'

But Origen only gives us a particularly clear formulation of an approach to the definition of heresy that had already been developed in the previous century. Clement, for example, had made much of the novelty of heretical beliefs and their discontinuity with Christian tradition (e.g. *Stromata*, 7. 16. 103, 17. 107). He also emphasized, against the heretics, the *antiquity* of the Church (with which, incidentally, he linked the consistency and unity of its teaching): the true and truly ancient Church is one, he says (*Stromata*, 7. 17. 107. 3: *μίαν εἶναι τὴν ἀληθῆ ἐκκλησίαν τὴν τῷ ὄντι ἀρχαίαν*); and he repeats the point more fully a little later in the same chapter: 'In substance, in purpose, in foundation, and in pre-eminence we say that the ancient and catholic church is one.'[11] A heretic is one who has *rejected* this ecclesiastical tradition (*ὁ ἀναλακτίσας τὴν ἐκκλησιαστικὴν παράδοσιν*: 7. 16. 95. 1): Clement accuses the Marcionites in particular of untimely *innovation* (*κεκαινοτομῆσθαι*: 7. 17. 107. 3). Even the earliest heresies, he says, only took their rise in the post-apostolic age, at the time of Hadrian's reign (7. 17. 106).[12]

[10] *Commentary on the Song of Songs*, 3. 4, 179. 4–8 Baehrens. Cf. Bauer (1964), 3: 'Die Entwicklung vollzieht sich in folgender Weise: Unglaube, Rechtglaube, Irrglaube.'

[11] *Stromata*, 7. 17. 107. 5: *κατά τε οὖν ὑπόστασιν, κατά τε ἐπίνοιαν, κατά τε ἀρχὴν κατά τε ἐξοχὴν μόνην εἶναί φαμεν τὴν ἀρχαίαν καὶ καθολικὴν ἐκκλησίαν*. Cf. Hegesippus, one of the earliest opponents of Marcion, who argued for the unity of the Church on the grounds that the same doctrine was to be found throughout its many branches, and that 'in all the lists of episcopal succession and in every city 'things are as *the Law, the prophets, and the Lord* preach [*ἐν ἑκάστῃ δὲ διαδοχῇ καὶ ἐν ἑκάστῃ πόλει οὕτως ἔχει ὡς ὁ νόμος κηρύσσει καὶ οἱ προφῆται καὶ ὁ κύριος*]' (Eusebius, *Ecclesiastical History*, 4. 22. 3).

[12] Some heretics seem to have thought that the Apostles adulterated the teaching of Jesus, and to that extent quite deliberately contrasted their own doctrines with those of the Apostles: cf. esp. Irenaeus, *Against Heresies*, 3. 2. 2, with Pelikan (1971), 92–3. But for Clement, and also for Irenaeus, the validity of any view of Jesus could not be established unless it could be traced through the open teaching of the Apostles. They were in a privileged position to know what Christ thought, and it

It should be emphasized once again that this obsession with the relative antiquity of the orthodox Church was not a merely rhetorical device, a *captatio benevolentiae* aimed at a nostalgic or atavistic audience. In logical terms it was (as it was for the Platonists) an argument that the truth might only be identified at all within Christianity if it were possible in the first place to identify objectively a single 'orthodox' tradition which stood out from the other positions. As with the Platonists, history provided the only means of doing this, allowing the position that came first to be distinguished as such from the welter of differences that followed.[13] And once the original form of Christianity had been isolated in this way, the Christians could go on to suggest that the heretics' *creation* of increasing disagreement where there had been unity before argued for the degeneracy of their philosophical approach—and argued as well for the superior plausibility of the original position, deviation from which was shown to have such negative philosophical results. In parallel with the assertion of the youth of all heresies, the Christians drew on exactly the same motifs as we saw in the last chapter were used by the Platonists to characterize the difficulties caused and encountered by the divergent schools of Greek philosophy. We find, for example, the frequent observation that the positions variously adopted by the 'heretics' led them to disagree with each other (Irenaeus, *Against Heresies*, 1. 11. 1; Clement, *Stromata*, 7. 16. 101; Tertullian, *Prescription of the Heretics*, 37. 7–38. 3); also the claim that they could each be seen to contradict themselves (Clement, *Stromata*, 7. 15. 92, 16. 97; Origen, *Commentary on St John*, 19. 14, 314. 18 Preuschen); and of course that they contradicted what is obviously true—which in the context of Christian discussion embraces contradiction with Scripture as well (Clement, *Stromata*, 7. 16. 97; cf. ps.-Justin, *Questions for the Orthodox*, 4, 394 B). And further, to provide an explanation for the impulse to heresy, and in

would be unintelligible for them to risk the loss or distortion of the truth by keeping it secret (*Against Heresies*, 3. 3. 1). (There are esoteric elements in Clement's own theology too, of course; but these relate rather to the nature of the *gnōsis* to which the Christian is supposed to be led than to the tradition which leads him there.)

[13] And compare Tertullian, *Against Hermogenes*, 1. 1, ii. 339. 1–5 Oehler: 'We tend, for the sake of abbreviation, to refute the heretics on the basis of their youth. For, as the rule of faith comes first, and even predicts future heresies, so the heresies which are predicted come later, because it is *future* heresies that were predicted by the more ancient rule of truth.' Also *On the Veiling of Virgins*, 1. 2, 1. 883. 11 Oehler: 'It is not so much their novelty as the truth that refutes heresies [*haereses non tam novitas quam veritas revincit*].'

support of the claim that the orthodoxy contained nothing in itself that could promote serious disagreement,[14] the heretics were credited with non-philosophical motives also familiar from Platonist texts to explain their emergence at all: love of contention (*aemulatio*: Tertullian, *Prescription of Heretics*, 38. 6), or the vain desire to attract followers of their own (Irenaeus, *Against Heresies*, 1. 28. 1; cf. 3. 23. 8 for the motive behind Tatian's conversion to Gnosticism in particular).[15] Concepts such as love of honour (*φιλοτιμία*: *Stromata*, 7. 16. 98. 2), love of glory (*φιλοδοξία*: *Stromata*, 7. 15. 91. 2, 16. 105. 5), and love of self (*φιλαυτία*: *Stromata*, 7. 15. 91. 2; 7. 16. 96. 5) are central to Clement's characterization of the heretics as they were to the Platonists' characterization of the Hellenistic schools.[16]

All of these arguments naturally had a profound impact on the internal politics of Christianity: but the immediate stimulus for their development seems to have been the need to construct a form of Christianity that could play its part as a recognizable character on the Greek philosophical stage. To oversimplify the matter a little (but not, perhaps, very much), the invention of orthodoxy as a matter of internal definition was a response to the external pressure

[14] Cf. Athenagoras, *On the Resurrection of the Dead*, 1. 1, stressing that heresy is sown by the heretics themselves: it is in no way, not even accidentally, a natural growth from the truth. The point is the same as that made by Numenius with reference to Plato: cf. again fr. 24. 67–73 des Places, quoted and discussed in ch. 7.

[15] It is worth noting that there are precedents for these motifs in much earlier Christian and Jewish polemic. Paul himself was accused by the Jews of being motivated to break with the Law in anger after being refused the hand of the high priest's daughter (Epiphanius, *Heresies*, 30. 16. 6–9), and polemical terms familiar from later Platonist and Christian arguments already occur in (especially Pauline) criticisms of the infidel. So for example *φιλονεικία*, already associated with faction at Luke 22. 24, is warned against by Paul at 1 Corinthians 11: 16. *φιλαυτία* is a vice of the eschatological age at 2 Timothy 3: 2. The term *κενοδοξία* makes a few appearances in the New Testament, which perhaps accounts for the characteristically Christian criticism of *κενὴ δόξα* among heretics and pagans: see Galatians 5: 26, Philippians 2: 3, and cf. Colossians 2: 8 (*κενὴ ἀπάτη*, associated with *φιλοσοφία*). For similar themes cf. e.g. Philippians 1: 14–18, a passage used by Tertullian at *Against Marcion*, 5. 20. Again, although these motifs do not take their place in the same kind of polemical structure as that provided by the Platonist model, the superficial similarities they set up with it must have assisted in the Christians' assimilation of it. It is interesting to note, by the way, that the word *φιλοτιμία* is only used positively in Paul, to refer to enthusiasm in promoting the Gospel (cf. Romans 15: 20, 2 Corinthians 5: 9, 1 Thessalonians 4: 11), and in later Christian writers it appears in this positive light as well as in its more negative aspect. Cf. e.g. Theophilus, *To Autolycus*, 1. 14. 16; Athenagoras, *On the Resurrection of the Dead*, 23. 6. 3; Clement, *Protrepticus*, 12. 121. 2.

[16] Cf. Opsomer (1998), 151–5, for the use of the word *φιλαυτία* in particular in Platonist polemic.

created by the Platonist attack on Christian sectarianism. Earlier, I mentioned that Clement gave us evidence for such attacks—I shall turn now briefly to consider his reply (*Stromata*, 7. 15. 89. 4–90. 2; but see all of *Stromata*, 7. 15):[17]

> That heresies would be sown among the truth, like tares among the wheat [Matthew 13: 24–30], was foretold by the Lord . . . So if someone should abandon his undertakings and stray from agreement, surely we are not to keep away from the truth ourselves?

Orthodox Christianity is not refuted because some of its members have gone astray. Note what Clement does in this passage: the various and equipollent battle-lines implied by the pagans' characterization of a sectarian Christianity have been replaced by a single division, between the orthodox and the rest. All of the 'heretical' divisions within Christianity are at once brought under a single heading in opposition to the 'orthodoxy'. The one division that is left (between the orthodox and the heretics) is denied equipollence by the historical observation that the heretics are manifest divergences—from their original agreement with the 'orthodoxy' (compare Origen as quoted above); and (what is also implied in Clement's skilfully ambivalent language) from the 'agreement' which characterizes the orthodox position. A diachronic survey of the question will, in other words, quickly pick out the true Christianity from the synchronic tangle of disagreement identified by the pagans. And Clement goes further than this: not only are we able to make out the true Christian tradition among the tangle of the heretics, but their squabbles actually help us to see its superior status (and compare again the Platonist argument that the disintegration of Hellenistic thought strengthens the hypothesis that Plato had been right all along). 'Indeed,' says Clement, citing 1 Corinthians 11: 19, '[Paul] says that it is for the "approved" that the heresies exist' (*Stromata*, 7. 15. 90. 5). Clement accepts his opponents' premiss that factionalism indicates that something has gone wrong in a philosophy; but by using historical analysis

[17] For simplicity's sake, I omit from the main text the *ad hominem* argument with which Clement's reply begins (*Stromata*, 7. 15. 89. 3): 'There are very many sects among the Jews and among the most respected of the Greek philosophers, but you do not think that you should hold off from philosophy or Judaism because of the mutual disagreement of these sects.' But Clement himself, of course, wishes precisely to use the sectarian nature of his opponents' philosophy to remove any justification for adherence to it.

to locate the causes of factionalism outside of the orthodox position, he can turn the pagans' argument against Christianity as a whole into a refutation of heresies in particular. Compare the Platonists' appropriation of the Argument from Disagreement to lead us away from the Hellenistic schools and back to Plato: so here, the pagans' criticism of Christianity is actually used to lead us away from the heresies, and thereby to support the claims of the orthodox.

> It is clear that the truth, being arduous and difficult, prompts questioning; and, when the enquirer does not learn or grasp truly, but merely acquires the impression of knowledge, the result is the self- and glory-loving heresies.[18]

Heretics are just too big-headed (the familiar words *φίλαυτοι καὶ φιλόδοξοι* occur here) to see that their researches have not led them to the truth. *The Church*, says Clement, *is not divided*: the causes of division lie with the heretics who *ipso facto* are located outside of the Church (cf. *Stromata*, 7. 17. 107).

2. *The Hebraeo-Christian Tradition and Pagan Divergence*

The identification of an orthodoxy distinct from heretical sects within Christianity is a crucial first stage in the Christians' response to their Platonist critics. But it is only a first stage. For, while it heads off the argument that no one position within the religion could be discerned to be superior to any of the many others, it does not yet deal with the wider issue. Strictly, the Platonists only drew attention to the divisions within Christianity to lend support to their hypothesis that their own tradition (through Plato, and the older theologies on which he drew) was the one in which the truth, if discernible at all, might be found. Sooner or later the disagreements within Christianity were *bound* to result, on the Platonists' hypothesis, because the religion was itself an innovative, divergent tradition. We have a number of texts dating from the second century onwards which attest to this strand of the Platonists' argument, from Theophilus (*To Autolycus*, 3. 4, but cf. the whole of book 3, which is largely devoted to refuting the point) to Eusebius (*Preparation for the Gospel*, 1. 5. 11, 16 B–C; 4. 1. 3, 130 B–C), with fragments of Porphyry's work *Against the Christians* in between (e.g. fr. 69.

[18] *Stromata*, 7. 15. 91. 2. Cf. also 7. 15. 92.

7–8, 25–7 Harnack). The following is the version, already alluded to in Chapter 6, which Origen found in the second-century treatise of Celsus (*Against Celsus*, 3. 5):

> Celsus imagines that the Jews were Egyptian by race, and left Egypt after revolting against the Egyptian community and despising the religious customs of Egypt. He says that what they did to the Egyptians, they suffered in turn through those who followed Jesus and believed him to be the Christ; in both cases a revolt against the community led to innovation.

If the truth were to be discernible in Christianity it might well have to be sought among the 'orthodox'; but the youth of the Christian tradition and the wider historical context in which it finds its place give us no reason to expect that the truth *would* be discernible there at all. Unless the Christians could answer this point, they would draw little benefit from an ability to distinguish between orthodox and heretic.

The Platonists' attack on Christianity through claims for its historical origins very obviously parallels the first-century Graeco-Egyptian polemic against the Jews which was discussed in Chapter 4—and the similarity is no coincidence either. As the Platonists took over and developed the Stoics' theory of the transmission of primitive wisdom, so they inherited their concern to isolate and reject what they thought could be shown to be derivative cultural traditions. It is reasonable, then, to suppose that the Christians could have looked to the Jewish apologists for help in deflecting it—at least for help in proving that the Hebrew tradition from which they took their rise was one of genuine antiquity. Origen, for example, refers his readers to Josephus, '*On the Antiquity of the Jews*' (that is, *Against Apion*) at *Against Celsus*, 1. 16. However, the Jewish apologists could *only* be of any use in helping to prove the antiquity of the Hebrew tradition: the Jews themselves would have concurred with the Greeks that Christianity was still a divergence from *this*. The Christians, on the other hand, needed to show that *Christianity itself* was the tradition of prior antiquity. And the way in which they did this—not to say the very fact that they did it at all—is one of the most interesting indications of how deeply the invention of orthodox Christianity was influenced by the Platonists' model of the history of philosophy. For by the early second century AD Christians had started to claim that the Hebrew tradition was philosophically identical with orthodox Christianity.

Christianity had to face the question of its historical origins long before it came into contact with pagan philosophy. Perhaps the most pressing question that the religion faced at its inception was just this: How should Christianity see its relationship with Judaism? Was it to be a religion which broke from its Jewish roots altogether? Would it acknowledge Judaism as merely a precursor of itself, or as an incomplete revelation of God, which was completed in Christ? Or would Christianity rather see itself in the role of the *true* Judaism: no addition, no new revelation, just a correct understanding of the original Covenant which the Jews themselves had lost sight of?

Christianity certainly does not seem to have been born in a deliberate attempt to break with Judaism: whatever Jesus' own view of Judaism,[19] his immediate followers were, essentially, *Jewish* Christians, who thought of Jesus in conformity with Old Testamental Judaism, either as a prophet, or, more radically, as the Messiah of Jewish expectation;[20] and their religious life was closely linked

[19] It has standardly been supposed that Jesus had a more or less ambivalent attitude towards the Law, rejecting a 'legalistic' interpretation of it even if he did not reject it as such, and putting his own teaching above it. Cf. e.g. Bousset (1911), 107–9, 199; Bultmann (1926), 52–8, 66; (1948–53), i. 10–15; Käsemann (1964), 38; Schweizer (1968), 34–8; Bornkamm (1975), 92–3. But against all of this see E. P. Sanders (1985), 55–6: 'The trouble with this thread is that the apostles in Jerusalem apparently did not know that the Torah had been abrogated: that was the contribution of Paul and possibly other apostles to the Gentiles.' (In fact Bultmann himself at 1948–53: i. 55 supposes that the question of the validity of the Law was not raised among the first followers of Jesus.) Sanders' own understanding places Jesus much more solidly within the context of the Law: according to him, Jesus may not have thought the Mosaic dispensation final or binding, but his only positive challenge to the Law was his injunction to 'let the dead bury their dead' (see 1985: 245–69, esp. 267; also 1–58 for a full doxographical survey of the issue).

[20] These accounts of Jesus were exemplified in the two major wings of Ebionite Christianity which persisted into the 4th cent., some time after the Pauline Church had gained ascendency and eclipsed their claim to be representatives of mainstream Christianity. For the Ebionites in general cf. Irenaeus, *Against Heresies*, 1. 26. 2; Origen, *Against Celsus*, 5. 61; Epiphanius, *Heresies*, 30. 16 (with esp. Lüdemann 1996: 52–3 for the Ebionites' roots in the earliest Jewish Christianity). One of the Ebionite sects, the 'Nazarenes', saw in Christ the Messiah and son of God (although their adherence to the Jewish Law and their rejection of Paul led them to be branded as heretics). The other (reflected later in the ps.-Clementine *Recognitions*) saw Christ as the 'true prophet', akin in his nature to Adam, Moses, and other prophets. The question of whether Jesus saw *himself* as a prophet or as the Messiah hinges in good part around the infinitely vexed question of whether he proclaimed himself to be the 'Son of Man' (Bultmann 1948–53: i. 2–9, cf. 25–33, and Macquarrie 1990: 41 argue, for example, that he rather used this phrase to point towards someone still to come, and Robinson 1956 suggests that this is how his early followers understood him), and whether the phrase has Messianic overtones anyway (cf. Vermes 1978,

to the Temple and based on observance of the Law.[21] But at the same time there were clearly those who thought that Christianity was a sect too far, whether because of the peculiar doctrines of the Christians, or perhaps rather because of their public and zealous advocacy of them; and we have early, although admittedly partisan, evidence for attempts at suppression.[22] Prominent in our view of anti-Christian activists is, of course, Saul (or Paul) of Tarsus.

Paul was converted in due course, and himself became a Christian. But whatever else it changed, Paul's conversion did not change his opposition to the belief that the proper home of Christianity was within Judaism. For the converted Paul, who believed in the Messiahship of Christ, Jesus' ministry, death, and resurrection were matters of such cosmological import that they could not but have changed matters considerably. If Jesus was divine,[23] it must (for Paul) follow that his importance was not restrained by the bounds of the Jewish Law. This position is reinforced by Paul's peculiar understanding of Jesus as the antitype of Adam: as Adam through his disobedience brought death into the world, and all our woe, with loss of Eden, so Jesus, in overcoming death by his perfect self-denial and submission to the will of God, opened the kingdom of heaven once again to all mankind. This belief in the renewal of humanity itself in Christ, and the promise of salvation for Gentile as well as Jew towards which it pointed, necessarily called into ques-

arguing that it is merely an Aramaic periphrasis for 'man'). For an overview of the enormous literature on the subject see Schürer, ii. 520–3, with n. 27.

[21] e.g. Acts 2: 46; 5: 42. Peter's close adherence to the Law notoriously earned him the criticism of Paul: Galatians 2: 11–14 (a passage which Origen uses to answer Celsus' charge that Jewish believers in Jesus abandoned their ancestral religion: *Against Celsus*, 2. 1). Cf. Bultmann (1948–53), i. 54: 'Selbsverständlich meint die eschatologische Gemeinde nicht eine neue Religionsgemeinschaft—also ein neues historisches Phänomen—zu sein und *grenzt sich nicht als neue Religion gegen das Judentum ab.* Sie hält am Tempel und seinem Kult fest' (Bultmann's emphasis).

[22] Cf. Acts 5: 27–42. James, the brother of Jesus, who appears to have been the first leader of the Jewish-Christian community, was condemned by the Sanhedrin and executed in the early 60s (Acts 7: 54–60; Josephus, *Jewish Antiquities*, 20. 200–1 with Lüdemann 1996: 49–52).

[23] Or if he *became* divine: there is some debate over whether Paul believed in the pre-existence of Christ as the son of God, or whether he held the 'adoptionist' position, that Jesus only earned divine sonship through the resurrection. For the latter position cf. Philippians 2: 6–11 (also Romans 1: 3–4) with e.g. Dunn (1989), 36–46; Macquarrie (1990), 55–65. But the former (and ultimately 'orthodox') position is supported by Romans 8: 3; 2 Corinthians 8: 9; Galatians 4: 4; Philippians 2: 6–7; and cf. DuBose (1907), esp. 293; Bultmann (1948–53), i. 185, and esp. 299–300; Schweizer (1966); A. T. Hanson (1975), 83.

tion the continuing relevance of the Covenant made by God with the Jewish people in particular. Paul never argued that Christianity had straightforwardly *replaced* or *superseded* the Law, but he did think that Judaism was 'renewed', and at least to that extent made something *different*, in Christ.[24] Jesus, properly speaking, fulfilled the Law, he did not replace it: but this is already enough for Paul to be able to speak as if there is a *new* Law—the 'law of faith' (Romans 3: 27), the 'law of the Spirit' (Romans 8: 2), or the 'law of Christ' (Galatians 6: 2).[25]

A trend to separate Christianity from Judaism started with Paul, then—indeed, it led him (ironically, perhaps) to become the first Christian to be thought of as in any sense and from any point of view a 'heretic' or 'apostate'.[26] But it gained currency as the first century progressed. The Gospel of John the Evangelist was thought, in some quarters, to have been written as an early response to the Gnosticism then being propounded by Cerinthus—and in particular to the Gnostic doctrine that the Gods of the Old and New Testaments were *different* Gods, the one the God of creation, the other the God of redemption announced to man by Christ.[27] St John

[24] The Law is new because its readers are renewed (2 Corinthians 3: 14), because the Spirit which lay behind the letter is now (apparently for the first time) revealed (Romans 3: 20–1).

[25] With all of this cf. Benoit (1962–3).

[26] Cf. esp. Irenaeus, *Against Heresies*, 1. 26. 2, and Epiphanius, *Heresies*, 30. 16. 8–9, with Bauer (1964), 238: 'So ist also, wenn man sich etwas zugespitzt ausdrücken darf, der Apostel Paulus das einzige Ketzerhaupt gewesen, das die apostolische Zeit kennt, das einzige, der in ihr—wenigstens von gewisser Seite her—so beurteilt worden ist.' Cf., more recently, Lüdemann (1996), esp. ch. 4. Due no doubt to his antipathy to Jewish Christianity, Paul (at least, a carefully edited version of Paul) became adopted by Gnostics who wished to stress the disjunction between Judaism and Christianity (cf. esp. Grant 1966: 36; cf. 88–9), a circumstance which may have retarded his final assimilation into 'orthodox' Christianity (cf. e.g. Lüdemann 1996: 55–6 for Justin's reluctance to appeal to Paul).

[27] Irenaeus, *Against Heresies*, 3. 11. 1. The claim is repeated by Jerome (*Commentary on Matthew*, prologue 42–9), and expanded by him to include Ebion, the eponymous (but probably mythical) founder of the Ebionites. Victorinus (*Commentary on the Apocalypse*, 11. 1) says that John had Valentinus in his sights as well as Cerinthus and Ebion. However, some modern scholars have identified Gnostic elements in John himself (e.g. Bultmann 1949: 220; Grant 1966: 166–75; and cf. Harnack 1894–7: i. 216, arguing that Gnosticism was a crucial element in the Hellenization of Christianity as a whole), and have argued that the first readers of the Gospel were Gnostics (e.g. J. N. Sanders 1943: 46–66; Barrett 1960: 95); and we know at least that it was a text extensively employed by them (it was the subject of a commentary by Heracleon, for example). If this is right (but cf. *contra* F.-M. Braun 1959: 394; Brown 1966, pp. liv–lvi, lxxxi–lxxxii), and especially if it is right that Irenaeus was the first 'orthodox' writer to make extensive use of John (so e.g. R. P. C. Hanson 1970: 426; Grant 1966: 36), it may be that Irenaeus' claim for

asserted the unity of the Christian and Jewish Gods in the strongest form possible, by making Christ both the agent of creation *and* the herald of redemption: 'All things were made by him and without him was not anything made that was made. In him was life, and the life was the light of men' (John 1: 3–4). It may or may not be the case that all of this was intended as a challenge to Gnosticism: what is undeniable, however, is that it constituted a challenge to Judaism. In making an overt and complete identification of the Christian with the Jewish God, John was in effect appropriating the God of the Jews in a way that allowed him to maintain the subordination of the Old to the New Covenant. If Jesus Christ, and he alone,[28] was the Word of God, then his voice was not only louder than those of Moses and the prophets, it might, when necessary, silence them altogether. Judaism became, in John's Gospel, God's preparation for Christianity, and Christianity in turn was established as the full revelation of what had only been partially available before. John did not argue for a straightforward *rejection* of the Law, nor did he deny that in times past God spoke through the prophets. But he certainly went some way towards distancing his Christianity from Jewish observance. He allowed, for example, Jesus to refer to the Law as '*your* Law' when speaking to the Jews (see 8. 17; 10. 34; and cf. 15. 25); and he drew, or at the very least implied, a distinction between the followers of Moses and the followers of Jesus (cf. 9. 28).[29] Above all, he was clear that Jesus brought *new* teaching (the teaching of 'him who sent me' at 7. 16, for example) in addition to, and perhaps even instead of, the Law. The Johannine Christ even more than the Pauline Christ did rather more than open our eyes to a new and proper understanding of the truth, he brought that truth into the world with him: 'For the Law was given by Moses, but grace and truth came by Jesus Christ' (1. 17).[30]

its original purpose was part of an attempt to (re)appropriate the Gospel for the orthodox Church.

[28] This clause is necessary because some Jewish Christians—as, for example, those whose beliefs are reflected in the ps.-Clementine *Recognitions*—believed the word of God to have been incarnate in Moses and others of the prophets as well.

[29] Cf. Brown (1966), pp. lxx–lxxv. Benoit (1962–3) cites John 7: 19 and 22–3, as evidence that the Evangelist actually advocated submission to the Law, but the context will not support this reading. Jesus' argument here is purely *ad hominem*: are his actions (he asks) a greater transgression of the Law than those of the Jews who accuse him? 'Did not Moses give you the Law? And none of you keep the Law. Why do you seek to kill me?' (7: 19).

[30] This verse is admittedly controversial. The phrase 'grace and truth' (ἡ χάρις

This disjunctive understanding of Judaism and Christianity seems to have gained ground outside of, and quite probably in response to, 'mainstream' Jewish Christianity. The letters ascribed to St John, for example, are clear that the teaching of Christianity should be dated, not from its Judaic roots, but from its 'beginning' in Christ (cf. 1 John 2: 8; 3: 11 with 23), and the letters of Ignatius of Antioch, written in the early second century AD, argued even more passionately that Christ is our *only* teacher. Ignatius allowed that the 'ancient Scriptures' spoke expectantly *of* Christ, but he was very clear that they were devoid of his teaching (*Magnesians*, 9). Judaism, for Ignatius, had come to a decisive full stop with the coming of Christ (*Magnesians*, 10).[31]

However, if there was an increasing tendency within the Pauline Christianity of the first century to make a distinction between the teaching of Christ on the one hand and the teaching of Moses and the prophets on the other, to assert not just that the advent of Christ was an important event in the divine economy, but that it brought *in addition* a Christian truth which had not been available to the Jews of the first Covenant, things changed radically in the century that

καὶ ἡ ἀλήθεια, at 1. 14 as well as 17) is clearly the Hebrew *ḥesed we'emet* (attributes of God e.g. at Exodus 34: 6–7), and might not, even in John, have the force that its literal translation into Greek might imply. So Brown (1966: 4), for example, takes the phrase to mean 'enduring love', and criticizes theologians such as Bultmann (see 1941: 49–50 with 50 n. 1; cf. 1932: 245–8), who argue that the word ἀλήθεια in John should be understood in Greek epistemological terms. It might be possible to find some middle ground here, but 'at any rate' (so A. T. Hanson 1975: 6) John's intention is clear: 'the same God who showed himself to Moses at the giving of the law has now manifested himself in Jesus'. John is clear that Jesus trumps the Jewish prophets and, as Brown himself acknowledges (1966, p. lxxii), Jewish Law is supposed to be 'superseded' by his teaching.

[31] It is true that Ignatius occasionally seems to encourage a spiritual observance of the Law, which might be taken to suggest that he thought appropriate exegesis could save the Old Testament for the Christians. Cf. e.g. *Philadelphians*, 6, where he criticizes 'Jews falsely so called' for accepting merely carnal circumcision: this might be taken to imply a contrast with '*true*' Jews, i.e. Christians, who engage in a spiritual circumcision instead. However, it is probably easier to suppose that Ignatius does not mean to distinguish Jews from Christians, but rather true from false Jews in the pre-Christian period. Judaism, he would be saying, is effectively defunct, but was, even in its own day, abused by its adherents. Again, at *Magnesians*, 9, Ignatius says that Christians should observe the Sabbath in a spiritual manner: but this does not on closer inspection seem to be so much an *interpretation* of Mosaic Law as an *appropriation* of the concept of the Sabbath. Indeed, by saying (in the same place) that Christians are bound to keep the day of the resurrection as a festival (a literal, not a 'spiritual', festival), Ignatius clearly implies that a new set of customs is appropriate to the new cast of mind required by the Christian faith. Cf. on this Pelikan (1971), 18.

followed. For at that point the Christian Apologists rather suddenly began to adopt a position that was almost diametrically opposed to this one, and went to some lengths to argue, not just (against extreme positions such as that of Marcion) that the Gods of the Old and New Testaments were the same God, and that Christ had been announced by the prophets, but even that the *wisdom* handed down through Judaism was in essence the *same* as the wisdom passed on through Christ. Indeed, this trend can already be seen emerging in the letter written in the late first or early second century and ascribed in antiquity to the Apostle Barnabas,[32] one of the earliest texts to give us evidence for the (re)appropriation of the Judaic Scriptures as *Christian* texts in this sense. Barnabas (as I shall, for convenience, refer to its author) says, it is true, that God's Testament never reached the Jewish people, who were 'unworthy to receive it' (esp. 14), and on the basis of this claim commentators have sometimes seen Barnabas as evidence for a continuing rift between the Jewish and Christian traditions.[33] But at the same time, and in the same place, Barnabas made it clear that Moses at least *did* receive and understand the Covenant. What is more, Barnabas is quite clear that this Covenant was the *same* as the Covenant which was passed on to, and received by, the Christians in Christ: no distinction between the Old and the New can be found in his letter. This already gives a very different picture of Christian philosophy from the one which we saw in Ignatius, or John, or even Paul, all of whom, in their different ways, were clear that Christ brought something that was quite new, that could not even in principle have been available to anyone living in the pre-Christian era.

Moses, then, received the Covenant, and although Barnabas does not say this explicitly, it must follow that he at least had understood the truth which was now to be found among the Christians. The question, then, is whether the expression of this truth was confined to Moses, or whether it became embodied in the Hebrew tradition itself. Did God withhold his Covenant again once the Jews at large had failed to 'receive' it? If this were so, then we could talk with Quasten (1950–60: i. 89) of Barnabas' 'absolute repudiation' of the Old Testament, and he would constitute late evidence for a trend

[32] See on the *Epistle* in general Paget (1994). It is normally dated to the reign of Trajan or Hadrian, but Paget (at 9–30) suggests a date as early as the reign of Nerva (AD 96–8).

[33] Cf. Pelikan (1971), 14; also Quasten (1950–60), i. 89, as cited below.

to distance Christian philosophy from its Jewish prehistory rather than early evidence for a trend in which Christianity was made historically continuous with the revelation of God to the Jewish prophets. But it seems to me that it was not so. For Barnabas engages in extensive Christian exegesis, in particular (but not only) allegorical and typological exegesis, of Moses and the prophets as if they do contain 'Christian' teaching (cf. esp. 7–12, 15–16). What is more, Barnabas pointedly characterizes the Jews as being in error, not in ignorance: it was not that they did not have access to the Covenant in the writings of Moses, it was rather that they *did not interpret it properly* (*Epistle*, 10). Barnabas did not 'absolutely repudiate' the Old Testament:[34] he rather repudiated the Jews' understanding of it. *It* he embraced, as expressing (to those who have been shown the way by Christ) what was, essentially, Christian teaching.[35]

Barnabas signals for us one of the most important shifts in the development of early Christian philosophy: increasingly we find that, when Christians call their religion a renewal, they mean something different from Paul: they mean not that it is *new* in any sense, not a development from Jewish thought, but rather that it is a *reversion* to an original philosophy which was preserved in the Jewish tradition, but from an understanding of which the Jews themselves had strayed.[36] And this extension of the argument for the antiquity

[34] Quasten's claim that he did sits uneasily with his own statement three pages earlier (1950–60: i. 85–6) that Barnabas thought the Jews only 'misunderstood the Law because they interpreted it literally'.

[35] Compare also *Epistle*, 9, where we learn that Abraham understood at least something of the Christian truth. He is said to have 'received the doctrines of the three letters', and to have circumcised 318 (Greek: TIH) men of his household as an allusion to the coming of Jesus (IH) and his death on the cross (T).

[36] Cf. e.g. Justin, *Dialogue*, 23 and 46; Tertullian, *Answer to the Jews*, 2, *Prescription of the Heretics*, 13; Irenaeus, *Against Heresies*, 4 (in its entirety, but esp. 2. 1–3, 7. 4, 21); and, later on, Eusebius, *Ecclesiastical History*, 1. 2. 1–16; 1. 4. 14. To read Scripture in the 'Jewish' fashion came to mean to interpret it literally—that is, to miss its true, Christian meaning: so Clement, *Pedagogue*, 1. 6. 34. 3; Eusebius, *Ecclesiastical History*, 7. 24. 1; cf. Justin, *Dialogue*, 14; Augustine, *On Christian Doctrine*, 3. 8–9. Origen says that Christ taught more than Solomon knew (*On First Principles*, 3. 3. 1, 256. 25–8 Koetschau); but the context of this claim is a discussion of the relationship between pagan philosophy (the 'wisdom of this world') and true Christian wisdom—the 'wisdom of God'. Since Solomon's wisdom is described by Origen in terms which relate it to Greek philosophy in particular (cf. Origen's *Commentary on the Song of Songs*, esp. prologue 3, where Origen says that Solomon provided the model for the Greek division of philosophy), Solomon cannot be taken to represent the Hebrew tradition at large in the passage from *On First Principles* cited. The claim that Christ taught more than Solomon knew cannot, for example,

of the Church considered narrowly earlier on as a means for the isolation of later, heretical positions finally enables us to see the full scope and significance of the historical model in terms of which the 'orthodox' defined themselves.[37] For the orthodox Christian tradition did not simply claim to be older than heretical schools; it claimed, through its appropriation to itself of the ancient Hebrew tradition, to be older than *all* competing philosophical traditions: it went back, in fact, to primitive antiquity. The claim to orthodoxy thus turns out to be of much wider importance than if it had been (as commentators often assume) restricted to use in the internal politics of Christianity.[38] In fact, the notion of 'orthodoxy' as it was developed was one of the most important philosophical weapons by which the Platonizing Western Church won the battle for Christianity against their external opponents as well. Christians were now able to argue that pagan theologies, just like the 'Christian' heresies later on, were divergences from their tradition[39]—and by doing so they were able to answer their pagan critics in kind. Christianity was not the deviant tradition: orthodox Hebraeo-Christianity was the original standard in terms of which all later branches of thought would have to be measured.

be extended to the claim that Christ (at least in his later incarnate form) taught more than Moses and the prophets had known. (For the acquaintance of Moses and the prophets with the pre-existent Christ see in any case Origen, *Commentary on John*, 1. 15, 19. 6–23 Preuschen. Cf. also Harl 1958: 337; Pelikan 1971: 110–11.)

[37] Against e.g. Lilla (1971: 31–7), who thinks that the antiquity achieved by the appropriation of Jewish Scripture serves a merely rhetorical cause.

[38] Indeed, commentators tend to assume something even weaker than this, namely that 'orthodoxy' was, in effect, merely the title of victory won by the dominant party in an internal struggle for followers. But that 'orthodoxy' was defined (and was supposed to be recognized) by means other than numerical or political supremacy is suggested already by, for example, Tertullian's suggestion that there had been a time when the orthodox were outnumbered by the heretics (*Against Marcion*, 5. 20. 2, ii. 333. 26–8 Oehler). Cf. also St Vincent of Lérins three centuries later: 'But what if some novel contagion tries to infect the whole Church, not merely a tiny part of it? He [the catholic, or orthodox, Christian] will take care to adhere to antiquity, which cannot now be led astray by any deceit of novelty' (*Commonitorium*, 4).

[39] Origen at one point actually says that heretical ideas lie at the basis of Greek philosophy: *Letter to Gregory*, 2. More common is the claim (also relevant for making the connection) that Christian heresies have their roots in pagan philosophy: so Irenaeus, *Against Heresies*, 2. 14; Hippolytus, *Refutation of All Heresies*, esp. 1, preface 9, 3. 23–6 Wendland; 9. 31, 264. 19–33 Wendland; 10. 32, 288. 23–289. 2 Wendland. Tertullian, *Prescription of the Heretics*, 7, 43. Later on, cf. e.g. Eusebius, *Ecclesiastical History*, 5. 28. 13–19. Justin explicitly links the manner by which the pagans and heretics divide into factions: he discusses the former at *Dialogue*, 2. 1–2, and the latter, with a back-reference to this passage, at *Dialogue*, 35.

There is, as it happens, nothing in the *Epistle of Barnabas* itself to spell out the attitude to pagan theology implied by his approach, and common among the 'orthodox' later on—nothing, for example, to suggest that its author linked the argument for the 'Christianity' of Hebrew Scripture with a belief in the youth of pagan traditions. But then we would not expect there to be much on the pagans in a letter which is framed as an attack on the Jews and addressed to the Christians in particular. But from roughly the same period the first concrete formulation of this kind of theme *is* found, in the surviving work of the first Christian Apologist: the Athenian philosopher Marcianus Aristides.[40] Aristides' belief that Hebrew Scripture needed to be reclaimed from the Jews as essentially Christian Scripture is evident in his claim that the Jews *strayed* from their knowledge of the wisdom it contains (*Apology*, 14). But Aristides went further than this (and so further than the *Epistle of Barnabas*), by speaking of the pagans as well. For Aristides suggested that the wisdom contained in the Old Testament predated the rise of traditional pagan theology: more specifically, he suggested that pagan theology was itself the result of a *straying* from it. What is important about this is that Aristides means something quite specific by his image of straying: not simply that the pagans were in error ('far from the truth'); but actually that their theology was, *historically speaking*, a divergence from the wisdom preserved in Christianity. He obviously thinks, for example, that the pagans' error was the same in kind as, only worse than, that of the Jews. They, he says, erred, notably by their lapses into idolatry and their rejection of Christ; but remained, nevertheless, closest to the truth of any non-Christian body.[41] The Chaldeans were worse: they 'did not know God', but 'went astray after the elements', and came to worship the celestial bodies, the created rather than the creator (*Apology*, 3). Worse still were the Greeks, who worshipped the absurd anthro-

[40] It was only in 1889 that the discovery of a Syriac translation of Aristides' *Apology* in the Monastery of St Catherine alerted scholars to the fact that the Greek original had been preserved as part of a medieval romance called the *History of Barlaam and Josaphat*. See Harris (1891) (including Syriac and Greek texts). Of Aristides himself we know little. Eusebius refers to him in his *Ecclesiastical History*, but adds nothing to what survives in the first few lines of the Syriac version of the *Apology* (lost in the Greek), where Aristides describes himself as an 'Athenian philosopher' and dedicates his work to the emperor Hadrian (thus placing it within AD 117–138).

[41] *Apology*, 14; the Syriac version at this point says more plainly that they have 'strayed from true knowledge', and adds that their religious practice shows that they serve angels, not the God whom they profess to worship.

pomorphisms we find in their poetry (8–11). Worst of all were the Egyptians, who were 'more stupid' and went 'further astray'. Not satisfied with the gods of other nations, they introduced (note the suggestion of an even worse *innovation*) animals and even plants as objects of their worship (12).

There is nothing in first-century Christianity to prepare us for this, the suggestion that pagan theology was a historical divergence from the primitive Christian truth: but it makes perfect sense—indeed, it is *needed*—as part of a broadly 'Platonic' representation of the place of Christianity in the history of philosophy. The Christians could have answered Platonist attempts to marginalize their tradition by asserting its historical independence from pagan philosophy; as long as the notion of orthodoxy held, this might at least have prevented them from falling under the terms of the Platonists' account of what happens to divergent traditions. But the Christians needed more than a *defence* of themselves, for, if they merely restored equipollence between their arguments and those of the Platonists, the Sceptical response to the whole debate would win. In order to go further and marginalize the pagans in their turn, in order to show thereby that the choice of (orthodox) Christianity as a path towards finding the truth was the only choice that could be reasonably justified, the Christians had to be able to show in addition that pagan traditions could be brought, along with Christian heresies, under the terms of *their* account of divergence. They had to be able to argue that the difficulties and disagreements evident in pagan theology (e.g. the 'ridiculous', 'absurd', and 'stupid' doctrines identified by Aristides at *Apology*, 8, 12) could only be explained in terms of this divergence—under the hypothesis, of course, that the original (i.e. Christian) theology was right.

The adoption of the Platonic model of philosophy which I have argued lies at the ultimate root of the Christian notion of 'orthodoxy' was presumably not such a deliberate affair as I might have made it sound—although it is hard, given the nature of our evidence, to talk about it in any other way. Perhaps 'assimilation' would be a better word than 'adoption': it came to form part of Christianity not, perhaps, because of any conscious decision on the part of the religion itself, but rather because of the preformed assumptions and outlook of a certain body of its recruits from the later first century AD. To put this more bluntly, the construction of Christian orthodoxy and the associated rewriting of the history of Christianity might be explained at its simplest by the work of men whose training in Platonism made this the only natural way of understanding its claim to provide a path to the truth at all.[42] But, however the model used to define the 'orthodoxy' came to be adopted, the important thing is the response it provided to attacks against Christianity such as those we have seen in Celsus. Celsus' attempt to undermine the Christian religion by calling it a corruption of a corruption of Egyptian tradition could be met by the 'orthodox' response, that Christianity was in reception of the truth preserved in Judaism, and that the Hebrew tradition it represented was in its turn very much older than any tradition that existed among the pagans. Just as the Platonists were arguing that their tradition preserved the most ancient philosophy, resurrected and expounded by Plato in particular, so the invention of Christian orthodoxy involved the claim that the Christians stood at the head of a tradition that had preserved the truth since the beginning. For the second-century Christians of the Western Church there was much that was important about Christ's coming: he fulfilled the prophecies, he played a vital soteriological role; but he was not a philosophical innovator. As far as doctrine went, Christ's importance was that he 'removed the veil' that had come to obscure the interpretation of Hebrew Scripture, and thus made available once again the *meaning* whose expression was preserved in the Judaic tradition. And, with this, orthodox Christianity was itself established as a philosophical tradition of the greatest antiquity. As long as this historical model could be maintained, the Platonists would no longer be able to use either the internal divisions of Christianity *or* its disagreement with pagan traditions to suggest that it was set on a path that led away from the truth; the heretics and pagans

[42] It is hard in most cases to comment with certainty on the training in Greek philosophy received by the Apologists; but Platonism features prominently where we can say anything at all. Justin, for example, describes at *Dialogue* 2 the journey he made through the various schools of Greek philosophy before his conversion and, whatever the historical accuracy of his account (some conventionalization is reasonably suspected by Goodenough 1923: 59), it is nevertheless significant that the last thinker with whom Justin claims to have studied, and the one for whose philosophy he expresses the highest regard, is the Platonist. Cf. Andresen (1952–3). For Platonist influences on Athenagoras cf. Malherbe (1970), arguing in particular that his *Embassy* is an 'exposition of the Christian faith that is carefully organized along the lines of a Middle Platonic epitome of Plato's philosophy' (214). For Clement's Platonism see Lilla (1971), esp. 41–51. And, more generally on this topic, Waszink (1957).

together were clearly isolated on the philosophical margins of the religion, whose original, orthodox expression had endured in its purest form since the beginning. As the final conclusion of all this, the orthodox were in a position to argue that the truth could be discerned nowhere at all, if it did not lie in the ancient tradition represented by orthodox Christianity.

Or at least they were now very *nearly* in a position to put this argument. One obstacle still, however, remained. For if Christians could show that traditional pagan theology (such, for example, as was expressed in the poems of Homer) was a corruption of the tradition which they maintained in its purest state, they had still to deal with the problem of pagan *philosophy* as developed, most notably, by Plato. For this, according to claims made by the Platonists, was a restored account of god and the world which went back *beyond* the mythological tradition. Indeed, the Platonists accepted that their own cultural tradition had suffered corruption, such that the restoration was needed (arguing only that the Jewish tradition, for example, was in worse or no better repair than their own). But to make their argument secure, the Christians needed to show that *all* pagan thought could be explained in terms of divergence from Christian thought, such that disagreements within it would prove that the truth was absent or indiscernible there. This was a question tackled by Christian thinkers later into the second century.

9

The 'Dependency Theme'

1. *The Need for the Argument*

As part of his response to Celsus' attack on the sectarian nature of Christian philosophy, Origen makes the following observation (*Against Celsus*, 3. 13; but see all of 12–13):

> Anyone who criticizes Christianity on account of its sects might also criticize the teaching of Socrates; for from his instruction many schools have come into being, whose adherents do not hold the same opinions. Furthermore, one might criticize Plato for his doctrines on the ground that Aristotle left his instruction and introduced new ideas.

It is a more pointed riposte than it looks. Celsus had presumably intended to criticize Christianity *as a whole* for the divisions within it; but the parallels that Origen draws with pagan philosophy show that he responds as if Celsus had attacked *orthodox* Christianity for the *heresies* which later arose. In other words, Origen's response to Celsus involves a tacit assertion that *Christianity*, properly speaking, is not divided at all, that the disagreements identified by Celsus arose only later and do nothing to make the orthodoxy less discernible.[1]

So much for the defence of Christian unity. But there is another subtlety here as well. By drawing not one but *two* parallels in Greek philosophy to the rise of heretical Christian sects, Origen is able to hint that it is not possible to separate out a single thread of Greek philosophy comparable in its own context with the orthodox school of Christianity. It is not possible, that is to say, to locate within Greek philosophy a *single* reference-point in terms of which one might identify and dismiss 'divergent' philosophical

[1] Compare Clement's strategy in answering a similar point (at *Stromata*, 7. 15. 89. 4–90. 2, discussed in ch. 8).

positions within it. Each Greek philosopher is already, he suggests, part of a multiform and fragmented philosophical landscape. This applies not least of all to the figurehead of Celsus' own philosophy, Plato, whom Origen places at the centre of a mini-history of Greek philosophical disagreement: Plato's pupils (as, of course, we know) disagreed with him; but Plato must in his own turn be implicated in dispute with the other 'Socratic' schools over the interpretation of Socrates (despite any claims that they might have made—compare my discussion in Chapter 6—for the effective irrelevance of these schools). Why should Greek philosophy be like this? When Origen insists that the rise of Christian heresies is *not* the result of a Christian tendency to factionalism and love of contention (*οὐ πάντως διὰ τὰς στάσεις καὶ τὸ φιλόνεικον*),[2] we might be expected to understand that it is precisely factionalism and strife, or some similar trait, which characterizes Greek philosophy and explains its essential disunity.

In the last chapter I looked at the arguments in early Christian philosophy corresponding to the first part of Origen's answer to Celsus just outlined: the demonstration that a 'true' Christianity around which heresies later clustered could be readily discerned in spite of them, that a tendency to division was no part of this primitive orthodoxy, and that, as a consequence, the objective observer had no reason to think that, if the truth lay in Christianity at all, its location would be indiscernible. (It would, of course, lie with the orthodoxy.) Furthermore, I showed that one of the consequences of the way in which this 'orthodoxy' was constructed was that traditional pagan theologies must also be considered later divergences from the Hebraeo-Christian tradition it represented—and could

[2] *Against Celsus*, 3. 12. Origen is here arguing that if Christian heresies are taken to have their impulse in 'true' Christianity at all, then they are only the result of attempts to interpret the Bible and seek for the truth as it quite rightly encouraged. I have shown that most Christians vigorously denied that the *source* of heresy lay within Christianity at all, maintaining that it sprang from the influence of pagan philosophy or the vices of the heretics themselves. However, Origen's relatively charitable account of the rise of Christian heresy here has parallels elsewhere in his work. He argues, for example, that heretics were inspired by demonic suggestion (*On First Principles*, 3. 3. 4, 260. 3–15 Koetschau), but is prepared to account for their actions by ignorance rather than malice (the actions, that is, both of the heretics and also of the daemons: see *On First Principles*, 3. 3. 3, 258. 15–259. 2 Koetschau). That is not to underestimate the danger of heresy: Origen identifies heretics as the 'foxes' described in the Song of Songs (*Commentary on the Song of Songs*, 3 [4], 236. 29–31 Baehrens); their doctrines, he says, were the building-blocks of the gates of hell (cf. *Commentary on St Matthew*, 12. 12, 91. 31–92. 5 Klosterman).

for this reason be safely ignored by the philosopher. The Christian argument against the pagans seems to be complete with this: but one difficulty still remains. For the Christian argument that pagan theological traditions (roughly speaking, pagan mythology) were corrupt divergences from the ancient Hebraeo-Christian orthodoxy demanded (this was the point of it) that these traditions could never come closer to the truth: as divergences from the truth, they would always tend to the worse. So the sudden emergence from them of Greek *philosophy*—that is to say, of the theological speculation of Plato, for example—comes as a very unwelcome surprise, however late in the day it appears. The Christians might well view this philosophy as superior to the mythological traditions which preceded it (although see further below for Origen himself); but in that case it looked like an *improvement*, and whether it was taken to represent the rise of a new tradition of thought *de novo* among the Greeks, or whether (as the Platonists themselves would have claimed) it was after all to be explained by their reconstruction of earlier wisdom through the older traditions available to them, it presented a historical turn of some embarrassment to the logic of the Christian argument. Pagan mythology might be a path leading *away* from the primitive truth; but pagan philosophy might look (even, or especially, to a Christian) like an attempt to overcome the faults inherent in their earlier tradition to build a road leading back there. The Christians as a whole had to explain this development, and they had to be able to do it in a way that would convince the objective observer that the same defects, the same essential weaknesses, which led to the divergences of the pagans' theological traditions remained present in their new philosophical study as well, so that someone travelling the Greek philosophical route would still stand no chance of actually reaching the truth. And one way in which they did it was to invoke the aid of a theme already (and conveniently) familiar from earlier Jewish apologetic. Greek philosophy, Christians argued, owed its rise to contact with the philosophy of the Hebraeo-Christian tradition: the inherent tendency towards disagreement among the pagans ensured that it could not have come about without this contact, and likewise that it could not but have gone seriously wrong once the contact was lost. In its own way, Greek philosophy was also a divergence from Hebraeo-Christian thought; and if its origins there explained what seemed positive in it, the Greeks' approach to its use remained as corrupt as ever—which accounts for the obvious difficulties it encountered. This, then, is the last of the three elements of the Christian response to Platonism that I outlined at the beginning of the last chapter: what one commentator (Ridings 1995: 24) has called the 'dependency theme'.

2. *Overview of the Theme*

The Christian argument for the dependency of pagan philosophy on Christian thought is one that has occasioned much interest, some debate, and not a little embarrassment. Henry Chadwick, for example, has said of it that it 'sounds too much like the quaint claim that the Greeks derived their culture from Ghana, or that St Paul founded the Church of England on his roundabout route to Spain' (1966: 14).[3] In a more recent study of the topic as it occurs in Clement, Eusebius, and Theodoretus, Daniel Ridings (1995), recognizing that the motif was too prevalent in Christian thought to be dismissed out of hand in this way, still concluded that the purpose of the dependency motif was more rhetorical than philosophical. The Christians, he argued, wished to show that the pagans, in imitating Christian wisdom, thereby accorded it the highest form of flattery. But even this, I think, misses much of the point of the argument—certainly as it was used by the Christians. It is true (as I suggested in Chapter 4) that the earliest accusations of pagan borrowing in *Jewish* apologetic—notably in the works of Artapanus and Aristobulus—probably were developed as part of an attempt to correct the negative characterization of Jewish culture by the Greeks. But I also showed that the polemical situation had already changed by the later Hellenistic and early Imperial periods: that, when Philo and Josephus accused the pagans of borrowing from Judaic philosophy, they must have done so for a far more substantive philosophical purpose. Philo and Josephus needed to show that Jewish wisdom was *older* than any that the pagans could pretend to, in particular that it was not just a debased form of Egyptian wisdom (as their detractors had started to claim), in order to show that it was worth taking seriously as philosophy at all.[4]

[3] Molland (1936: 63) simply says that the accusation of theft is 'rather unworthy of a thinker like Clement'—though, we would have to add, of thinkers like Justin, Tatian, Theophilus, Tertullian, Hippolytus, Origen, Eusebius, Theodoretus, Augustine, and, in a word, the whole of the Patristic tradition as well.

[4] A failure to distinguish the use made of the theme by writers such as Philo and

It is important to note that Greek philosophers used the theme in their attacks on the Christians as well. Celsus, for example, accused the Jews and Christians of theft on a number of occasions. He accused Moses of basing his narrative of the Tower of Babel on a story in Homer (Origen, *Against Celsus*, 4. 21, inviting us to compare Genesis, 11. 1–9, with Homer, *Iliad*, 5. 385–7, and *Odyssey*, 11. 305–20), Moses and the prophets of basing certain of their doctrines on a misunderstanding of Plato (*Against Celsus*, 6. 7), Jesus of stealing from Plato his doctrine that it is hard for the rich man to enter the kingdom of God (*Against Celsus*, 6. 16 with reference to Plato, *Laws*, 743 A), and the Christians generally of deriving their notion of heaven from 'certain ancient men of ancient times whom [Celsus] regards as divinely inspired, and in particular from Plato' (*Against Celsus*, 7. 28: Celsus cites Homer, *Odyssey*, 4. 563–5, and Plato, *Phaedo*, 109 A–B). We know that Celsus was not alone in making these kinds of accusation,[5] but it is worth concentrating on his witness because in his case alone we know a great deal about the context in which he made them, and can see what they added to his attack. Celsus' whole point was that pagan philosophy (Platonism in particular, one assumes) was validated by its reception and preservation of primitive wisdom through the ancient philosophical traditions, and that Christianity was philosophically discredited as an innovative form of a divergent offshoot of this tradition. So, when Celsus accused the Jews and Christians of stealing from pagan thought, we know that he was not (just) canvassing *respect* for his own beliefs: he was actually in the process of supporting his claims for their validity against the Christian alternative. Presumably, Celsus believed that the innate corruption of the Christian tradition meant that such positive features as it did contain could only be explained by appealing to forces lying outside of it: it could not have developed these insights unaided, so it must have bor-

Josephus from that made of it by earlier Jewish writers seems to lie behind Hengel's claim that the Jews 'do not know the later Christian polemical idea of the "Theft of the Philosophers"'. See Hengel (1974), 166 n. 387, quoted approvingly at Ridings (1995), 232 (cf. 38). Cf. also Roth (1978), 66.

[5] Tertullian, at *Apology*, 47. 2, i. 286. 7 Oehler (quoted below), suggests that the similarities caused by the pagans' dependency on Christian philosophy led *them* to accuse the *Christians* of theft. Later on, the Platonist Amelius, a pupil of Plotinus, apparently argued that St John the Evangelist 'stole' his account of the divine Logos from Heraclitus: see Eusebius, *Preparation for the Gospel*, 11. 19. 1, 540 B–C. This claim, at least, has been repeated more recently: cf. in particular Kelber (1958), 35–7.

rowed them from the prior tradition of the Greeks. If this is right, then it should also be clear that the dependency theme was of great philosophical importance to the Christians—or, rather, that it was an important part of a wider argument for the philosophical validity of Christian orthodoxy. For the Christians needed to provide an account of pagan philosophy that would enable the objective observer to compare it with Christian thought and see that the latter might, but that the former could not, help one discover the truth. The dependency theme assisted them in doing this. Providing evidence for the dependence of Greek on Christian philosophy, the Christians were able to show that the pagans just were not, by nature, philosophers in a true or rigorous sense, that their philosophy could only be explained in terms which made it subordinate and inferior to the Hebraeo-Christian tradition. Furthermore, the factions and disagreements which arose among pagan philosophers could be taken to show that they did not, even at this stage, shake off their love of disputation for a love of the truth instead. The Christian hypothesis of dependency explains seductive similarities between pagan and Hebraeo-Christian thought: but it also, more importantly, explains why we should not suppose that the former might ever lead us closer to the truth.

3. *Tertullian on Pagan Philosophy*

In the foregoing I have outlined the Christian dependency theme in a way that generalizes across what is, in fact, a very varied collection of arguments. I have done this, however, to emphasize the unity of purpose that lay behind these various attempts to account for pagan philosophy—and the common root they have within a broadly 'Platonic' approach to the history of philosophy and the vindication of Christian thought. In what follows, I shall attempt to add some refinement to this account by taking as object-studies the individual cases of Justin and Clement (who have been the subject of particular misunderstanding on this score); and I shall look finally at the approach to the question and the wider context of his answer to Celsus adopted by Origen himself. But to start with, and to set the scene, I want to look first at the argument to be found in Clement's Latin contemporary, Tertullian. The following quotation comes abbreviated—long though it is—from *Apology*, 47. 1–14 (i. 286. 1–290. 17 Oehler):[6]

The truth is older than everything, unless I'm mistaken; and the antiquity of divine literature, previously demonstrated [cf. Tertullian, *Apology*, 19], helps me here: it makes it more easily believed that it was the storehouse for all later wisdom—and if I were not moderating the weight of the present volume, I would run through this proof as well. What poet or sophist has not drunk at the fountain of the prophets at all? From it the philosophers have slaked the thirst of their intellect (so that it is the things they have of ours which lead them to compare *us* to *them*). This is why, I think, philosophy has also been driven out by some—by the Thebans, I mean, and the Spartans and Argives: while they try to imitate our doctrines, these men who, as I have said, lust after glory and eloquence only, turned to serve their own purposes anything they stumbled on in the collection of sacred Scripture through their own habitual curiosity . . . [4] For wherever there was simplicity of truth, so much the more would human scruples alter it, disdaining faith, so that they mixed uncertainties even into those certainties they found. Having found just God, they did not discuss him as they found him, so that they disputed over his quality and nature and place.

Tertullian here gives examples of pagan philosophical disagreement, not only over the nature of god, but also over the nature of the universe and of soul. He continues at 47. 10:

But to those who debase what is ours, we at once object that the criterion of truth is that which has been transmitted from Christ through his companions, by whom these various 'interpreters' will be proved to be somewhat later. Everything opposed to the truth has been built from the truth itself . . . [13] From where, I ask you, do such similarities with poets or philosophers come? Nowhere but from our mysteries. And if they come from our mysteries, which are earlier, then our philosophy is more reliable, and more believable, since even its imitations find faith among you.

Tertullian's argument in this passage is focused on twin claims, for the antiquity of Christian thought, and for the essentially disputatious nature of pagan philosophy. But, while Tertullian refers the reader elsewhere for substantiation of the former claim, he still need to justify the latter. That pagan philosophy contains disagreement is certain, but that it is *essentially* factional such that none of the paths it offers could lead to the truth needs to be argued. Tertullian, then, uses the hypothesis that the pagans borrowed from

[6] And cf. Tertullian, *To the Nations*, 2. 2, for something rather similar.

Christianity to weave a much tighter account of philosophical history and to argue more fully that Christianity is not only worth considering in its own terms, but is objectively *preferable* to pagan philosophy for someone seeking the truth. He notes that the pagan philosophical tradition has very recent roots, and he notes that there are remarkable similarities between some Greek doctrines and elements of very ancient Hebraeo-Christian thought; then he asks the obvious questions: *Why so late and how so similar?*

It should be noted that Tertullian (not alone among Christian writers who accused the pagans of theft) was well aware of the possibility and even the plausibility of appealing to the kinds of explanation that his twentieth-century critics would rather he had used at this point: he was, for example, prepared to countenance the possibility that *chance* played a role in the similarity between Christian and pagan philosophy; he also acknowledged that, in so far as the Greeks were rational animals as all men are, they might have been capable of working towards the same kinds of truth for themselves (both of these possibilities are raised at *On the Soul*, 2. 1, ii. 558. 8–13 Oehler). Tertullian realizes that it is a bold move to accuse the pagans of theft, that however much Christian-seeming wealth they have about them, it would never be possible now to catch them with their hands in the till. But neither of these options, he thinks, answers the facts of the case so well or so fully as the hypothesis that the pagans borrowed from Hebrew Scripture—a hypothesis for which he can, by the way, find some corroboration in the Greeks' own claim that the early geniuses of their philosophical tradition had travelled the world in search of barbarian wisdom.[7] In particular, what neither option does is to explain the late appearance of philosophical wisdom among the Greeks. The hypothesis of theft provides a much better starting-point for an explanation of this. But it is not on its own quite enough. For Tertullian's argument is not simply that if Greek philosophy arose later than Hebrew thought it must have arisen from contact with it (*post hoc ergo propter hoc*)—it would be too weak to command much attention if it were. It is rather (and crucially) conjoined with the suggestion that the Greeks' approach to philosophy was essentially corrupt—that they were driven by a love of glory rather than a love

[7] Compare the reference to the Greeks' 'curiosity' at *Apology*, 47. 3, i. 287. 1 Oehler, with *On the Soul*, 2. 4, ii. 559. 9–10 Oehler: 'It is believable that a man in search of wisdom may, out of curiosity, have gone to the prophets themselves.'

of the truth.[8] It is this addition to the hypothesis, suggested by the observable fact that Greek philosophy is full of disagreement,[9] which allows the full hypothesis to provide the real explanation for why the pagans did not develop philosophy earlier. Quite simply, they lacked the necessary qualities. If they had possessed a love of the truth, they would have developed philosophy earlier, and they would not have fallen into disagreement in the way that they did. But, driven instead by a love of glory and dispute, they could only have acquired philosophical ideas from elsewhere, and it was inevitable that they should fall into debate about even them. This hypothesis is the only way in which Tertullian is able to explain what seems positive in Greek philosophy, while also explaining the late genesis of the tradition and the fractious course of its subsequent history. And, as the end result of all this, it guarantees for the objective observer that, despite its apparently positive components, Greek philosophy is *essentially* rotten, that it could not be *even* as likely as the Christian orthodoxy to constitute a path to the truth.

4. *Justin on Pagan Philosophy*

Tertullian considered that 'chance' or 'shared rationality' could in principle be used to explain similarities between pagan and Christian philosophy: though, as we have seen, neither of these possibilities had for him sufficient explanatory power to recommend themselves strongly. Justin, however, seems at times more optimistic for the potential of pagan rationality. He refers on various occasions to an 'inborn seed of reason' (*logos*), or (what seems to be a related concept) 'seminal reason', at least a 'part' of which is present in every man.[10] And the presence of this fragment of *logos*

[8] And cf. Tertullian, *To the Nations*, 2. 2. 4, i. 352. 8 Oehler; also *Against Marcion*, 5. 20. 1, ii. 333. 8–15 Oehler, quoting Paul, Philippians 1: 14–17.

[9] And see further on the disagreement of Greek philosophers Tertullian, *On the Soul*, 2. 4, ii. 559. 11–12 Oehler: 'You will find in them more diversity than community, since even in community their diversity is discernible.'

[10] Cf. *I Apology*, 44. 8–10 (as quoted below); *II Apology*, 8. 1, 13. 3. The source of Justin's terminology here has been hotly (and fruitlessly) debated. One camp links it with the Stoic term 'spermatic reason' (σπερματικὸς λόγος): cf. H. Meyer (1914), 87 ff.; Pohlenz (1959), i. 412–13; Dillon (1996), 137. But there is no evidence for the use of this phrase in an epistemological context in the Stoa: 'spermatic reason' is rather used by the Stoics in a broadly biological sense to refer to the creative and generative principle of the cosmos (e.g. D.L. 7. 136, S.E. *M.* 9. 101) or, in the plural, to generative principles of animals or things more generally within the cosmos (*SVF* ii. 717, 739, 986, 1027; Cornutus, *Introduction*, 27, 49. 10 Lang; cf. Plutarch, *Table-*

in every person allows people to discover the rational order of the universe: allows them, in fact, to gain the truth by the practice of philosophy. So *II Apology*, 10. 2 (and cf. 13. 3):

Whatever was properly maintained and discovered by philosophers or law-givers had been worked out by them from the discovery and contemplation of part of the *logos*.

And, famously, Justin thinks that some pagan authors have made such good use of their rationality that they became Christians in all but name. So *I Apology*, 46. 3:

Those who live by reason [*logos*] are also Christians, even if they were considered to be godless: among the Greeks, Socrates and Heraclitus and men like them; among barbarians, Abraham, Ananias, Azarias, Misael, Elias, and many others.

But what do these passages actually tell us? Not as much as has often been supposed. For commentators have been tempted to read Justin's ascription of *logos* to the Greeks as a theory explaining their philosophy as the product of divine dispensation—even of divine inspiration; in any case, of the unaided contact that their reason allowed them with the truth.[11] However, if we are told that the pagans possessed (seeds of) *rationality*, it would be very wrong to conclude

talk, 2. 3, 637 A). Other commentators have given the phrase a Middle Platonist origin, or see a fusion of Stoic and Platonist elements in the term (so Andresen 1952–3: 157 ff., 170–7; Holte 1958; Dawson 1992: 191–2), or say (as Price 1988) that it is a standard term in the philosophical vocabulary of the age. There are suggestive parallels with Philo (cf. *Who is the Heir?*, 119, *Allegory of the Laws*, 3. 150), but it is not clear that the phrase is a technical (rather than a descriptive) term for him, and Dawson (loc. cit.) may be too optimistic in linking these references with Numenius' image of the Demiurge, as a 'planter' who 'plants' souls in individual men (fr. 13 des Places with n. 2 on p. 108 of his edition; and cf. Krämer 1964: 83 n. 213 as cited there).

[11] Cf. e.g. Price (1988), 20, who thinks that the passages under question indicate that all men (pagans included) have 'innate knowledge of the divine truth'. Lilla (1971: 23–5) suggests, rather cumbersomely, that the pagans have been vouchsafed their own *revelation* of Christ. But these passages only say that all men, *qua* rational beings, have reason—the potential to access the truth. It might be objected that this is too weak a position to maintain in the face of an identification of reason (*logos*) with Christ (the Logos). But there is a close and familiar analogy to this in Greek thought: many Greek philosophers (from Heraclitus onwards) supposed that the subjective possession of reason involved precisely sharing in the objective rationality of the universe—which might itself be identified with god (as in the case of the Stoics). Yet no Greek writer ever thought, when he said this, that all rational animals *understand* the universe (or at least, understand it correctly) merely by virtue of being rational in this way.

that this guaranteed them an insight into the truth. There are, after all, innumerable ways of being rationally wrong: to have reason is not yet to have *right* reason, or truth. Nor do the 'Christian' lives of Socrates and Heraclitus support the idea that the pagans (that any pagans) had been granted a philosophical revelation. This is something that becomes clear when the passage quoted above is seen in its proper context. For Justin is here not discussing the general state of pagan philosophy, but considering the following *moral* objection that someone might raise against Christianity:[12] If a knowledge of Christ is necessary for a virtuous life (so the objection goes), then it would seem that no one who lived before the advent of Christ could be properly responsible for his actions: he would have lacked the knowledge necessary to be virtuous, and, under the circumstances, his vice could hardly be counted as culpable. In answer to this objection, Justin says (at *I Apology*, 46. 2) that 'Christ is the first-born of God, and we have declared above [cf. e.g. *I Apology*, 5; also 63] that he is Reason [*logos*] of which every race of men were partakers: and so those who lived by reason are also Christians' (and so on as in the passage already quoted). In other words, Justin answers *first* (as we ought by now to have expected) that Christianity represents no *new* revelation of truth (something which may, by the way, account for the virtue at least of Abraham, who already had knowledge of Christ);[13] but then *second* that Christian morality is essentially reasonable anyway. Someone who lives according to reason is to that extent living *as a Christian would live*—and a moral distinction can be drawn between this individual and a person who lives contrary to reason. But the fact that Socrates and Heraclitus led, according to Justin, *reasonable* lives emphatically does not suggest that they had profited from divine revelation of the truth—and certainly not, to move the question beyond that of ethics, that their wider philosophy (let alone the philosophy of the pagan world as a whole) was equal to a Christian understanding of the universe. Justin thinks that the 'seed of reason' in the Greeks enabled some of them to live rational lives (and to that extent Christian lives *de facto*); but it did

[12] Such an accusation is attested for Porphyry: cf. *Against the Christians*, frr. 81–2 Harnack.

[13] Cf. *I Apology*, 63 (with reference to Exodus 3: 6), from which it appears that the truth (i.e. Christ) appeared in full to Jacob and to Isaac as well. Justin emphasizes, against the understanding of the (later) Jews, that it was Christ and *not* God the Father and Creator who appeared.

not (at least, not directly) explain the growth of *philosophy* as such among them.[14]

The presence of a 'seed of reason' in man does not *directly* explain the development of philosophy in the Greeks: but it turns out that it does so *indirectly*. This seed of reason does not *give* the Greeks the truth, but it allows them to *recognize* it when they see it—and where might they have seen it, except in Hebrew Scripture? *I Apology*, 44. 8–10:

And so too Plato, when he said 'The blame is his who chooses: God is blameless' [*Republic*, 10, 617 E 4–5], said it having taken it from the prophet Moses—for Moses is more ancient than all Greek writers. And everything that the philosophers and poets have said concerning the immortality of the soul, or its punishment after death, or the contemplation of the heavens, or similar doctrines, they have been able to grasp and expound because they took their starting-points from the prophets.[15] *Hence there seem to be seeds of truth among all men*; but they are proved not to understand it accurately when they contradict themselves.

Note the *hence* (ὅθεν) in this passage: here, at least, Justin does not posit direct inspiration as the means by which pagan came to have similarities with Christian philosophy. Rather the opposite: he *deduces* the presence in it of what he here calls 'seeds of truth' from the fact that the Greeks *must* have borrowed from the Christians. These 'seeds of truth' (by which Justin presumably means again the innate seeds of *logos*, or rationality, from which the truth can grow) do not obviate the need for the Greeks to steal from the Hebraeo-Christian

[14] Justin elsewhere draws a contrast between the philosophy of even the best Greeks and the perfect philosophy of the Christians. At *II Apology*, 8. 1–3, he argues *a fortiori* that, if the daemons were moved to inspire persecution of the Stoics, of Heraclitus, and, 'more recently', of Musonius (presumably the 1st-cent.-AD Stoic; cf. also *I Apology*, 5, for the daemons' vicarious persecution of Socrates), then it is no wonder that they also inspired persecution of the Christians, who had a perfect knowledge of Christ (i.e. by contrast with even the best of the pagans).

[15] Cf. *I Apology*, 59–60, where Justin argues that Plato's account of the creation of the world by God from unformed matter derives from Genesis, 1; and the poetical notion of Erebus is ascribed to Moses in this passage (a reference to Deuteronomy, 32. 22). Justin takes Plato's reference to the letter chi in his account of God's formation of the universe (*Timaeus*, 36 B–C) to be a reference to the 'cross' set up by Moses in the wilderness (Numbers, 21. 8–9, although the Hebrew says 'pole', *nēs*; cf. LXX σημεῖον)—which is in turn a type of the Cross of Calvary (cf. already the Gospel of John at 3: 14 and the *Letter of Barnabas*, 12. 5–7 with Daniélou 1958–78: i. 106–7). In this case, however, Justin believes that Plato copied the symbol while missing the symbolism of it.

tradition, but rather allow them to do it.[16] It seems most satisfactory to suppose that Justin's strategy is much the same as Tertullian's: that he is also prompting us to ask why Greek philosophy only began when it did, why it came about much later than the first revelations of Christian thought—and that *despite* the possession of rationality by the Greeks. The answer, again, is that the Greeks tended to *misuse* their reason—which explains the disagreement and contradiction prevalent in their tradition.[17] The history of pagan philosophy—including its chronology, its apparent strengths, and its obvious weaknesses—can again only be understood if we ascribe its origins to contact with Hebraeo-Christian thought, and see that its practitioners are essentially driven by the wrong motives. Once again, the hypothesis, for so long as it holds, gives the objective observer a reason to suppose that Greek philosophy could never improve on Christian thought: that it owes everything of real value to it, and tends to corrupt what it has. There is no reason to suspect even equipollence between the two traditions.

5. *Clement of Alexandria on Pagan Philosophy*

According to Justin and Tertullian, the very existence of pagan philosophy could only be explained by the hypothesis of contact

[16] This goes some way towards meeting Harnack, who, believing that Justin attributes a direct revelation of Christ to the pagans, finds it inconsistent that he posits additional sources of dependency on Hebraeo-Christian thought. Given the role of the Logos, he says, there should have been no need at all for the pagans to steal from Scripture, and no advantage for Justin in claiming that they did. See Harnack (1894–7), i. 384 n. 2; cf. Puech (1928–30), i. 128; also Holte (1958), 112–13. But on my reading Justin's accusation of theft is only in *theory* an independent source of the truth for the pagans: in practice it is actually a *counterpart* to the claim for their direct acquaintance with Hebrew Scripture: reason (*logos*) shows that there is something worth stealing here in the first place. (One might also note that Harnack's account of Justin could at best imply that his theory is otiose, not that it is actually contradictory; and it may not even be able to do that, since Plato's supposed adoption of the symbol of the cross in the *Timaeus*—see again n. 15—would be poorly explained by 'revelation' if, as Justin says, he copied the symbol, but had no inkling of its real symbolic value.) There is a third route of dependency suggested by Justin, and considered by Harnack as part of the 'inconsistency': Justin says that pagan mythology was inspired by daemons who wanted to parody the Christian message (*I Apology*, 54, 62; *II Apology*, 5). I shall not discuss these passages further here, since I am interested in the explanation of pagan philosophy, not mythology; it is, however, enough to say against Harnack that Justin makes a clear distinction between the two things, and finds the achievements of the former more problematic than the degeneracies of the latter, so that there is no inconsistency or even superfluity here either.

[17] For which see *I Apology*, 44. 10; *II Apology*, 10. 3, with *Dialogue*, 2. 1–2.

with the Hebraeo-Christian tradition. There simply *was* no pagan philosophy to speak of before the pagans came into contact with Hebrew Scripture, nor is it likely that there could have been. But while it might be the case that suggestively 'Christian' theological doctrines only surfaced among Greek philosophers of the fifth century, this theory ignores the fact that the pagans as a whole had developed certain other branches of philosophy (notably, for example, mathematics and astronomy) to a very high level, and very early on. One could, of course, accommodate this fact into the theory by distinguishing between truths that matter and truths that do not—the truths, in Tertullian's famous distinction, of Jerusalem and Athens respectively.[18] Nevertheless, if Christ is identified with reason—if, that is, all truth is Christian truth, because the world was created through Christ who is Reason and Truth—one cannot afford to be utterly dismissive even of 'Athenian' wisdom. And according to Clement of Alexandria, it was possible to take its achievements quite seriously, but to use even them in confirming the essential degeneracy of the pagan philosophical tradition.

Like Justin, again, Clement acknowledged that the pagans had rationality too; but unlike Justin, he allowed that they discovered a great deal on the basis of it. The Egyptians developed geometry, for example, the Babylonians developed astronomy, and the Thracians were noted for their development of medicine (see especially *Protrepticus*, 6. 70. 1; and cf. *Stromata*, 1. 14–16). And so, through these more ancient traditions, he allowed that the Greeks might ultimately trace their philosophical tradition back to the very first men (*Stromata*, 6. 7. 57. 3):

> . . . if I come to Pythagoras and Pherecydes and Thales and the first wise men [i.e. among the Greeks], I come to a stand in my search for their teacher. Should you say the Egyptians, the Indians, the Babylonians, or the Magi themselves, I will not stop from asking who their teacher was. And I lead you back to the first generation of men.

But the enquiry has still not gone far enough. 'From *that* point,' says Clement (picking up where the quotation above leaves off), 'I begin to investigate who is their teacher.' *Who taught the first generation of men?* Rather like Cornutus (as we saw in Chapter 3), Clement was not prepared to suppose that philosophy arose spontaneously in man—possibly because, like Cornutus, he thought that the pas-

[18] Cf. *Prescription of Heretics*, 7, ii. 10. 1–2 Oehler.

sions of man would not, without external help, naturally encourage the development of philosophy (that is, a search for the truth, as opposed to a more self-serving employment of rationality). In any case, Clement's answer to the question was similar in its own way to Cornutus' answer as well: primitive man, if he practised philosophy, must have been led to do so by the divine.[19] In particular, he must have been led to it by Christ—who is Reason, who gave rational order to creation, and who is (therefore) the fountainhead and end point of rational enquiry.[20]

The Greeks, of course, were not likely to accept that Christ was ultimately at the head of their tradition: nevertheless, with an appropriate pagan substitution, the Platonists might well find much to agree with in this picture of the history of their philosophy. Indeed, it looks as if Clement has conceded everything to them: their tradition was of the highest antiquity, developed independently, and developed from roots which were (at least) as good as those at the basis of Hebraeo-Christianity. But this very concession is now the basis for Clement's demonstration of the inherent decadence of the pagan tradition. According to Clement, the fact that pagan philosophy has such ancient roots only draws attention to the very late (and then not very systematic) development of a more

[19] *Stromata*, 6. 7. 57. 4: 'No *man* could have originated philosophy, *for men had not yet been taught* [οὐδέπω γὰρ μεμαθήκεσαν].' Cf. also *Stromata*, 6. 18. 166. 4: 'The only wisdom is God-taught, on which all the springs of wisdom depend which aim at the truth.' For Cornutus see *Introduction*, 20, 39. 12–40. 4 Lang.

[20] We should not, with Clement any more than with Justin, be tempted to think that an attribution of shared *logos* to men in any way leads to the claim that even the pagans are *inspired* by God—*pace* Lilla (1971), 16–27, but especially 17. For a critical discussion of Lilla's proof-texts ('in all cases . . . he ignores the context in which they are found, with one exception . . . where the context is so problematic, that he explains it away with a radical emendation of the text'), see Ridings (1995), 41–5. Ridings does not tackle Lilla's use of *Stromata*, 5. 5. 29, to show that Plato and Pythagoras were inspired with a spirit of prophecy, but here too the context refutes his claim. The passage is actually concerned with the Greeks' encounter with Hebrew thought, and it seems far more likely that the references to 'prophecy' relate to the Hebrews than to the pagans. Finally, Daniélou (1958–78: ii. 54–5) cites *Stromata*, 6. 5. 42. 3, where God gave as 'prophets' to the Greeks those men of their nation 'most distinguished in dialectic in proportion as they were capable of receiving the goodness of God'. But in this passage Clement is referring simply to the fact that a philosopher becomes useful to his fellow men *to the extent that* he achieves true philosophical insight. That the Greek philosophers are called 'prophets' in this context is exceptional, and clearly metaphorical: but Clement wants to emphasize the function which Greek philosophy has as a *surrogate* and preparation for the Christian revelation. He calls the philosophers 'prophets' in exactly the same spirit as that in which, at another point, he calls philosophy itself 'a sort of covenant' (*Stromata*, 6. 8. 67. 1).

'Christian' conception of god such as was to be found, for example, in Plato. In fact, he argues, a survey of earlier pagan philosophy shows that the pagans did not have it within their own approach to philosophy at all to elevate themselves to these higher realms of thought: while the course of true philosophy lies towards the heavens, pagan thought had remained instead essentially earth-bound.[21] Instead of theology, the pagans had developed only a crude mythology, which (drawing on Euhemeristic and allegorical exegesis of a kind employed by the Greeks themselves) Clement characterizes as a form of idolatry, aiming at worship of the created, not the Creator.[22] The pagans' own philosophical tradition might be ancient and independent, but they had still known 'nothing beyond this world' (*Stromata*, 6. 7. 56. 1). Any hints at a higher conception of god in later stages of their historical development could *only*, Clement argued, be explained by forces outside of their own tradition: could only be explained by theft. And so Clement, like Justin and Tertullian, accused the philosophers of Classical Greece of stealing from Hebrew Scripture: indeed, he claimed that all of the 'higher' philosophy of Greece, notably their advances in the fields of ethics and theology, must have been taken from the Jews (*Protrepticus*, 6. 70. 1–5; cf. also e.g. *Stromata*, 1. 22. 150; 1. 25. 165).[23] The pagan tradition gave no hint of a development towards higher levels of theological understanding; yet, just at the moment in history when we know that Greek thinkers were travelling the world (but in particular to Egypt) in search of ancient wisdom, Plato suddenly introduced a much more sublime notion of godhead than anything that pagan mythology had prepared us for, a notion of a monotheistic, even a trinitarian god which is really rather close to that supposedly contained very much earlier in Hebrew texts.[24]

[21] Compare Augustine, *City of God*, 18. 39; also Eusebius, *Ecclesiastical History*, 1. 2. 1–22; and something similar already in Tatian, *Oration*, 1.

[22] See all of *Protrepticus*, 2–4. Cf. similar characterizations of traditional pagan theology at e.g. Aristides, *Apology*, 13; Tatian, *Oration*, 21; Athenagoras, *Embassy*, 28–30; Lactantius, *Divine Institutes*, 1. 8–23; 2. 1–7; cf. Hippolytus, *Refutation*, 10. 32, 288. 23–5 Wendland.

[23] Clement focuses particular attention on Plato, whom he describes as a 'zealous admirer of Moses' (*Pedagogue*, 3. 11. 54. 2; cf. also 1. 8. 67; 2. 10. 100; *Stromata*, 1. 15. 66–9)—a fact which presumably reflects his own conviction that Plato is the best of Greek philosophers (*Pedagogue*, 3. 11. 54. 2), and so in need of the most explanation. A comprehensive list of the Hebraeo-Christian thought found by Clement in pagan philosophy can be found at Ridings (1995), 112–17.

[24] Clement, like other Christian thinkers, sees evidence of trinitarianism in Plato's

It should be noted that Clement's argument works the other way round as well. For if the sudden appearance in pagan philosophy of theological insights which cannot be explained in terms of their earlier tradition proves that these insights were the result of dependency on the Hebraeo-Christian tradition, and not of their own philosophical abilities, the fact that thinkers such as Plato felt the *need* to steal from the Hebrews likewise provides evidence that the pagans themselves could acknowledge the defects of their own prior tradition. Once again, the hypothesis of theft is closely bound up with the demonstration (which is, after all, the real point of the argument) that the pagans are in themselves incapable of pursuing philosophy towards its proper conclusion.

Clement often characterizes pagan philosophy as a *propaedeutic*, and it sometimes sounds as if the pagans were only ever supposed to be prepared by it for the coming of Christ—one of whose functions was to make the theology once restricted to the Hebrew tradition available to the whole of mankind (cf. *Stromata*, 6. 17. 153 with 7. 3. 20). Given this, it might seem strange of Clement to criticize the pagans for failing to attain (except, on occasion, by theft) the theological insights that their philosophy was only intended to prepare them for. But, as we have seen, Clement's point was not just that the pagans had failed to reach the end of philosophy, and had become trapped in the mundane: his point was rather that the extent of their failure was the result of their *abuse* of philosophy, the fact that, beyond a certain point, they were no longer even, as it were, pointing in the right direction. And if the idolatrous byroads down which their own theologies had variously strayed drew attention to this negative trait in pagan philosophy, the history of later Greek school philosophy made it clear that it was a trait that they never overcame, even after the remedial injections of Hebrew theology into their systems of thought. It is significant that Clement applies to the pagans exactly the same image as Numenius had used of the Hellenistic successors of Plato (*Stromata*, 1. 13. 57. 1):[25]

Second Epistle: see *Stromata*, 5. 14. 103 (and compare e.g. Justin, *I Apology*, 60; Athenagoras, *Embassy*, 23. 7). Clement adds plausibility to his claim that the Greeks stole from the Jews by associating the 'theft' with their admitted borrowings from other of the ancient nations. If, as we shall see below, the Greeks could have taken geometry from the Egyptians, astronomy from the Babylonians, and medicine from the Thracians (to employ only the most important examples), then why not the notion of God from the Jews? See *Protrepticus*, 6. 70. 1, and cf. *Stromata*, 1. 15–16.

[25] See Numenius fr. 24. 71–3 des Places with my discussion in ch. 7. Clement

There being, then, one truth (for falsehood has ten thousand bypaths), the sects [αἱρέσεις] of barbarian and Greek philosophy are just like the Bacchae tearing apart the limbs of Pentheus, and each boasts that the portion which has fallen to it is the whole truth.

God, in his providence, made philosophy—and potentially, through that philosophy, the knowledge of God—available to the Greeks; but the Greeks' *use* of philosophy had been, and remained, exactly the opposite of what it should have been. What truth they discovered through reason (or, presumably, theft) they sooner or later tore apart, and in doing so stunted the progress of their tradition. The development of their philosophical history was doomed to increasing fragmentation of just the kind already identified among the Hellenistic schools by Numenius.[26]

And all of this is what allows Clement, at another point in the *Stromata*, to characterize the *whole* of pagan philosophy as a 'theft' (see all of *Stromata*, 1. 17). He says this not because he thinks that every aspect of Greek philosophy was stolen from, or developed on the basis of contact with, Hebrew Scripture—as we have seen, this is not what he thinks at all. Nor does he say it because the tradition has its ultimate roots in Christ—there is nothing wrong with that. He rather says it precisely because the pagans had come to *misuse* the reason that they derived in the first place from Christ. The *purpose* of reason, says Clement, is to achieve an understanding of God: all other wisdom is the means towards this final purpose,[27]

of Alexandria is the earliest author to cite Numenius (*Stromata*, 1. 22. 150: cf. des Places 1973: 7), and it may be that he had direct knowledge of his use of this image. But cf. also Clement of Rome at I Clement 46, where the schisms within Christianity are said to 'divide and tear to pieces the members of Christ' (and compare Cyprian, *On the Unity of the Church*, 7, employing the image of the seamless garment divided by the soldiers).

[26] And so Clement suggests as a remedial measure an 'eclectic' approach to pagan thought that attempts to reunite these fragments: see *Stromata*, 1. 7. 37; cf. 1. 13. 57; something similar at Lactantius, *Divine Institutes*, 7. 7; and cf. again ch. 7 n. 20 for Numenius.

[27] Hence the *apparent* ambivalence over whether philosophy is something providential (as when Clement suggests that philosophy was deliberately handed to the Greeks by angels: cf. *Stromata*, 1. 17. 81; 5. 1. 10) or whether it is incidental (as when he says that it 'came from God to man, not as his primary purpose, but in the way that rain falls on good ground and on the rubbish heap and on the houses': *Stromata*, 1. 7. 37). In fact there is no conflict or ambivalence here at all: the gift of philosophy was providential in so far as it prepared the Greeks for the day when the full truth of Christianity would be made available to them (*Stromata*, 6. 8. 67; 6. 17. 153; 7. 2. 11); but incidental in so far as the Greeks would (until then) not use it for the

and it is because the pagans failed to use reason for this end that the fact that they used it at all can be characterized as a 'theft'. If the pagans had used reason well, as a means to find God, they would have used it as God had intended; but in appropriating it for ends it was never primarily intended for, they have, at the very least, breached the conditions of sale.

According to Clement, then, the pagan philosophical tradition was ancient, it was founded on reason—indeed, at one stage in history it was presumably right, as far as it went. But it diverged from the truth and its proper pursuit, as can be seen from the fact that thinkers such as Plato felt moved to turn their back on the theology it had come to represent and, as it were, tried to make a clean break for the truth by borrowing in elements of Hebraeo-Christian theology directly. Clement's account differs in details from those of Justin and Tertullian; but the point is very much the same, and the accusation of theft central to his argument that the truth, if discernible at all, would not be discernible in the corrupted environment of pagan philosophy. The occasional doctrine, stolen later on from the Jews, and the relative success of some of the older Greek philosophers who profited from this theft, might mislead one into thinking that pagan philosophy as a whole had the potential to lead one to the truth. But the wider history of pagan philosophy, both prior to but also (perhaps especially) since these thefts, shows that it remained essentially driven, not by a sincere desire for the truth, but by a selfish love of honour and contention.[28]

end for which it was intended. Cf. with this also *Stromata*, 1. 5. 28, where Clement begins by drawing a distinction between those things that are given 'primarily' (*κατὰ προηγούμενον*) on the one hand—he mentions the Old and New Testaments—and those that come as a consequence of something else (*κατὰ ἐπακολούθημα*). Although he gives philosophy as an example of the latter class, he goes on immediately to wonder whether philosophy was given to the Greeks in particular as a *primary* intention (*τάχα δὲ καὶ προηγουμένως τοῖς Ἕλλησιν ἐδόθη*). From this again we can see that Clement thought philosophy itself was a providential (i.e. deliberate) gift; but that the pagans' use of it made it a matter of chance (and to this extent 'incidental') that they gained any benefit from it at all.

[28] Cf. esp. *Stromata*, 8. 1. 1. 1–2. For love of honour (*φιλοτιμία*) and love of contention (*φιλονεικία*) see e.g. Clement, *Stromata*, 2. 21. 130. 1; 7. 11. 67. 6; for self-love (*φιλαυτία*) cf. *Stromata*, 6. 7 (esp. 56, where self-love is put down as the cause of all pagan error). Clement also uses this word in respect of the supposed 'theft' of Hebraeo-Christian material by Greek philosophers: so e.g. 1. 17. 87. 7, where the word comes from 2 Timothy 3: 2; cf. also 2. 1. 2; 6. 2. 27.

6. *Origen on Pagan Philosophy: An Alternative Approach*

The 'dependency' theme in its most familiar form—as an accusation of pagan 'theft' from the Christians—is used by thinkers such as Tertullian, Justin, and Clement to explain apparent reversals in pagan philosophical fortune during the Classical age, and to show in particular that the positive philosophical insights achieved by certain thinkers at that time did not represent the advance of their tradition, but had rather to be explained within the context of a model which confirmed its essential degeneracy. As I started this chapter with Origen's reply to Celsus' attacks, I shall end by considering an alternative approach suggested by him for the demonstration of the same ultimate position. For Origen did not accuse the pagans of theft (at least, such accusations did not form part of his general strategy against them).[29] He did not even believe that there was a reversal of fortune in the Classical pagan tradition (as we shall see, he accepted the validity of its older 'mythological' reflections more or less under the model offered by the Platonists). Nevertheless, he believed that that tradition could still be *best* explained as one that depended on the prior existence and superiority of the Christian truth. Most important of all, however, Origen wished, like all of his orthodox predecessors, to show thereby that the divisions apparent within the pagan tradition were endemic, and indicative of its incapacity to attain to the highest truth.

According to the Platonists, the ancient pagan traditions (subject to adequate exegesis) collectively preserved the philosophy and theology with which man was originally endowed by the gods. Origen largely concurs with them. That is to say, Origen allows that pagan philosophy embraced what (following the language of Paul at 1 Corinthians 2: 6–8) he refers to as 'the wisdom of this world'—

[29] Origen does consider the possibility of theft in other contexts: he suggests that the similarity between a passage in Plato's *Symposium* (Origen quotes from 203 B–E) and the Hebrew description of Paradise, if not the result of chance, might be explained by Greek acquaintance with Scripture (*Against Celsus*, 4. 39). Cf. also, again, *Commentary on the Song of Songs*, prologue 3, for the pagans' derivation of their threefold division of philosophy from Solomon. However, it might perhaps be the case that, having conceded third place to pagan philosophers in his ranking of theological achievement (after, that is, the 'mass of Christians' but before the idolaters: *Commentary on St John*, 2. 3, 56. 29–57. 7 Preuschen), Origen is reluctant to allow the pagans any kind of further insight which would encourage us to think that they might have risen further. For example, he explicitly passes up the opportunity at *Against Celsus*, 6. 18, to take the celebrated passage from Plato, *Epistle* 2, 312 E, as a reference to the trinitarian nature of God. The Hebrews, he says, did rather better than this.

such matters as 'poetry, grammar, rhetoric, geometry, and music, and, perhaps, medicine';[30] and also what he refers to (again, basing himself on Paul) as 'the wisdom of the princes of this world'[31]—which includes 'such things as the secret and hidden philosophy of the Egyptians, the astrology of the Chaldeans and Indians which promises knowledge of exalted matters, and also the manifold and various opinions of the Greeks about the divine'.[32] Origen readily concedes the validity of both of these traditions. The 'wisdom of this world' was, as developed by the pagans, valuable enough to be of service to the Christians themselves (*Letter to Gregory*, 2);[33] and the 'wisdom of the princes of this world' amounted, at least in Origen's somewhat heterodox outlook, to a relatively valid theology, since he himself believed in the divinity of the objects of its piety, the stars.[34] Furthermore, Origen allowed that both of these forms of wisdom came to the pagans from privileged and celestial sources: indeed, that they came from the 'gods'—or rather, to put this in Christian terms, from various classes of 'daemon'.[35] Origen's theory of pagan

[30] In short, he says, any study which does not concern itself with theological, moral, or (meta)physical issues: *On First Principles*, 3. 3. 2, 257. 19–25 Koetschau. Compare the list of subjects—also referred to as 'worldly wisdom'—which the Greek philosophers themselves consider 'ancillary' (ὡς συνερίθων φιλοσοφίᾳ) according to Origen, *Letter to Gregory*, 1: geometry, music, grammar, rhetoric, and astronomy. Astronomy is omitted from the list in *First Principles*, perhaps because in this context it would blur the distinction with pagan theology, the 'wisdom of the princes of this world', which Origen believed to be based on a recognition of the divinity of the stars (cf. below and n. 34).

[31] Origen argues that the 'rulers of this world' does not refer to *men*, but to the daemons who are appointed to the various nations: see *On First Principles*, 3. 3. 2, 257. 29–32 Koetschau; and cf. 4. 3. 12, 341. 11–14 Koetschau. The notion of daemons acting in this office is not novel to Origen: cf. e.g. Clement, *Stromata*, 6. 17. 157. The idea also occurs in the Jewish Christian *Recognitions* at 2. 42, and Daniélou (1951; 1958–78: i. 176–7, ii. 397–8) sees the origin of its belief in early Jewish Christian exegesis of the Babel narrative. However, parallels can be found in Greek thought as well: cf. e.g. Plato, *Statesman*, 271 D–E.

[32] *On First Principles* 3. 3. 2, 257. 25–8 Koetschau.

[33] Although elsewhere (and not necessarily inconsistently) Origen emphasizes the antiquity of all forms of Christian philosophy relative to Greek: cf. e.g. *Against Celsus*, 4. 11, 6. 7. Feldman (1990: 110) sees here an argument merely *ad hominem*; but no such explanation can be given of, for example, *Commentary on the Song of Songs*, prologue 3. 4, 75. 23–76. 4 Baehrens (and cf. 2. 5. 1–2, 141. 19–24 Baehrens).

[34] Origen's belief in the divinity of the stars (for which in general see Scott 1991) was formally anathematized in the 6th cent. See especially Justinian's *Letter to Menas* at *Acta Conciliorum Oecumenicorum*, iii. 213. 27–8 Schwarz; also the third of the fifteen anathemas against Origen and his followers promulgated by the Council of Justinian (at Straub 1971: 248. 14–16).

[35] See all of *On First Principles*, 3. 3. 2–3. For Christian identification of daemons

philosophy looks thus far—very much more even than Clement's—like the Platonists' own theory in Christian dress. So how did he derive from it a demonstration of the essential dependency of pagan on Christian wisdom? Or, more importantly, of the essential weakness of pagan philosophy such dependency might imply?

The answer, of course, lies in the fact that the 'gods' of Greek philosophy are themselves (as 'daemons') subordinate creatures within the Christian hierarchy. In so far as the pagans derived their philosophy from the 'gods', it must be dependent on and inferior to the highest Christian truth, which even these daemons could not have known: what Origen, completing his account of the different types of wisdom, calls the 'wisdom of God'.[36]

Origen, it should be noted, does not invoke the daemons as another way of asserting the 'theft' of Hebrew philosophy by the pagans: indeed, Origen never presents the work of the daemons in the light of a 'theft' at all. As we have seen, the accusation of theft as such was only of use to Origen's predecessors to explain the sudden emergence of 'philosophy' among the pagans after a long tradition of degenerate idolatry; but Origen has rejected the view that pagan philosophy did emerge in sudden opposition to their earlier theology, accepting the Platonists' claims of continuity between their theological and philosophical traditions. There was, for Origen,

with (or at least as the powers behind) the pagan gods cf. e.g. Athenagoras, *Embassy*, 23–6; Justin, *I Apology*, 5, 21, 62; Lactantius, *Divine Institutes*, 2. 15–18; also Origen himself at e.g. *Exhortation to Martyrdom*, 45; and further, for the generally negative assessment of the action of these daemons: Theophilus, *To Autolycus*, 2. 8. 56–61; Justin, *I Apology*, 54; ps.-Clement, *Recognitions*, 4. 13–19; *Homilies*, 4. 12. Origen himself believed that the daemons lurked as a malicious presence behind pagan idolatry (cf. again *Exhortation to Martyrdom*, 45). However, it is important to note that, so far as philosophical theology is concerned, the worst that he thinks can be said of the daemons is that they failed to pass on the 'wisdom of God'—and only then because they lacked knowledge of it themselves. He considers and rejects the possibility that they deliberately intended to deceive, at *On First Principles*, 3. 3. 3, 258. 15–259. 2 Koetschau. (And cf. already Clement, *Stromata*, 1. 17. 81.)

[36] *On First Principles*, 3. 3. 1, 256. 6–15 Koetschau. Origen's threefold distinction of wisdom is already foreshadowed in Clement, who, as we have already seen, distinguished between mundane and supra-mundane forms of wisdom, and posited in addition a Christian *gnōsis*—which, for him, was the end point of philosophical study. The most significant difference between the two schemes is that, while the 'supra-mundane' wisdom of the Greeks embraced what Clement believed the Greeks to have stolen from the Hebrews, the 'wisdom of the princes of the world' included for Origen a more autonomous level of theological insight, whose roots in the pagan tradition were essentially the same in kind as the roots of 'mundane' philosophy—in Origen's terminology, the 'wisdom of this world'.

very little that an accusation of 'theft', in the sense that Tertullian, Justin, and Clement had meant it, could help to explain. Rather, then, Origen posits a more general hypothesis of dependency as a means of undermining the impasse an objective observer might see between the claims of the pagans and Christians. Instead of challenging the pagans' historical model as such, asserting a distinction between their 'divergent' theological traditions and the appearance of philosophical insights among them, Origen rather *accepts* their model—arguing only that it needs to be supplemented by the recognition of a further and superior layer of philosophical insight unavailable in the pagan tradition. (The accommodation of the pagans' history of philosophy into his own, by the way, should not properly be viewed as a 'concession' to them by Origen. Rather, it represents a redrawing of the battle-line between him and the pagans, one that works very much to his advantage. For by claiming that the pagans were not so much *wrong* as only partially right, Origen will be able to say, at a later stage of his argument, that the objective observer's initial attraction to the pagan model is no reason for him to maintain suspension of judgement in the face of the conclusions that Origen will draw from his own. Never mind for now whether one or the other is right: the fact that Origen's model accommodates the pagans' account of their tradition ensures that the mere plausibility of the latter cannot provide reasons for doubting the former, so long as Origen succeeds in showing that it has the superior explanatory power. If he does succeed in doing this, then it will turn out that everything that contributed to the plausibility of the pagans' model will actually contribute as well to the plausibility of Origen's.)

Origen, then, sets up a slightly different form of disagreement between himself and the pagans from that presupposed in the accounts of his predecessors, presenting himself as offering, not a different model altogether, but rather a *fuller* version of the model developed by the pagans themselves. The question he formulated for the objective observer by doing this was thus not so much which of the two models was *more likely to be right*, but which of the two models was *likely to be more right*: not, that is, whether the pagans provided a reasonable account of the phenomena, but whether they provided an *adequate* account. The pagans, naturally, thought that they did, that the 'additional' layer of wisdom posited by Origen over and above the theology of their own tradition was (to put it most charitably) otiose, and unjustifiable as part of any hypothesis to explain the course of philosophical history. But Origen did not just assert the existence of the 'wisdom of God' as something above what the pagans knew; he argued that this wisdom *was* needed to form part of an adequate hypothesis. The pagans themselves could explain what was positive in their traditions; but what they failed to explain (or glossed over) was the extent of the diversity to be found in them—diversity already, as Origen stresses, in the expression of their ancient theological accounts, never mind in the later history of their schools.[37] If they really were in possession of the full truth, so Origen argues, such diversity would not have arisen so persistently throughout their history; if there exists a higher truth of which they remained in ignorance, on the other hand, then such diversity would be very easily explicable indeed. The pagans, he suggests, acquired from their 'gods', i.e. from the daemons, exactly what one would acquire from a plurality of rational creatures, namely *rational opinions* (plural).[38] To use the language of Origen's *Commentary on St John* (see all of 2. 2–3), theirs was a theology of λόγοι—and all the more incapable of achieving unity in a higher principle because none of these various opinions was actually irrational or obviously wrong. By contrast (as proved in the earlier thread of the argument which I examined in Chapter 8), it was possible to discern a stable, orthodox Christian tradition of the highest antiquity, and Origen explains this, in the same passage, as a consequence of its foundation in λόγος, in *reason* in the singular; or, more emphatically in the case of the truest Christians, in ὁ λόγος, *the Reason* (*Commentary on St John*, 2. 3, 56. 29–32 Preuschen).

And this is the ultimate basis of Origen's answer to Celsus. Celsus had accused Christianity of being essentially factional: but, having shown that true Christianity was not divided and did not tend to division at all, Origen completes his response by demonstrating that the explanation he can give for the coherence and unity of the Hebraeo-Christian tradition can be used in addition to give the fullest explanation available for pagan philosophy. He tackles

[37] See again *On First Principles*, 3. 3. 2, 257. 28 Koetschau for the 'manifold and diverse opinions of the Greeks concerning the divine', which form part of the 'wisdom of the princes of this world'.

[38] From the diversity in pagan theology Origen concludes that they were not taught the 'wisdom of God' by the daemons; and from the daemons' essential good faith in passing on wisdom to the pagans, the fact that they themselves lacked this wisdom as well: cf. esp. *On First Principles*, 3. 3. 1, 256. 15–18 Koetschau, for the individual opinions they necessarily formed in its absence.

any apparent contrast between the pagan traditions of theology and philosophy by adopting the Platonists' own answer to this (that the traditions are really the same)—and in doing so defuses the danger that someone who found it a plausible answer in its own right might for that reason maintain his suspension of judgement even when presented with a seductive alternative to it. But then Origen shows in addition that the pagan account does not cover all of the phenomena, that his extended model can better explain the weaknesses in the pagan tradition (it lacks the stability that comes with knowledge of the highest principles), *as well as* explaining its strengths (it is rational, and even, to a large degree, right). The objective observer has, after all, justification for thinking that Origen's answer is *preferable* to that of the Platonists, just in so far as it has the greater explanatory power; and he has no positive reason to doubt that it might be true, since nothing that made the alternative, Platonist model plausible constitutes any serious objection to it. In consequence of all this, the objective observer has every reason to suppose that the divisions within pagan thought emerge from an inherent instability explained by its subordinate philosophical status. The *ultimate* truth, if discernible at all, will be discernible in Christianity: pagan philosophy can act as a propaedeutic in Origen's scheme[39]—but is essentially locked in plurality and division which prevents it from reaching any further than this.

7. *Conclusion*

In this chapter I have illustrated the argument of dependency by reference to the works of four writers who figure prominently in the remains of early Christian philosophy: Tertullian, Justin, Clement, and Origen. The evidence for many of their contemporaries does not allow such a detailed reconstruction of their views on the matter: but again and again the appearance of the same and cognate themes guarantees for us that they must have viewed the subject in much the same terms. The use of Hebrew Scripture by Greek philosophers was posited early on by Hippolytus and Tatian, in addition to the writers already discussed;[40] the *antiquity* of the Hebraeo-Christian tradition relative to any pagan tradition was in any case

[39] Cf. *Letter to Gregory*, 1; and *Commentary on St John*, 2. 3, 56. 19–21 Preuschen.

[40] See Tatian, *Oration*, 40 (with Hawthorn 1964 for a different view of the motif's antecedents); Hippolytus, *Refutation of All Heresies*, 9. 27. Cf. also e.g. ps.-Justin, *Exhortation*, 26–33; Minucius Felix, *Octavius*, 34. 5; Theophilus, *To Autolycus*,

universally assumed by Christians who wrote as self-consciously 'orthodox'.[41] Similarly universal were the vices—all, again, familiar from the Platonist model explored in Chapter 7—identified as inherent in, or at the root of, pagan philosophy, vices which explain its decadent course: love of honour, glory, contention, and the like;[42] disagreement and self-contradiction as consequences of these.[43] As a final example, which shows how the themes of the antiquity of the Hebraeo-Christian tradition and the absurdity and self-contradiction of the pagans were united in the Christians' writing, here is a précis of two books against pagan philosophy (themselves now lost) which were written by Hippolytus of Rome—the second-century heresiologist most familiar to us for his *Refutation of All Heresies*:[44]

2. 8. 56–61 (suggesting that the pagans had derived elements of the Hebraeo-Christian truth from daemons). Augustine too believed that the Greeks must have drawn on Hebrew Scripture, but found it hard to explain how they did it. In his work *On Christian Doctrine* (at 2. 43) he was able to assume that Hebrew Scripture had already been translated into Greek, and that Plato had access to these translations when in Egypt; he also thought that Plato might have met Jeremiah at this time. Later on, he withdrew both of these suggestions as historically untenable: see *Retractationes*, 2. 4. But he was left with the possibility that Plato learnt Hebrew philosophy orally from its exponents: after all (Augustine notes at *City of God*, 8. 11), we know that he learnt about Egyptian philosophy, and he certainly needed interpreters for that.

[41] See e.g. Tatian, *Oration*, 29, 31, 36–41; Theophilus, *To Autolycus*, 2. 30, 3. 16–30; Hippolytus, *Refutation of All Heresies*, 10. 31, 287. 21–4 Wendland. Later on, compare e.g. Lactantius, *Divine Institutes*, 4. 5; Eusebius, *Ecclesiastical History*, 1. 2. 1–16; 1. 4. 10, etc.; *Preparation for the Gospel*, 1. 2 with 1. 6; Augustine, *City of God*, 18. 37.

[42] e.g. Theophilus, *To Autolycus*, 3. 1. 1–2; 3. 3. 1–3; Athenagoras, *On the Resurrection of the Dead*, 1. 1; ps.-Justin, *Exhortation*, 1, 1A; 7, 8C; cf. Irenaeus, *Heresies*, 2. 26. 2.

[43] Cf. e.g. Athenagoras, *On the Resurrection of the Dead*, 1. 2; Tatian, *Oration*, 25 with 29; Theophilus, *To Autolycus*, 3. 3. 3–4; ps.-Justin, *Exhortation*, 7, 8A; *Questions for the Christians*, 13, 211 B–C. Naturally, emphasis is placed on the consistency of the Hebraeo-Christian tradition in contrast: cf. e.g. Theophilus, *To Autolycus*, 2. 10. 1, 3. 17. 9–10.

[44] Photius, *Library*, 48, 11^{b}17–22 for this extract. Photius says that the work was called *On the Universe* or *On the Cause of the Universe* or *On the Substance of the Universe*—this latter title being one which Hippolytus claims for a work of his own (see *Refutation of All Heresies*, 10. 32, 288. 22–3 Wendland). The copy of the work read by Photius ascribed it to Josephus, but the implausibility of this (the work contained, apparently, a reference to Christ as the 'son of God' which Josephus would hardly have made) was already apparent to Photius—and indeed, to a scribe who had inserted in the margins of his copy the claim that the work was actually by one 'Gaius'. The brief description given of 'Gaius' fits what we know of Hippolytus—and so it seems extremely likely that he was, in fact, the author. See further Quasten (1950–60), ii. 195–6; and especially Marcovich (1986), 12–15.

[The author] showed in them that Plato contradicted himself and that Alcinous[45] spoke absurdly and falsely concerning the soul, matter, and the resurrection; put forward his own views on these subjects instead; and proved that the Jewish race was much older than the Greek.

The argument that pagan philosophy depended on Hebraeo-Christian thought is in some ways extremely complex. Different authors identified dependency at different points, and different channels for the transmission of Hebraic influence were suggested[46] (Origen proving his point without resorting to claims of direct later contact at all). But viewed in terms of the wider strategy of which it forms a part, the whole issue starts to look much more straightforward. The Christians needed to show to an objective observer that pagan theology *and* (despite its occasional moments of insight) pagan philosophy were *essentially* driven by the wrong motives, that, as a consequence, they were *necessarily* riven by faction; that to seek for the truth through pagan tradition was probably to start from the wrong place, and certainly to head in the wrong direction. The most Sceptical observer is invited to conclude at least that *if* the truth might be discernible anywhere at all it could only be in the ancient and consistent tradition of Hebraeo-Christian orthodoxy. If it might have seemed that the 'dependency theme' took us away from the Platonist model of argument for the unique preferability of a particular course in philosophy, it should now be clear that it was, on the contrary, essential to the Christian adoption of that model. And the topic is far from being a quaint byway in the history of Christian apologetic: as part of the model in whose terms Christian orthodoxy was defined and asserted as a philosophical tradition of unique standing in the history of thought, it played a vital role in establishing the Christian Church as, arguably, the most historically successful achievement of the Platonists' model itself.

[45] It is not at all clear who this 'Alcinous' was. He has been identified with the homonymous author of the 2nd-cent.-AD handbook of Platonism, the *Didaskalikos*: see e.g. Witt (1937), 104–5. But there is hardly more than the homonymy itself to support the identification, and caution is rightly urged by Whittaker (1990), pp. xi–xii; cf. also Göransson (1995), 135–6.

[46] Clement lists many of them in *Stromata*, 1. 17–18 and 19.

References

1. *Ancient Authors*

The editions listed below are used for ease of reference, although in some cases their text has been superseded by newer editions. I note the more important of the latter below ad locc.: bibliographical details (if not otherwise given here) will be found in L. Berkowitz and K. A. Squitier, *Thesaurus Linguae Graecae: Canon of Greek Authors and Works from Homer to* AD *200*, 2nd edn. (New York and Oxford: Oxford University Press, 1986), to which the reader is also referred for details of editions employed in this book but not mentioned below.

ALCINOUS, *Didaskalikos*. Cited according to the edition of Hermann; but for the text see now Whittaker (1990).

Anonymous Commentary on Plato's Theaetetus, ed. Bastianini and Sedley (1995).

CASSIODORUS, *On Orthography*, ed. H. Keil, *Grammatici Latini*, vii (Leipzig: Teubner, 1878), 143–210.

CEDRENUS, GEORGE, *Compendium of Histories*, ed. I. Bekker (Corpus Scriptorum Historiae Byzantiae; Bonn: Weber, 1938).

CHAEREMON, fragments, ed. van der Horst (1987).

CHARISIUS, *Art of Grammar*, ed. H. Keil, *Grammatici Latini*, i (Leipzig: Teubner, 1857), 1–296.

DERVENI PAPYRUS, trans. A. Laks and G. W. Most, 'A Provisional Translation of the Derveni Papyrus', in Laks and Most (eds.), *Studies on the Derveni Papyrus* (Oxford: Clarendon Press, 1997), 9–22. Column numbers are given as in this translation; for line numbers and text of columns I–VII see K. Tsantsangolou, 'The First Columns of the Derveni Papyrus and their Religious Significance', in Laks and Most, *Studies on the Derveni Papyrus*, 93–128 at 93–5; and, for the remainder, see the text printed anonymously at *Zeitschrift für Papyrologie und Epigraphik*, 47 (1982), after 300.

HIPPOLYTUS, *Refutation of All Heresies*. Cited according to the edition of Wendland; but cf. now Marcovich (1986) for the text.

IAMBLICHUS, *On the Mysteries of Egypt*, ed. G. Parthey, *Jamblichi de mysteriis liber* (Berlin: Friedrich Nikolaus, 1857). But for the text cf. the edition of É. des Places.

Malalas, John, *Chronographia*, ed. L. Dindorff (Corpus Scriptorum Historiae Byzantiae; Bonn: Weber, 1931).

Maximus of Tyre. ed. M. B. Trapp, *Maximus Tyrius: Dissertationes* (Stuttgart and Leipzig: Teubner, 1994).

Origen, *On First Principles*, ed. P. Koetschau, *Origenes: Werke*, vol. v (Die griechischen christlichen Schriftsteller der ersten drei Jahrhunderte, 22; Leipzig: Hinrichs, 1913). For the text, see now Görgemanns and Karpp.

Philodemus, *On the Stoics*, ed. T. Dorandi, 'Filodemo: Gli Stoici (PHerc. 155 e 339)', *Cronache ercolanesi*, 12 (1982), 91–133.

—— *Index of Stoics*, ed. T. Dorandi, *Filodemo: Storia dei filosofi. La Stoà da Zenone a Panezio (PHerc. 1018)* (Philosophia Antiqua, 60; Leiden, Cologne, and New York, NY: 1994).

Plutarch, fragments, ed. F. H. Sandbach, *Plutarchus: Moralia*, vol. vii (Leipzig: Teubner, 1967). Also, with English translation, in *Plutarch's Moralia*, vol. xv (Loeb Classical Library; Cambridge, Mass.: Harvard University Press, 1969).

Porphyry, fragments (except fragments in Harnack's edition of Porphyry, *Against the Christians*), ed. A. Smith, *Porphyrius: Fragmenta* (Leipzig: Teubner, 1993).

Posidonius, fragments, ed. L. Edelstein and I. G. Kidd, *Posidonius*, vol. i. *The Fragments*, 2nd edn. (Cambridge: Cambridge University Press, 1989). Cf. also Theiler (1982).

Proclus, *On the First Alcibiades*, ed. and trans. A. Ph. Segonds, *Sur le premier Alcibiade de Platon* (2 vols.; Paris: Belles Lettres, 1985–6).

Sophocles, fragments. In addition to Radt: A. Nauck, *Tragicorum Graecorum fragmenta*, 2nd edn. (Leipzig: Teubner, 1889).

Syncellus, George, *Chronographia*, ed. W. Dindorff (Corpus Scriptorum Historiae Byzantiae; Bonn: Weber, 1829).

Tertullian. References are to *Quinti Septimii Florentis Tertulliani Quae Supersunt Opera*, ed. F. Oehler (3 vols.; Leipzig: T. G. Weigel, 1853). For the text see *Quinti Septimi Florentis Tertulliani Opera* (various editors) (2 vols.; Corpus Christianorum, Series Latina, 1–2; Turnholt: Brepols, 1954).

Theophrastus, fragments, ed. and trans. W. W. Fortenbaugh, P. M. Huby, R. W. Sharples, D. Gutas, *et al.*, *Theophrastus of Eresus: Sources for his Life, Writings, Thought and Influence*, 1–2 (Leiden, New York, and Cologne: Brill, 1993).

Thrasyllus, testimonia, in Tarrant (1993), 215–49.

Varro, *Divine Antiquities*, in M. Terentius Varro, *Antiquitates rerum divinarum*, ed. B. Cardauns (Mainz: Akademie der Wissenschaften und der Literatur, and Wiesbaden: Steiner, 1976).

2. *Modern Authors*

ALGRA, K. A. (1997), 'Chrysippus, Carneades, Cicero: The Ethical *Divisiones* in Cicero's *Lucullus*', in Inwood and Mansfeld (1997), 107–39.

ALLEN, J. (1994), 'Academic Probabilism and Stoic Epistemology', *Classical Quarterly*, NS 44: 85–113.

ANDRESEN, C. (1952–3), 'Justin und der mittlere Platonismus', *Zeitschrift für die Neutestamentliche Wissenschaft*, 44: 157–95.

AUCHER, J. B. (1822), *Philonis Judaei Sermones Tres Hactenus Inediti* (Venice: Typis Coenobii Patrum Armenorum in Insula S. Lazari).

BABUT, D. (1969), *Plutarque et le Stoïcisme* (Paris: Presses Universitaires de France).

BALDRY, H. C. (1952), 'Who Invented the Golden Age?', *Classical Quarterly*, NS 2: 83–92.

—— (1956), 'Hesiod's Five Ages', *Journal of the History of Ideas*, 17: 553–4.

BARCLAY, J. M. G. (1996), *Jews in the Mediterranean Diaspora from Alexander to Trajan (323 BCE–117 CE)* (Edinburgh: T. & T. Clark).

BAR-KOCHVA, B. (1996), *Pseudo-Hecataeus* On the Jews: *Legitimizing the Jewish Diaspora* (Berkeley, Los Angeles, and London: University of California Press).

BARNES, J. (1989), 'Antiochus of Ascalon', in Griffin and Barnes (1989), 51–96.

—— (1990), *The Toils of Scepticism* (Cambridge: Cambridge University Press).

—— (1992), 'Metacommentary', *Oxford Studies in Ancient Philosophy*, 10: 267–81.

—— and GRIFFIN, M. (eds.) (1997), *Philosophia Togata*, ii. *Essays on Philosophy and Roman Society* (Oxford: Clarendon Press).

BARRETT, C. K. (1960), *The Gospel according to St John: An Introduction with Commentary and Notes on the Greek Text* (London: SPCK).

BASTIANINI, G., and SEDLEY, D. (1995), 'Commentarium in Platonis "Theaetetum"', *Corpus dei papiri filosofici greci e latini*, 3: 227–562.

BAUER, W. (1964), *Rechtgläubigkeit und Ketzerei im ältesten Christentum*, 2nd edn. (Beiträge zur historischen Theologie, 10; Tübingen: J. C. B. Mohr).

BELTRAMI, A. (1927), *L. Annaei Senecae ad Lucilium Epistularum Moralium Libri XIV–XX* (Bologna: Zanichelli).

BENOIT, P. (1962–3), 'Paulinisme et Johannisme', *New Testament Studies*, 9: 193–207.

BERCHMAN, R. M. (1984), *From Philo to Origen: Middle Platonism in Transition* (Brown Judaic Studies, 69; Chico, Calif.: Scholars Press).

BERTOLI, E. (1982), 'L'età dell'oro in Posidonio e Seneca', *Quaderni di lingue e letterature*, 7: 151–79.

BICKERMAN, E. J. (1975), 'The Jewish Historian Demetrios', in J. Neusner (ed.), *Christianity, Judaism and Other Greco-Roman Cults*, iii (Leiden: Brill), 72–84.

BIELER, L. (1935–6), *Θεῖος ἀνήρ: Das Bild des 'göttlichen Menschen' in Spätantike und Frühchristentum* (2 vols.; Wien: Höfels).

BLANKERT, S. (1940), *Seneca (Epist. 90) over Natuur en Cultuur en Posidonius als zijn Bron* (diss., Amsterdam).

BORNKAMM, G. (1975), *Jesus von Nazareth*, 2nd edn. (Stuttgart: Kohlhammer).

BOUSSET, W. (1911), *Jesus*, English trans. by J. P. Trevelyan (London: Williams & Northgate).

—— (1915), *Jüdisch-christlicher Schulbetrieb in Alexandria und Rom: Literarische Untersuchungen zu Philo und Clemens von Alexandria, Justin und Irenäus* (Forschungen zur Religion und Literatur des Alten und Neuen Testaments, NS 6; Göttingen: Vandenhoeck & Ruprecht).

BOYANCÉ, P. (1955), 'Sur la théologie de Varron', *Revue des études anciennes*, 57: 57–85.

BOYS-STONES, G. R. (1997), 'Thyrsus-bearer of the Academy or Enthusiast for Plato? Plutarch's *De Stoicorum repugnantiis*', in J. Mossman (ed.), *Plutarch and his Intellectual World* (London: Duckworth), 41–58.

—— (2002*a*), 'The Stoics' Two Types of Allegory', in Boys-Stones (2002*b*).

—— (ed.) (2002*b*), *Metaphor and Allegory: Classical Studies in Theory and Practice* (Oxford: Oxford University Press, forthcoming).

BRAUN, F.-M. (1959), *Jean le théologien*, i. *Jean le théologien et son évangile dans l'église ancienne* (Paris: Gabalda).

BRAUN, M. (1938), *History and Romance in Graeco-oriental Literature* (Oxford: Basil Blackwell).

BRÉHIER, É. (1925), *Les Idées philosophiques et religieuses de Philon d'Alexandrie*, 2nd edn. (Études de Philosophie Médiévale, 8; Paris: Vrin).

BRITTAIN, C. F. (1996), 'Philo of Larissa and the Fourth Academy' (diss. Oxford). Forthcoming as *Philo of Larissa: The Last of the Academic Sceptics* (Oxford: Oxford University Press).

BROWN, R. E. (1966), *The Gospel according to John (Introduction, Translation and Notes)*, vol. i (Garden City, NY: Doubleday).

BRZOSKA, J. (1896), 'Apollonius (85)', in *RE* ii. 141–4.

BUFFIÈRE, F. (1956), *Les Mythes d'Homère et la pensée grecque* (Paris: Belles Lettres).

BULTMANN, R. (1926), *Jesus* (Berlin: Deutsche Bibliothek).

—— (1932), '*Ἀλήθεια*', in G. Kittel (ed.), *Theologisches Wörterbuch zum Neuen Testaments*, i (Stuttgart: W. Kohlhammer), 239–48.

—— (1941), *Das Evangelium des Johannes* (Göttingen: Vandenhoeck & Ruprecht).

—— (1948–53), *Theologie des Neuen Testaments* (3 vols.; Tübingen: J. C. B. Mohr).

—— (1949), *Das Urchristentum im Rahmen der antiken Religionen* (Zurich: Artemis).

Chadwick, H. (1965), *Origen:* Contra Celsum. *Translated with an Introduction and Notes* (Cambridge: Cambridge University Press).

—— (1966), *Early Christian Thought and the Classical Tradition: Studies in Justin, Clement, and Origen* (Oxford: Clarendon Press).

—— (1970), 'Philo and the Beginnings of Christian Thought', in A. H. Armstrong (ed.), *The Cambridge History of Later Greek and Early Medieval Philosophy*, corrected edn. (Cambridge: Cambridge University Press), 133–92.

Charlesworth, J. H. (1983–5), *The Old Testament Pseudepigrapha* (2 vols.; Garden City, NY: Doubleday).

Charrue, J. M. (1978), *Plotin, lecteur de Platon* (Paris: Belles Lettres).

Cizek, A. (1963), 'Sur les traces de Zénon dans les "Lettres à Lucilius"', *Helikon*, 3: 196–208.

Cohn, L. (1894), 'Apion (3)', in *RE* i. 2803–6.

Cole, T. (1990), *Democritus and the Sources of Greek Anthropology* (American Philological Association Monograph Series, 25; Atlanta, Ga.: Scholars Press).

Collins, J. J. (1974), *The Sibylline Oracles of Egyptian Judaism* (Missoula, Mont.: Society of Biblical Literature).

—— (1983), *Between Athens and Jerusalem: Jewish Identity in the Hellenistic Diaspora* (New York, NY: Crossroad).

Cooper, J. M. (1998), 'Posidonius on Emotions', in Sihvola and Engberg-Pedersen (1998), 71–111.

Daniélou, J. (1951), 'Les sources juives de la doctrine des anges des nations chez Origène', *Recherches de science religieuse*, 38: 132–7.

—— (1958–78), *Histoire des doctrines chrétiennes avant Nicée* (3 vols.; Paris: Éditions du Cerf).

Dawson, D. (1992), *Allegorical Readers and Cultural Revision in Ancient Alexandria* (Berkeley, Los Angeles, and London: University of California Press).

Decharme, P. (1898), 'Note sur un fragment des "Daedala" de Plutarque', in *Mélanges Henri Weil: Recueil de mémoires concernant l'histoire et la littérature grecques dédié à Henri Weil* (Paris: Thorin), 111–17.

Desjardins, M. (1991), 'Bauer and Beyond: On Recent Scholarly Discussions of *αἵρεσις* in the Early Christian Era', *The Second Century*, 8: 65–82.

des Places, É. (1973) (ed. and trans), *Numénius: Fragments* (Paris: Belles Lettres).

—— (1977) (ed. and trans.), *Atticus: Fragments* (Paris: Belles Lettres).

DÉTIENNE, M. (1962), *Homère, Hésiode et Pythagore: Poésie et philosophie dans le pythagorisme ancien* (Brussels: Latomus).

DIELS, H. (1879) (ed.), *Doxographi Graeci* (Berlin: Reimer).

DILLON, J. M. (1981), 'Ganymede as the Logos: Traces of a Forgotten Allegorization in Philo', *Classical Quarterly*, NS 31: 183–5.

——(1988), '"Orthodoxy" and "Eclecticism": Middle Platonists and Neo-Pythagoreans', in Dillon and Long (1988), 103–25.

——(1992), 'Plato and the Golden Age', *Hermathena*, 153: 21–36.

——(1995), 'The Neoplatonic Exegesis of the *Statesman* Myth', in C. J. Rowe (ed.), *Reading the* Statesman (Proceedings of the Third Symposium Platonicum; Sankt Augustin: Academia Verlag), 364–74.

——(1996), *The Middle Platonists 80 B.C. to A.D. 220*, rev. edn. (London: Duckworth).

——and LONG, A. A. (eds.) (1988), *The Question of 'Eclecticism': Studies in Later Greek Philosophy* (Berkeley, Los Angeles, and London: University of California Press).

DODDS, E. R. (1960), 'Tradition and Personal Achievement in the Philosophy of Plotinus', *Journal of Roman Studies*, 50: 1–7.

——(1973), 'The Ancient Concept of Progress', in id., *The Ancient Concept of Progress and Other Essays on Greek Literature and Belief* (Oxford: Clarendon Press), 1–25.

DONINI, P.-L. (1982), *Le scuole, l'anima, l'impero: La filosofia antica da Antioco a Plotino* (Turin: Rosenberg & Sellier).

——(1986), 'Plutarco, Ammonio e l'Accademia', in F. E. Brenk and I. Gallo (eds.), *Miscellanea Plutarchea: Atti del I convegno di studi su Plutarco* (Quaderni del giornale filologico ferrarese, 8; Ferrara: Giornale filologico ferrarese), 97–110.

——(1994), 'Testi e commenti, manuali e insegnamento: La forma sistematica e i metodi della filosofia in età postellenistica', *ANRW* ii. 36.7: 5027–100.

DORNSEIFF, F. (1938), 'Antikes zum Alten Testament, 4. Die Abfassungszeit des Pentateuchs und die Deuteronomiumsfrage', *Zeitschrift für die Alttestamentliche Wissenschaft*, 56: 64–85.

DÖRRIE, H. (1944), 'Der Platoniker Eudoros von Alexandreia', *Hermes*, 79: 25–39.

——(1967), 'Die platonische Theologie des Kelsos in ihrer Auseinandersetzung mit der christlichen Theologie auf Grund von Origenes c. Celsum 7. 42 ff', in *Nachrichten der Akademie der Wissenschaften in Göttingen: Philologisch-historische Klasse*, Jahrgang 1967, no. 2 (Göttingen: Vandenhoeck & Ruprecht), 19–55.

——(1972), 'Die Wertung der Barbaren im Urteil der Griechen: Knechtsnaturen? Oder Bewahrer und Künder heilbringender Weisheit?', in

R. Stiehl and G. A. Lehmann (eds.), *Antike und Universalgeschichte* [Festschrift Hans Erich Stier] (Münster: Aschendorff), 146–75.

—— (1976), *Von Platon zum Platonismus: Ein Bruch in der Überlieferung und seine Überwindung* (Rheinisch-Westfälische Akademie der Wissenschaften: Geisteswissenschaften, Vorträge G 211; Opladen: Westdeutscher Verlag).

—— and BALTES, M. (1990), *Der Platonismus in der Antike: Grundlagen, System, Entwicklung*, ii. *Der hellenistische Rahmen des kaiserzeitlichen Platonismus* (Stuttgart-Bad Cannstatt: Frommann-Holzboog).

DUBOSE, W. P. (1907), *The Gospel according to St Paul* (New York: Longmans, Green & Co.).

DUNN, J. D. G. (1989), *Christology in the Making: A New Testament Inquiry into the Origins of the Doctrine of the Incarnation*, 2nd edn. (London: SCM Press).

EDELSTEIN, L. (1967), *The Idea of Progress in Classical Antiquity* (Baltimore: John Hopkins Press).

EDWARDS, M. J. (1990), 'Numenius, Pherecydes and *The Cave of the Nymphs*', *Classical Quarterly*, NS 40: 258–62.

ELTER, A. (1893–5), *De gnomologiorum Graecorum historia atque origine commentatio* (Bonn: E. C. Georgi Typographeum Academicum).

ÉON, A. (1970), 'La notion plotinienne d'exégèse', *Revue internationale de philosophie*, 24: 252–89.

ERSKINE, A. (1990), *The Hellenistic Stoa: Political Thought and Action* (Ithaca, NY: Cornell University Press).

FELDMAN, L. H. (1990), 'Origen's *Contra Celsum* and Josephus' *Contra Apionem*: The Issue of Jewish Origins', *Vigiliae Christianae*, 44: 105–35.

—— (1993), *Jew and Gentile in the Ancient World: Attitudes and Interactions from Alexander to Justinian* (Princeton, NJ: Princeton University Press).

FÉVRIER, J. G. (1924), *La Date, la composition et les sources de la Lettre d'Aristée à Philocrate* (Paris: É. Champion).

FLAMMAND, J.-M. (1994), 'Dioclès de Cnide', in Goulet (1994–), ii. 774–5.

FOWLER, R. L. (1987), *The Nature of Early Greek Lyric: Three Preliminary Studies* (Toronto: University of Toronto Press).

FRANKEL, Z. (1851), *Über den Einfluß der palästinischen Exegese auf die alexandrinische Hermeneutik* (Leipzig: Barth).

FRASER, P. M. (1972), *Ptolemaic Alexandria* (3 vols.; Oxford: Clarendon Press).

FREDE, M. (1984), 'The Sceptic's Two Kinds of Assent and the Question of the Possibility of Knowledge', in R. Rorty, J. B. Schneewind, and Q. Skinner (eds.), *Philosophy in History: Essays on the Historiography of Philosophy* (Cambridge: Cambridge University Press), 255–78.

—— (1987), 'Numenius', *ANRW* ii. 36.2: 1034–75.

FREDE, M. (1989), 'Chaeremon der Stoiker', *ANRW* ii. 36.3: 2067–103.

——(1994), 'Celsus philosophus Platonicus', *ANRW* ii. 36.7: 5183–213.

——(1997), 'Celsus' Attack on the Christians', in Barnes and Griffin (1997), 218–40.

——(2002), 'Non-verbal Allegory', in Boys-Stones (2002*b*).

FREUDENTHAL, J. (1874–5), *Alexander Polyhistor und die von ihm erhaltenen Reste jüdischer und samaritanischer Geschichtswerke* (2 vols.; Hellenistische Studien; Breslau: H. Skutsch).

FRITZ, K. VON (1947), 'Pandora, Prometheus and the Myth of Ages', *Review of Religion*, 11: 227–60.

FROIDEFOND, C. (1987), 'Plutarque et le platonisme', *ANRW* ii. 36.1: 184–233.

FRUIN, R. (1847), *Manethonis Sebennytae Reliquiae* (Leiden: Gebhard & Co.).

GAGER, J. G. (1969), 'Pseudo-Hecataeus Again', *Zeitschrift für die Neutestamentliche Wissenschaft*, 60: 130–9.

——(1972), *Moses in Greco-Roman Paganism* (Nashville: Abingdon Press).

GAISER, K. (1983), 'La biografia di Platone in Filodemo: Nuovi dati dal PHerc. 1021', *Cronache ercolanesi*, 13: 53–62.

——(1988), *Philodems Academica: Die Berichte über Platon und die Alte Akademie in zwei herkulanensischen Papyri* (Stuttgart-Bad Cannstatt: Frommann-Holzboog).

GATZ, B. (1967), *Weltalter, goldene Zeit und sinnverwandte Vorstellungen* (Spudasmata, 16; Hildesheim: G. Olms).

GAUTHIER, H. (1935), *Les Nomes d'Égypte depuis Hérodote jusqu'à la conquète arabe* (Cairo: Institut Français d'Archéologie Orientale).

GELZER, T. (1982), 'Plotins Interesse an den Vorsokratikern', *Museum Helveticum*, 39: 101–31.

GERCKE, A. (1896), 'Aristobulos (15)', in *RE* ii. 918–20.

GIGLIONI, G. B. (1986), 'Dicearco e la riflessione sul passato', *Rivista storica italiana*, 98: 629–52.

GILL, C. (1998), 'Did Galen Understand Platonic and Stoic Thinking on Emotions?', in Sihvola and Engberg-Pedersen (1998), 113–48.

GLIBERT-THIRRY, A. (1977), 'La théorie stoïcienne de la passion chez Chrysippe et son évolution chez Posidonius', *Revue philosophique de Louvain*, 75: 393–435.

GLUCKER, J. (1978), *Antiochus and the Late Academy* (Hypomnemata, 56; Göttingen: Vandenhoeck & Ruprecht).

——(1997), 'Socrates in the Academic Books and Other Ciceronian Works', in Inwood and Mansfeld (1997), 58–88.

GOODENOUGH, E. R. (1923), *The Theology of Justin Martyr* (Jena: Frommann).

Göransson, T. (1995), *Albinus, Alcinous, Arius Didymus* (Studia Graeca et Latina Gothoburgensia, 61; Göteborg: University of Göteborg).

Görler, W. (1994), 'Philon aus Larisa', in F. Ueberweg, *Die Philosophie der Antike*, rev. edn. (Die hellenistische Philosopie, ed. H. Flashar, 4; Basel: Schwabe & Co.), 915–37.

Goulet, R. (1994), 'Aristoboulos', in Goulet (1994–), i. 379–80.

——(1994–), *Dictionnaire des philosophes antiques* (Paris: CNRS).

Grant, R. M. (1966), *Gnosticism and Early Christianity*, rev. edn. (New York: Columbia University Press).

Griffin, M., and Barnes, J. (1989), *Philosophia Togata: Essays on Philosophy and Roman Society* (Oxford: Clarendon Press).

Griffiths, J. G. (1956), 'Archaeology and Hesiod's Five Ages', *Journal of the History of Ideas*, 17: 109–19.

——(1958), 'Did Hesiod Invent the Golden Age?', *Journal of the History of Ideas*, 19: 91–3.

Grilli, A. (1953), 'La posizione di Aristotele, Epicuro e Posidonio nei confronti della storia della civiltà', *Rendiconti dell'Istituto Lombardo di Scienze e Lettere* (*classe di lettere e scienze morali e storiche*), 86: 3–44.

Gudeman, A. (1928), 'Lysimachos (20)', in *RE* xiv. 32–9.

Guthrie, W. K. C. (1957), *In the Beginning: Some Greek Views on the Origins of Life and the Early State of Man* (London: Methuen).

Hadas-Lebel, M. (1973), *De Providentia I et II* (Les Oeuvres de Philon d'Alexandria, ed. R. Arnaldez, J. Puilloux, and C. Mondésert, 35; Paris: Éditions de Cerf).

Hanson, A. T. (1975), *Grace and Truth: A Study in the Doctrine of the Incarnation* (London: SPCK).

Hanson, R. P. C. (1959), *Allegory and Event: A Study of the Sources and Significance of Origen's Interpretation of Scripture* (London: SCM Press).

——(1970), 'Biblical Exegesis in the Early Church', in P. R. Ackroyd and C. F. Evans (eds.), *The Cambridge History of the Bible*, i. *From the Beginnings to Jerome* (Cambridge: Cambridge University Press), 412–53.

Hardie, P. R. (1992), 'Plutarch and the Interpretation of Myth', *ANRW* ii. 33.6: 4743–87.

Harl, M. (1958), *Origène et la fonction révélatrice du verbe incarné* (Patristica Sorbonensia, 2; Paris: Éditions du Seuil).

Harnack, A. von (1894–7), *Lehrbuch der Dogmengeschichte*, 3rd edn. (3 vols.; Freiburg and Leipzig: J. C. B. Mohr).

Harris, J. R. (1891), *The Apology of Aristides on Behalf of the Christians: From a Syriac MS Preserved on Mount Sinai* (Texts and Studies: Contributions to Biblical and Patristic Literature, 1.1; Cambridge: Cambridge University Press).

HAWTHORN, G. F. (1964), 'Tatian and his Discourse to the Greeks', *Harvard Theological Review*, 57: 161–88.

HAYS, R. S. (1983), 'Lucius Annaeus Cornutus' "Epidrome" (Introduction to the Traditions of Greek Theology): Introduction, Translation and Notes' (diss. University of Texas, Austin).

HEINEMANN, I. (1919), 'Poseidonios über die Entwicklung der jüdischen Religion', *Monatsschrift für Geschichte und Wissenschaft des Judentums*, 63: 113–21.

—— (1921–8), *Poseidonios' metaphysische Schriften* (2 vols.; Breslau: M. & H. Marcus).

HENGEL, M. (1974), *Judaism and Hellenism: Studies in their Encounter in Palestine during the Early Hellenistic Period*, trans. J. Bowden (London: SCM Press).

HINE, H. (1995), 'Seneca, Stoicism and the Problem of Moral Evil', in D. Innes, H. Hine, and C. Pelling (eds.), *Ethics and Rhetoric: Classical Essays for Donald Russell on his Seventy-fifth Birthday* (Oxford: Clarendon Press), 93–106.

HIRZEL, R. (1877–83), *Untersuchungen zu Ciceros philosophischen Schriften* (3 vols.; Leipzig: S. Hirzel).

HOFFMANN, R. J. (1987), *Celsus On the True Doctrine: A Discourse against the Christians* (New York: Oxford University Press).

HOLTE, R. (1958), 'Logos Spermatikos: Christianity and Ancient Philosophy according to St Justin's Apologies', *Studia Theologica*, 12: 109–68.

IGAL, J. (1981), 'The Gnostics and "The Ancient Philosophy" in Porphyry and Plotinus', in J. Blumenthal and R. A. Markus (eds.), *Neoplatonism and Early Christian Thought: Essays in Honour of A. H. Armstrong* (London: Variorum), 138–49.

INWOOD, B., and MANSFELD, J. (eds.) (1997), *Assent and Argument in Cicero's* Academic Books (Proceedings of the 7th Symposium Hellenisticum; Leiden and New York: Brill).

JACOBSON, H. (1977), 'Apion's Nickname', *American Journal of Philology*, 98: 413–15.

JACOBY, F. (1912), 'Hekataios (4)', in *RE* vii. 2750–69.

JAEGER, W. (1938), *Diocles von Karystos: Die griechische Medizin und die Schule des Aristoteles* (Berlin: de Gruyter).

—— (1948), *Aristotle: Fundamentals of the History of his Development*, 2nd edn., trans. R. Robinson (Oxford: Clarendon Press).

JÄGER, H. (1919), *Die Quellen des Porphyrios in seiner Pythagoras-Biographie* (diss. Zurich).

JONES, H. S. (1926), 'Claudius and the Jewish Question at Alexandria', *Journal of Roman Studies*, 16: 17–35.

Käsemann, E. (1964), 'The Problem of the Historical Jesus', *Essays on New Testament Themes*, ch. 1 (*Studies in Biblical Theology*, 41: 15–47).

Kasher, A. (1985), *The Jews in Hellenistic and Roman Egypt: The Struggle for Equal Rights* (Texte und Studien zum antiken Judentum, 7; Tübingen: J. C. B. Mohr).

Keim, T. (1873), *Celsus' Wahres Wort: Älteste Streitschrift antiker Weltanschauung gegen das Christentum vom Jahr 178 n. Chr.* (Zurich: Orell, Füssli & Co.).

Kelber, W. (1958), *Die Logoslehre von Herakilt bis Origenes* (Stuttgart: Urachhaus).

Kidd, I. G. (1971), 'Posidonius on Emotions', in A. A. Long (ed.), *Problems in Stoicism* (London: Athlone Press), 200–15.

—— (1978), 'Philosophy and Science in Posidonius', *Antike und Abendland*, 24: 7–15.

—— (1988), *Posidonius*, ii. *The Commentary* (Cambridge: Cambridge University Press).

—— (1999), *Posidonius*, iii. *The Translation of the Fragments* (Cambridge: Cambridge University Press).

Kindstrand, J. F. (1973), *Homer in der zweiten Sophistik: Studien zu der Homerlektüre und dem Homerbild bei Dion von Prusa, Maximos von Tyros und Ailios Aristeides* (Acta Universitatis Upsaliensis: Studia Graeca Upsaliensia, 7; Uppsala: Uppsala University).

Kirk, G. S., Raven, J. E., and Schofield, M. (1983), *The Presocratic Philosophers*, 2nd edn. (Cambridge: Cambridge University Press).

Kleingünther, A. (1933), *Πρῶτος Εὑρετής: Untersuchungen zur Geschichte einer Fragestellung* (*Philologus*, suppl. 26; Leipzig: Dieterichische Verlagsbuchhandlung).

Kleve, K. (1983), 'Scurra Atticus: The Epicurean View of Socrates', in *Συζήτησις: Studi sull'epicureismo greco e romano offerti a Marcello Gigante*, i. (Naples: Gaetano Macchiaroli), 227–53.

Krämer, H. J. (1964), *Der Ursprung der Geistmetaphysik: Untersuchungen zur Geschichte des Platonismus zwischen Platon und Plotin* (Amsterdam: Schippers).

Laffranque, M. (1964), *Poseidonios d'Apamée: Essai de mise au point* (Paris: Presses Universitaires de France).

Laqueur, R. (1928), 'Manethon (1)', in *RE* xiv. 1060–101.

Lamberton, R. (1986), *Homer the Theologian: Neoplatonist Allegorical Reading and the Growth of the Epic Tradition* (Berkeley, Los Angeles, and London: University of California Press).

Leo, F. (ed.) (1879), *L. Annaei Senecae Tragoediae*, vol. ii (Berlin: Weidmann).

Lévy, I. (1907), 'Moïse en Éthiopie', *Revue des études juives*, 53: 201–11.

LEWY, H. (1932), 'Hekataios von Abdera περὶ Ἰουδαίων', *Zeitschrift für die Neutestamentliche Wissenschaft*, 31: 117–32.

—— (1938), 'Aristotle and the Jewish Sage according to Clearchus of Soli', *Harvard Theological Review*, 31: 205–35.

LILLA, S. R. C. (1971), *Clement of Alexandria: A Study in Christian Platonism and Gnosticism* (London: Oxford University Press).

LONG, A. A. (1988), 'Socrates in Hellenistic Philosophy', *Classical Quarterly*, NS 38: 150–71.

—— (1992), 'Stoic Readings of Homer', in R. Lamberton and J. J. Keaney (eds.), *Homer's Ancient Readers: The Hermeneutics of Greek Epic's Earliest Exegetes* (Princeton: Princeton University Press), 41–66.

LOVEJOY, A. O., and BOAS, G. (1935), *Primitivism and Related Ideas in Antiquity* (A Documentary History of Primitivism and Related Ideas, ed. A. O. Lovejoy, G. Chinard, G. Boas, and R. S. Crane, 1; Baltimore: Johns Hopkins University Press).

LÜDEMANN, G. (1996), *Heretics: The Other Side of Early Christianity*, trans. J. Bowden (London: SCM Press).

MACQUARRIE, J. (1990), *Jesus Christ in Modern Thought* (London: SCM Press).

MALHERBE, A. J. (1970), 'Athenagoras on the Poets and Philosophers', in P. Granfield and J. A. Jungmann (eds.), *Kyriakon* [Festchrift Johannes Quasten], i (Münster: Aschendorff), 214–25.

MANSFELD, J. (1991), 'Two Attributions', *Classical Quarterly*, NS 41: 541–4.

MARCOVICH, M. (ed.) (1986), *Hippolytus: Refutatio Omnium Haeresium* (Berlin: de Gruyter).

MARTINI, E. (1905), 'Dikaiarchos (3)', in *RE* v. 546–63.

MARTINI, G. J. (1825), *Disputatio Literaria Inauguralis de L. Annaeo Cornuto Philosopho Stoico* (diss. Leiden).

MARX, F. (1894), 'Annaeus (9)', in *RE* i. 2226–36.

MEYER, E. (1904), *Ägyptische Chronologie* (Berlin: Königlich Akademie der Wissenschaften).

—— (1908), *Nachträge zur ägyptischen Chronologie* (Berlin: Königlich Akademie der Wissenschaften).

MEYER, H. (1914), *Geschichte der Lehre von den Keimkräften von der Stoa bis zum Ausgang der Patristik* (Bonn: Hanstein).

MOLLAND, E. (1936), 'Clement of Alexandria on the Origin of Greek Philosophy', *Symbolae Osloenses*, 15–16: 57–85.

MOMIGLIANO, A. (1971), 'The Hellenistic Discovery of Judaism', in id., *Alien Wisdom: The Limits of Hellenization* (Cambridge: Cambridge University Press), 74–96.

MORESCHINI, C. (1978), *Apuleio e il platonismo* (Florence: Olschki).

Most, G. (1989), 'Cornutus and Stoic Allegoresis: A Preliminary Report', *ANRW* ii. 36.3: 2014–65.

—— (1993), 'Die früheste erhaltene griechische Dichterallegorese', *Rheinisches Museum*, 136: 209–12.

—— (1997), 'The Fire Next Time: Cosmology, Allegoresis and Salvation in the Derveni Papyrus', *Journal of Hellenic Studies*, 117: 117–35.

—— (1999), 'The Poetics of Early Greek Philosophy', in A. A. Long (ed.), *The Cambridge Companion to Early Greek Philosophy* (Cambridge: Cambridge University Press), 332–62.

Motzo, B. (1912–13), 'Il *κατὰ Ἰουδαίων* di Apione', *Atti della Reale Accademia delle Scienze di Torino*, 48: 459–68.

Murray, O. (1970), 'Hecataeus of Abdera and Pharaonic Kingship', *Journal of Egyptian Archaeology*, 56: 141–71.

—— (1973), 'Hecataeus of Abdera and Theophrastus on Jews and Egyptians', *Journal of Egyptian Archaeology*, 59: 159–68.

Napolitano, L. M. (1985), 'Il platonismo di Eudoro: Tradizione protoaccademica e medioplatonismo alessandrino', *Museum Patavinum*, 3: 27–49.

Nikiprowetzky, V. (1973), 'L'exégèse de Philon d'Alexandrie', *Revue d'histoire et de la philosophie religieuse*, 53: 309–29.

Nock, A. D. (1931), 'Kornutos', in *RE* suppl. v. 995–1005.

Obbink, D. (1992), 'What All Men Believe—Must Be True: Common Conceptions and *Consensio Omnium* in Aristotle and Hellenistic Philosophy', *Oxford Studies in Ancient Philosophy*, 10: 193–231.

—— (1994), 'A Quotation of the Derveni Papyrus in Philodemus' *On Piety*', *Cronache ercolanesi*, 24: 111–35.

O'Brien, M. J. (1985), 'Xenophanes, Aeschylus and the Doctrine of Primeval Brutishness', *Classical Quarterly*, NS 35: 264–77.

O'Meara, D. J. (1989), *Pythagoras Revived: Mathematics and Philosophy in Late Antiquity* (Oxford: Clarendon Press).

Opsomer, J. (1998), *In Search of the Truth: Academic Tendencies in Middle Platonism* (Brussels: Paleis der Academiën).

Paget, J. C. (1994), *The Epistle of Barnabas: Outlook and Background* (Wissenschaftliche Untersuchungen zum Neuen Testament, 2.64; Tübingen: J. C. B. Mohr).

Pearson, A. C. (1891), *The Fragments of Zeno and Cleanthes* (London: C. J. Clay & Sons).

Pelikan, J. (1971), *The Christian Tradition: A History of the Development of Doctrine*, i. *The Emergence of the Catholic Tradition (100–600)* (Chicago and London: University of Chicago Press).

Pépin, J. (1958), *Mythe et Allégorie: Les origines grecques et les contestations judéo-chrétiennes* (Paris: Aubier, Éditions Montaigne).

PÉPIN, J. (1966), 'Porphyre, exégète d'Homère', in *Porphyre* (Entretiens sur l'Antiquité Classique, 12; Geneva: Vandœuvres-Genève), 229–66.

PFEIFFER, R. (1968), *History of Classical Scholarship: From the Beginnings to the End of the Hellenistic Age* (Oxford: Clarendon Press).

PFLIGERSDORFFER, G. (1982), 'Fremdes und Eigenes in Senecas 90. Brief an Lucilius', in J. Stagl (ed.), *Aspekte der Kultursoziologie: Aufsätze zur Soziologie, Philosophie, Anthropologie und Geschichte der Kultur. Zum 60. Geburtstag von Mohammed Rassem* (Berlin: Reimer), 303–26.

POHLENZ, M. (1959), *Die Stoa: Geschichte einer geistigen Bewegung*, 2nd edn. (2 vols.; Göttingen: Vandenhoeck & Ruprecht).

PRICE, R. M. (1988), '"Hellenization" and Logos Doctrine in Justin Martyr', *Vigiliae Christianae*, 42: 18–23.

PUECH, A. (1928–30), *Histoire de la littérature grecque chrétienne depuis les origines jusqu'à la fin du IVe siècle* (3 vols.; Paris: Belles Lettres).

QUASTEN, J. (1950–60), *Patrology* (3 vols.; Utrecht and Antwerp: Spectrum; Wesminster, Md.: The Newman Press).

RAJAK, T. (1978), 'Moses in Ethiopia: Legend and Literature', *Journal of Jewish Studies*, 29: 111–22.

REGENBOGEN, O. (1940), 'Theophrastos (3)', in *RE* suppl. vii. 1354–562.

REINACH, T. (ed.) (1930), *Flavius Josèphe: Contre Apion*, with translation by L. Blum (Paris: Belles Lettres).

REINHARDT, K. (1921), *Poseidonios* (Munich: Beck).

—— (1953), 'Poseidonios (3)', in *RE* xxii. 558–826.

REPPE, R. (1906), *De L. Annaeo Cornuto* (diss. Leipzig).

REYDAMS-SCHILS, G. (1997), 'Posidonius and the *Timaeus*: Off to Rhodes and Back to Plato?', *Classical Quarterly*, NS 47: 455–76.

REYHL, K. (1969), *Antonios Diogenes: Untersuchungen zu den Roman-Fragmenten der 'Wunder jenseits von Thule' und zu den 'Wahren Geschichten' des Lukian* (diss. Tübingen).

RIDINGS, D. (1995), *The Attic Moses: The Dependency Theme in Some Early Christian Writers* (Studia Graeca et Latina Gothoburgensia, 59; Göteborg: University of Göteborg).

ROBINSON, J. A. T. (1956), 'The Most Primitive Christology of All?', *Journal of Theological Studies*, 7: 177–89.

ROTH, N. (1978), 'The "Theft of Philosophy" by the Greeks from the Jews', *Classical Folia*, 32: 53–67.

RUDBERG, G. (1918), *Forschungen zu Poseidonios* (Skrifter utgifna af K. Humanistiska Vetenskaps-Samfundet i Uppsala, 20.3; Uppsala and Leipzig: Harassowitz).

RUNIA, D. T. (1995), 'Why Does Clement of Alexandria Call Philo "The Pythagorean"?', *Vigiliae Christianae*, 49: 1–22.

RUNNALLS, D. (1983), 'Moses' Ethiopian Campaign', *Journal for the Study of Judaism*, 14: 135–56.

Sanders, E. P. (1985), *Jesus and Judaism* (London: SCM Press).

Sanders, J. N. (1943), *The Fourth Gospel in the Early Church: Its Origin and Influence on Christian Theology up to Irenaeus* (Cambridge: Cambridge University Press).

Schäfer, P. (1997), 'Die Manetho-Fragmente bei Josephus und die Anfänge des antiken "Antisemitismus"', in G. W. Most (ed.), *Collecting Fragments/Fragmente sammeln* (Aporemata, 1; Göttingen: Vandenhoeck & Ruprecht), 186–206.

Schaller, B. (1963), 'Hekataios von Abdera über die Juden: Zur Frage der Echtheit und der Datierung', *Zeitschrift für die Neutestamentliche Wissenschaft*, 54: 15–31.

Schlunk, R. R. (1993), *Porphyry, The Homeric Questions: A Bilingual Edition* (Lang Classical Studies, 2; New York: Peter Lang).

Schürer, E. (1973–87), *The History of the Jewish People in the Age of Jesus Christ*, rev. edn. ed. G. Vermes, F. Millar, and M. Black (3 vols.; Edinburgh: T. & T. Clark).

Schwartz, E. (1885), 'Hekataeos von Teos', *Rheinisches Museum*, 40: 223–62.

—— (1896), 'Artapanus', in *RE* ii: 1306.

—— (1897), 'Chairemon (7)', in *RE* iii. 2025–7.

—— (1905), 'Diodorus (38)', in *RE* v. 663–704.

Schweizer, E. (1966), 'Zum religionsgeschichtlichen Hintergrund der "Sendungsformel" Gal. 4. 4f. Rm. 8. 3f. Joh. 3. 16f. I John 4. 9', *Zeitschrift für die Neutestamentliche Wissenschaft*, 57: 199–210.

—— (1968), *Jesus Christus im vielfältigen Zeugnis des Neuen Testaments* (Munich and Hamburg: Siebenstern-Taschenbuch).

Schwyzer, H.-R. (1932), *Chaeremon* (Leipzig: Harrassowitz).

Scott, A. (1991), *Origen and the Life of the Stars: A History of an Idea* (Oxford: Clarendon Press).

Sedley, D. (1989), 'Philosophical Allegiance in the Greco-Roman World', in Griffin and Barnes (1989), 97–119.

—— (1997), 'Plato's *Auctoritas* and the Rebirth of the Commentary Tradition', in Barnes and Griffin (1997), 110–29.

—— (1998), 'Theophrastus and Epicurean Physics', in J. M. van Ophuijsen and M. van Raalte (eds.), *Theophrastus: Reappraising the Sources* (Rutgers University Studies in Classical Humanities, 8; New Brunswick, NJ, and London: Transaction Publishers), 331–54.

Sihvola, J., and Engberg-Pedersen, T. (eds.) (1998), *The Emotions in Hellenistic Philosophy* (Dordecht, Boston, and London: Kluwer).

Snodgrass, A. M. (1998), *Homer and the Artists: Text and Picture in Early Greek Art* (Cambridge: Cambridge University Press).

Speyer, W. (1971), *Die literarische Fälschung im heidenischen und christlichen Altertum: Ein Versuch ihrer Deutung* (Munich: Beck).

STADEN, H. VON (1982), 'Hairesis and Heresy: The Case of the *haireseis iatrikai*', in B. F. Meyer and E. P. Sanders (eds.), *Jewish and Christian Self-definition*, iii. *Self-definition in the Greco-Roman World* (London: SCM Press), 76–100.

—— (1989), *Herophilus: The Art of Medicine in Early Alexandria. Edition, Translation and Essays* (Cambridge: Cambridge University Press).

STEINMETZ, P. (1986), 'Allegorische Deutung und allegorische Dichtung in der alten Stoa', *Rheinisches Museum*, 129: 18–30.

STERN, M. (1973), 'The Chronological Sequence of the First References to Jews in Greek Literature', Eng. trans. by T. Rajak at Murray 1973: 159–63.

—— (1974–84), *Greek and Latin Authors on Jews and Judaism*, edited with Introductions, Translations and Commentary (3 vols.; Jerusalem: Israel Academy of Sciences and Humanities).

STONE, M. E. (1984), *Jewish Writings of the Second Temple Period: Apocrypha, Pseudepigrapha, Qumran, Sectarian Writings, Philo, Josephus* (Assen: Van Gorcum).

STRAUB, J. (ed.) (1971), *Acta Conciliorum Oecumenicorum*, iv/1. *Concilium Universale Constantinopolitanum sub Iustiniano Habitum* (Berlin: De Gruyter).

SUSEMIHL, F. (1891–2), *Geschichte der griechischen Litteratur in der Alexandrinerzeit* (2 vols.; Leipzig: Teubner).

TARRANT, H. (1980), 'Academics and Platonics', *Prudentia*, 12: 109–18.

—— (1983), 'The Date of Anon. *In Theaetetum*', *Classical Quarterly*, NS 33: 161–87.

—— (1985), *Scepticism or Platonism? The Philosophy of the Fourth Academy* (Cambridge: Cambridge University Press).

—— (1993), *Thrasyllan Platonism* (Ithaca, NY, and London: Cornell University Press).

TATE, J. (1929*a*), 'Cornutus and the Poets', *Classical Quarterly*, 23: 41–5.

—— (1929*b*), 'Plato and Allegorical Interpretation', *Classical Quarterly*, 23: 142–54.

—— (1930), 'Plato and Allegorical Interpretation', *Classical Quarterly*, 24: 1–10 [continuing Tate 1929*b*].

TCHERIKOVER, V. (1959), *Hellenistic Civilization and the Jews* (Philadelphia: Jewish Publication Society of America).

—— and FUKS, A. (1957–64), *Corpus Papyrorum Judaicorum* (3 vols.; Jerusalem: Magnes Press; Cambridge, Mass.: Harvard University Press).

THEILER, W. (1930), *Die Vorbereitung des Neuplatonismus* (Problemata, 1; Berlin: Weidmann).

—— (1982), *Poseidonios: Die Fragmente* (2 vols.; Berlin: de Gruyter).

TURNER, E. G. (1954), 'Tiberius Iulius Alexander', *Journal of Roman Studies*, 44: 54–64.

van der Horst, P. W. (1987), *Chaeremon: Egyptian Priest and Stoic Philosopher*, 2nd edn. (Leiden: Brill).

Vander Waerdt, P. A. (1985), 'Peripatetic Soul-division, Posidonius and Middle Platonic Moral Psychology', *Greek, Roman and Byzantine Studies*, 26: 373–94.

Vergote, J. (1939), 'Clément d'Alexandrie et l'écriture égyptienne: Essai d'interprétation de Stromates V. 4, 20–21', *Muséon*, 52: 199–221.

Vermes, G. (1978), 'The Present State of the "Son of Man" Debate', *Journal of Jewish Studies*, 29: 123–34.

Vlastos, G. (1946), 'On the Pre-history in Diodorus', *American Journal of Philology*, 67: 51–9.

Wacholder, B. Z. (1974), *Eupolemus: A Study of Judaeo-Greek Literature* (Cincinnati: Hebrew Union College/Jewish Institute of Religion).

Waddell, W. G. (ed.) (1940), *Manetho* (Loeb Classical Library; Cambridge, Mass.: Harvard University Press).

Walter, N. (1964), *Der Thoraausleger Aristobulos: Untersuchungen zu seinen Fragmenten und zu pseudepigraphischen Resten der jüdisch-hellenistischen Literatur* (Texte und Untersuchungen, 86; Berlin: Akademie-Verlag).

Waszink, J. H. (1957), 'Der Platonismus und die altchristliche Gedankenwelt', in *Recherches sur la tradition platonicienne* (Entretiens sur l'Antiquité Classique, 3; Geneva: Fondation Hardt), 137–74.

Wehrli, F. (1928), *Zur Geschichte der allegorischen Deutung Homers im Altertum* (diss. Borna-Leipzig).

—— (1944), *Die Schule des Aristoteles*, i. *Dikaiarchos* (Basel: Schwabe & Co.).

—— (1968), 'Dikaiarchos (3)', in *RE* suppl. xi. 526–34.

Weill, R. (1918), *La Fin du moyen empire égyptien: Étude sur les monuments et l'histoire de la période comprise entre la XIIe e la XVIIIe dynastie* (2 vols.; Paris: Imprimerie Nationale).

West, M. L. (1978) (ed.), *Hesiod: Works and Days*, edited with Prolegomena and Commentary (Oxford: Oxford University Press).

—— (1983), *The Orphic Poems* (Oxford: Oxford University Press).

Whittaker, J. (1990) (ed.), *Alcinoos: Enseignement des doctrines de Platon*, with French translation by P. Louis (Paris: Belles Lettres).

Wifstrand, A. (1941–2), 'Die wahre Lehre des Kelsos', *Bulletin de la Société Royale des Lettres de Lund* (Lund: Gleerup), 391–431.

Willrich, H. (1900), *Judaica: Forschungen zur hellenistisch-jüdischen Geschichte und Litteratur* (Göttingen: Vandenhoeck & Ruprecht).

—— (1924), *Urkundenfälschung in der hellenistisch-jüdischen Literatur* (Forschungen zur Religion und Literatur des Alten und Neuen Testaments, NS 21; Göttingen: Vandenhoeck & Ruprecht).

Witt, R. E. (1937), *Albinus and the History of Middle Platonism* (Transactions of the Cambridge Philological Society, 7; Cambridge: Cambridge University Press).

Wolfson, H. A. (1947), *Philo: Foundations of Religious Philosophy in Judaism, Christianity and Islam* (2 vols.; Cambridge, Mass.: Harvard University Press).

Zeegers-vander Vorst, N. (1972), *Les Citations des poètes grecs chez les apologistes chrétiens du IIᵉ siècle* (Recueil de Travaux d'Histoire et de Philologie, 4.47; Louvain: Bibliothèque de l'Université, Bureau de Recueil).

Zeller, E. (1876), 'Der Streit Theophrasts gegen Zeno über die Ewigkeit der Welt', *Hermes*, 11: 422–9.

—— (1892), *Die Philosophie der Griechen in ihrer geschichtlichen Entwicklung*, 5th edn. (4 vols.; Leipzig: O. R. Reisland).

Index of Passages Cited

General Index

Printed and bound by CPI Group (UK) Ltd, Croydon, CR0 4YY